Confident Child

THE BANK STREET COLLEGE OF EDUCATION

Joanne Oppenheim
Betty Boegehold
Barbara Brenner

PANTHEON BOOKS · NEW YORK

Grateful acknowledgment is made to Nan Graham for her help in forming this book; to Dan Cullen for his insightful editorial assistance; to Dr. Richard Ruopp and the Bank Street faculty who supported us in the venture; and to Joan Auclair for manuscript preparation.

Manufactured in the United States of America
First Edition

Library of Congress Cataloging in Publication Data

Oppenheim, Joanne.
Raising a confident child.

Bibliography: p.
Includes index.
1. Child rearing.   2. Socialization.   3. Social skills—Study and teaching.   4. Child development.
I. Boegehold, Betty Virginia Doyle.   II. Brenner, Barbara.   III. Hooks, William H.   IV. Bank Street College of Education.   V. Title.
HQ769.O64   1985   649'.1   84-25450
ISBN 0-394-72719-3

Raising a Confident Child

THE BANK STREET YEAR-BY-YEAR GUIDE

Raising a

Consultant: Leah Levinger, Ph.D.
Editor: William H. Hooks

CONTENTS

FOREWORD

This is a deceptively simple book. Ostensibly it deals on a practical, commonsense level with the process of a child's becoming a social being, and with the daily challenges and rewards that this process provides for parents. Yet the most predictable, well-known, and everyday stuff of life can be and usually is more complicated than it might seem. *Raising a Confident Child* maintains a balance in its recognition of the matter-of-fact aspects of child development and child rearing, the more subtle hidden feelings of parents and children alike, and the added complexities of raising children in our rapidly changing society of conflicting values.

This book follows in chronological order the challenges that must be met by both parent and child as the latter becomes a member of the community. As each age of the child is considered, one becomes aware of three major and interrelated issues underlying the practical discussions of method:

- The gap between adult expectations and child behavior.
- The struggle between individual freedom and the demands of society.
- The balance between interpersonal relationships and solitary, contemplative experiences.

Each of these issues has been dealt with in psychology and in philosophy for the last two or three hundred years, and still there is no agreement on how to respond to them. Hence, it might be well to consider each at some length before we introduce the wealth of examples and principles suggested for specific behavior.

First, there is the recognition that there must inevitably be a gap

between what the adult wishes the child could do and what he expects
him to do, and what the child is actually able to do and wishes to do,
at each age. This conflict was pithily stated by Robert Louis Stevenson:

> A child should always say what's true
> And speak when he is spoken to,
> And behave mannerly at table;
> At least as far as he is able.

Our society, as scores of child development psychologists and popu-
larizers have recently pointed out, may put particularly strong pressures
on the child to grow up in a hurry. But there was stress in other periods
of history, too: the frontier child had to face hard physical labor and
the dangers of life almost as an adult would; the middle-class Victorian
child was expected at an exceedingly early age to be a model of deco-
rum. The concept of "age appropriate" behavior varies today. Some
parents, perhaps trying to relive their own nostalgic dreams of what
childhood ought to be, will say, "Why frustrate him? Why not let him
be a child for as long as he can?" Others, perhaps having to deal with
inner-city tensions, or with the burdens of single parenthood, may be
living on their own frontier. They may say, "It's time he learns how to
look after himself! He has to fit into my working schedule in order for
us to exist." In many families the issues are not this extreme or clear-
cut. Parents may in certain areas push the child to become more mature,
in other areas let him go at his own pace, and in still others discourage
maturity and indulge his staying infantile, dependent, and helpless. But
there are few times when the rate at which the child is growing perfectly
matches the rate at which the family hopes he will grow.

The second major issue is whether there is an inevitable battle between the spontaneous, free individual and the demands of the civilized
human community that mold and restrain her; or whether a person
best grows into her own self as she grows in her awareness of being
part of that community.

There is a long tradition in romantic poetry such as Wordsworth's
and Blake's, which had been enunciated by philosophers such as Rous-
seau and then clearly stated in the works of Freud, that a child, in order
to grow and be acceptable in the community, must pay the price of

giving up many of the early delights of his own body and desires. Premature or overly harsh demands for this process to take place were believed to result in emotional damage to the individual. Thus, until the middle of this century, one of the focal issues in the application of child development theory to actual child rearing, in home or in school, was the question of a timetable for recognizing and meeting the conventions of society.

But in the last forty years psychologists have emphasized that the child is striving to master her own body and her own relation with the environment, and achieves more of a sense of self as she does so. Thus when she can make her wants known, not by grunting and pointing, but by actual words, she has entered a new world of power as well as of communication.

The very young child may be self-absorbed, but she is not really self-aware. The great psychiatrist and neurologist Paul Schilder points out that awareness of self develops along with awareness of other people until, in later childhood or beginning adolescence, a sensitivity to reciprocal relations emerges (provided that the modeling and the support have been given). This latter view was stated by Schilder: "Emotions are directed towards others. Emotions are always social. Similarly, thinking is a social function, even in a lonely person. Humanity is the unseen listener to his thinking."

I share this point of view with Schilder, as I believe also do the authors of this book. It is because they see and support the positive aspects of mastering the ways of human society that this book can be useful and supportive, rather than prescriptive.

One of the more puzzling and complex issues of child development is that of competition. How does the child balance a sense of his own unique worth with a sense of membership in the common human stream? A distinction must be made between the useful role of measuring oneself and one's skills against those of others, and the destructive role of pitting oneself against others. The authors do well to caution parents and child rearers not only about inflating competitive desires in children but also about measuring them against each other. They point out how this emphasis may turn the joy of play into a grim battle for scores, and be less an expression of a child's desire to master skills than of an adult's vain desire to see her win. But the question still remains whether the "natural" competitiveness that does tend to emerge in the middle years is the child's own incorporation of the competitive tone of this society, or whether the adults in her immediate world have encouraged or discouraged competitive needs.

The final issue is one that has been met by poets more often than by any other observers of the human condition. What portion of a human being lives through the interactive social world, and what portion exists in the solitary and contemplative world? This is always subject to individual differences: temperamentally, certain people, even as children, seem to be more highly gregarious, more attuned to the bustling world of the nursery school discussion group or the adult marketplace, and others to discoveries and experiences on their own. The great burgeoning in the past few years of backpacking in the wilderness is an expression of the desire to maintain a certain part of the self away from highly socialized urban settings. William Blake formulated such an idea at the beginning of the nineteenth century:

> Great things are done when men and mountains meet;
> This is not done by jostling in the street.

And almost two hundred years before him, Andrew Marvell had written of the Garden of Eden:

> Two paradises 'twere in one
> To dwell in paradise alone.

One wants to aid the child in mastering the skills of observing the world around him and adapting to the varied requirements of many different situations. But in order to help him become an autonomous being and also one who may be able ultimately to alter the world and make it a better place, as well as adapting to it, something else is needed. This something else is the ability to contemplate, to wonder, and to nurture one's own thoughts.

The authors emphasize, as one of the constant challenges of parenting, the goal of raising a child who will get along with others. But it also recognizes the need for children to draw upon their own resources and to discover ways of life that do not necessarily demand interchange. This alternative may be easier for children of certain ages and temperaments. Particularly between the ages of eight and eleven, when the peer group is so important to children, an emphasis upon gregariousness may be the enemy of building the skill for intimacy. Intimacy between people grows and flourishes when each person can turn back to himself and then emerge toward a loved one. Children, in this often callous and embittered world, must be helped to develop what D. H. Lawrence called "the courage of one's own tenderness."

LEAH LEVINGER, PH.D.
Bank Street College of Education

Raising a Confident Child

1

The Meaning of Confidence and Sociability

Social Beings

We are all social beings. Almost everything we do depends on a network of social contracts—agreements we make with our families, friends, teachers, lovers, employers, even strangers. We couldn't live without a social framework; at least you couldn't call it living.

This delicate and intricate social fabric isn't something we stitched up overnight. It's a complicated tapestry, and it took us a while—thousands of years—and many experiments with design. But clearly, it was worth it. For one thing, it enables us to be civilized—a society rather than a tribe of savages. It gives us an anchor and a purpose. And it enables us to deal with each other. As the biologists put it, being social "conveys an advantage" for humans.

Is everyone social? Not to the same extent. Some people overdo the social—they can be cloying or overbearing and a burden on the rest of us. Then there are those who underdo sociability. As a result, they're sometimes isolated and lonely. They may not function well and can become a burden on themselves. At the extreme are the people who are antisocial, who have to be isolated from the rest of society. These deviations teach us that it seems to be crucial that one be not only social, but social to the right extent.

We all know this, in some unspoken way. That's why we value sociability—why we want it for ourselves and why we want to pass it along to our children. We want them to have a set of social skills because we know that they're a must for leading a civilized and productive life. We understand that these skills are a bridge to the mastery of things we know are important, and that what we share as social beings becomes *more* than what it is *because* of the sharing.

How does one go about raising a sociable child?

It doesn't happen by accident. Growing up social is a learned thing, and the first persons the child learns from are his parents. What they do, and what they say, is what they teach. In this context, *not* paying any attention to socialization can be a lesson in itself.

Social Codes

How do we show what kinds of social creatures we are? By what we say. By how we act toward other people. By the company we keep, the way we talk to strangers, the way we react to social situations, even the way we treat our pets.

We also send social signals in a hundred smaller ways. Some of them may be noticeable only by their absence. In fact, little things define us just as surely as big ones. Things like how we eat, what we wear, what we say by way of greeting, how we reveal our feelings. These little signals are the forms that reveal the substance of our social mores. They go by various code names—manners, etiquette, respect, politeness. They're all part of our social fabric, and they make some important statements about us, *and* about our children.

Every culture has its own set of social signals, although they are by no means the same everywhere. For instance, eating with the fingers is not considered polite in our culture. In some other places it's not only acceptable but proper. In certain countries it's the custom to belch at the end of a meal to show that you've enjoyed what you ate. In our society a burp gets a frown. And we shake hands to say hello, but there are places where a handshake is considered rude.

By the time we've grown up, we've learned a set of social codes from our parents. In most cases, we try hard to hand them down to our kids. But even what we hand down changes from generation to generation. A hundred years ago, rigid instruction in "the social graces" was considered vital to every child's proper upbringing. Children's books were laced with instructions on good manners. Then came a period when the idea of manners seemed to have gone out of fashion; they were equated with phoniness or with the trappings of the "establishment." Many parents thought that children would somehow learn the small social signals automatically, without being told.

But they didn't. Lately manners seem to be coming into their own again. We're recognizing how much we've missed them. We're appreciating how pleasant *please* and *thank you* sound and how much family life is improved when all members learn to respect one another's rights. It's a great thrill to hear your child say to his sister voluntarily, "It's your turn to go first."

COMMONSENSE RULES

The effect of this revival has been a new and more appropriate set of social signals. We've kept the manners that are relevant and rejected those that are outmoded. Curtsies are out. But *real* consideration is in. The new manners, like many other social rules, are based on common sense. Certain subjects are taboo at the dinner table not because they're "disgusting," but because we respect our dinner companions' digestion. You don't shout in the library, because it disturbs other readers. And it's a bad idea to talk with your mouth full, not because it isn't "polite," but because the person you are talking to can't understand what you're saying. It's also the easiest way to choke on your food and make yourself a candidate for the Heimlich maneuver.

TALKING MANNERS

"The way a person speaks absolutely classifies him," said Henry Higgins in *My Fair Lady*. Professor Higgins may have been a snob, but there's no denying that what he said contains more than a germ of truth. Besides revealing whether you're from Oshkosh or Orlando, your speech manner gives away your social secrets.

Every parent knows this. That's why we teach our children to listen, to speak politely, to think before they speak, to avoid foul language, and to refrain from saying things that may be hurtful to others. Learning how to talk and when to talk, how to listen and how to relate to what one hears, is a large part of becoming a social creature.

ACTION MANNERS

What else should be considered acceptable social responses? Respect for other people's space and property. Consideration for strangers in public places. Manners don't crop up only in how we talk, they also surface in actions. "Excuse me" doesn't mean much if you're being shoved aside by the person who says it to you. Manners, to be meaningful, have to include not only what people say but what they do. Pushing, shoving, disregarding, littering, are all manifestations of poor manners.

SHOULD WE TEACH MANNERS?

It's not only possible to teach manners and for children to learn them; in fact, it's essential. Whether we are aware of it or not, we're doing it all the time—the way we act, talk, and interact with other people is a powerful teaching tool for children. They are apt to mimic what they see and hear. The question is what manners to get involved with at what age. You can't teach your toddler the fine points of table manners when he's just learning how to hold a spoon. And diplomacy comes only after you have a body of language to be diplomatic with. Rudeness at a certain age may be a lack of control, due to a lack of maturity. Manners, like other aspects of socialization, have a timetable.

The Social Side of Sex and Gender

Biology defines some aspects of children's social development. One of the big "definers" is gender—whether a child is born male or female. Aside from the obvious physical differences between boys and girls, differences in personality and sociability assert themselves very early. It's hard to know whether these traits are gender-related, since no society brings up boys and girls with a uniform set of rules and expectations. What we can say is that many of the roles assigned to boys and girls affect very deeply the social fabric of their lives.

Beginning in the cradle, babies are imprinted in ways that are related to their gender. This imprinting has bearing on how they develop —on how they establish self-concepts of their male- or femaleness in toddlerhood. In the preschool years, their play and their fantasies will be shaped by continuing role and gender identification. As children grow older, family standards will show direct cause-and-effect relationships between expectations and resulting behavior. For instance, a family may expect a girl to be neat, polite, cooperative, quiet (a "little lady"), while their expectations for a boy in that same family may be that he will be boisterous, sloppy, even rude (a "regular rascal"). Obviously, these gender-related expectations will have social consequences for children.

Although many parents are making a conscious effort to avoid such stereotyping, old attitudes are deeply ingrained. A recent magazine ad for clocks featured two young adults side by side: "he" is the graduate in cap and gown; "she" is the bride in white veil and lace. Such messages delineating gender are pervasive, even subliminal. Research in the past decade has done much to reshape our previous views about the differences between men and women. Yet the leap from research to reality is still painfully slow. We still tend to assume that a woman in the green medic uniform is the scrub nurse, not the doctor. These instant assumptions about gender are learned early in life and reinforced by subtle, everyday events. Parents play the first and most significant role in shaping their children's sexual identity and long-lasting attitudes about themselves and others.

While *gender* identification influences children's socialization, it is its sexual expression that may bring a child face to face with some of society's strongest taboos. All children explore their sexuality in various ways as they grow. They may examine themselves and other children. They may ask "embarrassing" questions and do "embarrassing" things. How to allow healthy expressions of normal urges that still square with community mores can be a difficult assignment for a parent. It helps to know that sexuality is not simply a facet of biology. It is an integral part of the social self. What's appropriate at four may be a trouble signal at nine. It's important for parents to know when and how to respond to children's natural curiosity about themselves and others. Guiding children's sexual development goes beyond telling them the facts of life. It involves loving and caring and the capacity for tenderness and intimacy.

Social Steps

Growing up social is a step-by-step process—small steps for small children, larger strides as a child grows. There are major characteristics that set each developmental stage apart from the next, and special social learnings that need to accompany each stage. For this reason, we've followed a developmental timetable in this book, with suggestions for everyday activities and socializing experiences for each stage of childhood.

In the body of the book you'll discover that:

- *Infants* come into the world with considerably more social equipment than we used to think. They develop patterns of sociability as a result of how their parents, caregivers, and the children around them behave. There are definitely things you can do that will have long-lasting effects on your baby's social development. Talking and singing games, rocking, cuddling, and even just holding the baby are enormously important.
- *Toddlers* (1½ to 3) need a safe stage for creative exploration. This is a great time of exploration—first steps into the outside world of the playground, the supermarket, the dentist, as well as the thrilling beginnings of language. There's some behavior that you can expect from toddlers, and some that is beyond their social capabilities at ages 1½ to 3. They need support for their growing sociability and understanding when they slip back into babyhood.
- *Preschoolers* are on the road to being competent. They can play many kinds of games, can visit and be host or hostess. Social events like a movie or a restaurant are not beyond the preschooler's social capability. But you'll find that home is still the center of his universe, even though he is ready and able to form ties outside the family circle.
- During *early school years* (6, 7, 8), children are trying to understand two social worlds—the home and the school. A parent's job is to help the child make smooth transitions to greater independence and to encourage learning to live by the rules.

• In the *intermediate school years* (9, 10, 11), the dominant teachers of your child are other children. Not only do parents have to understand this, they must support or challenge it as it becomes necessary. This is no time to abandon the teaching of social skills and values, but on the contrary, to continue them so they are firmly fixed.

Each age group, as you will see, has its stamp. Many of them you will recognize: "Why, that's just what Sara does," or, "I'm glad to know that someone else's child does (or doesn't do) that." Sometimes you'll notice that your child's timetable is a little different from ours. That doesn't mean that your child is faster or slower than normal. It simply means that every child is unique, and that children who develop quickly in one area may develop slowly in another.

Social Styles

One of the points we will make over and over in this book is that the best way to insure that your child will grow up to be sociable is to work with his or her strengths. Some children are born quiet and somewhat shy; that's their temperament. Others seem to be born vivacious and outgoing. You can bring Quiet Tom out of his shell a bit, but you probably won't make him into the life of the party, and you shouldn't try. On the other hand, Bouncy Amy, the tot who tears around the playground, may not, at least for a long while, be ready to sit still for a Youth Symphony performance. Tom needs a little encouragement, Amy needs a little toning down. But the trick is to make sure that socializing doesn't knock out what's unique in both of them.

Perhaps this would be a good place to put in a word about solitude. Solitude is the flip side of sociability. It, too, needs to be recognized and valued as not only desirable but also necessary at times. It's as important for Amy and Tom to learn to enjoy times of solitary quiet and reflection as it is for them to learn to have interactive social experiences. To be truly social is to be comfortable with people and, when without them, to be comfortable with oneself.

What should you, the parent, be aiming for? Probably a course that makes the most of your child's individuality or, as one thoughtful parent said, "I'd like to raise a kid who is spunky but not rude, polite but not a snob, mannerly but not obsequious, affable but not fawning, assertive but not aggressive, individual but still a member of the group." A difficult ideal, but certainly worth striving for.

How to Use This Book

You may find that the best way to use this book is to read it all the way through. This will give you a good general picture of a child's social growth from infancy to the onset of adolescence. With this overview you can see what stage your own child is in. If you're having a social problem, you may find that it's just because your youngster is stuck in one of those "growing pains" stages and you'll relax. If you're having smooth sailing, you'll find out why. In any case, reading it through will give you perspective.

Another way you may want to use the book is to dip into it when you feel your child is approaching a new developmental stage. Looking ahead may be a very good way to orient yourself to what is coming.

A third way to use *Raising a Confident Child* is to select a subject that's puzzling you, whether it's homesickness, table manners, or traveling. Look it up in the Index, and then follow the subject through the various stages in the book.

Whether you use this book to learn about a developmental stage or a specific topic, you'll find something to guide you. We'll give you advice and support, but not prescriptions. We'll try to tell you what it's like from the child's point of view, as well as from the parent's. And we'll explore with you the physical and verbal activities that support social development at every stage.

By the time your child approaches adolescence, much of the foundation for social behavior has been laid. This doesn't mean that nothing can be changed, but it does mean that change comes harder. By this time you want your child to be the kind of person of whom neighbors and friends say, "Your kid is welcome in my house anytime."

2

Infancy—
The Beginning
of Social Life

BIRTH TO EIGHTEEN
MONTHS OLD

Infants as Social Beings

An infant is a social being by necessity. Essentially helpless, the new-born comes into the world with needs that only others can provide. Without caring adults to feed, cleanse, and comfort them, infants could not survive. So, from the start all basic needs are met by other people.

Yet a newborn does not know one person from another. An infant doesn't even know where he himself begins or ends. It is in the arms of those who care for him that an infant learns about the world of people and things. How he is cared for and the social setting that surrounds him will shape the child's long-lasting feelings about himself and others. In the day-to-day business of feeding, changing diapers, cuddling, rocking, singing, talking, and touching, an infant comes to feel more safe or unsafe, more comforted or uncomfortable, more loved or un-loved. It is in these everyday events that an infant learns what to expect from the people in his life. What he learns will color his future relationships with others for years to come.

What They're Like

During the first months of life an infant is more dependent than she will ever be again. Yet even a newborn is not without social resources. In addition to eating, sleeping, and wetting her diapers, an infant plays an active role right from the start.

Some babies are very energetic and demanding, while others are calm and quiet. Some sleep a lot, others sleep hardly at all. Some are snugglers, others squirmers. Because every infant is unique, there can be no single formula for how much rocking, holding, sleeping, feeding, or patting each baby needs. Trying to put a baby on a preconceived routine schedule is apt to be more frustrating than rewarding for both you and your baby. Infants are not lumps of clay waiting to be molded. From the start an infant is an active partner with her parents in shaping her social circle. The trick for the parents is to "read" her signals and follow her lead.

What They Can Do

Until recently most books about infants have focused on their helplessness and dependency. Yet current research indicates that people have been underestimating how much the infant can do to socialize with those who care for him. It's not that babies have gotten smarter. Rather, our understanding of what they can do keeps growing.

Less than five years ago a survey of mothers in the United States showed that 70 percent of them believed that infants are born blind. In fact, not only can infants see at birth, they are able to imitate exaggerated facial expressions almost at once. When held ten inches from an adult tester, babies only thirty-six hours old mirrored the tester's distinct facial expressions. Long before they can take hold of things with their hand, infants begin to take in a great deal of information with their eyes. Of all the things in the newborn child's world there is no sight more interesting or stimulating than a human face, with its moving eyes and interesting sounds.

In his design, the infant is ideally adapted to get a good look at the important faces in his small social circle. During the first month infants focus best on things seven to ten inches from their faces. In effect, the infant's early visual limitations screen out the visual overload of a world full of new sights and zoom in on the faces of those who care for him. In a matter of weeks his visual world will expand, and he will see as well as an adult.

How They Become Attached to Primary Caregivers

Although newborns cannot distinguish one face from another at first, they gradually learn to distinguish between the familiar and unfamiliar, the expected and unexpected. They form an attachment to the familiar and the expected. At four weeks old they will smile at the sound of Mother's voice. At two months an infant will usually stop crying at the sound of familiar footsteps, the sound of a familiar voice, or the sight of a familiar face. In the coming months the infant will not only distinguish between the familiar and the unfamiliar, but will clearly show her preference for some people over others.

At between five months and a year, the infant's attachment to her primary caregivers becomes even more evident. Suddenly, even the best-loved visiting Grandmother had better go slowly with her advances or be prepared for screams of protest. To avoid hurt or confrontation in such a situation, it is best to give the infant some time to watch her grandmother from a distance. Usually the infant's natural curiosity will outweigh her anxiety about being handled by someone other than her primary caregiver. But some clinging at this stage is a positive sign that the baby is really beginning to know who's who in her world.

This growing bond of attachment is a two-way street: the baby's responses trigger the parents' responses. A cuddly, friendly baby tends to elicit more loving and cooing than a baby who frets and frowns. So the baby puts in motion a set of parental actions and reactions; thus the baby is both sender and receiver. And the result is usually a deep and caring bonding between parent and child that is necessary for healthy development. It is from this attachment that the infant gathers a sense of security that will eventually grow into the freedom to explore beyond the close-knit relationship. But during infancy the need to hold on is real. Parents should recognize it and encourage the child's attachment. During these early months of dependency, parents remain the well-anchored security base from which all goodness, comfort, and protection flows.

How They Communicate

Right from the start an infant comes into the world with a full set of sensory equipment. He can see, hear, smell, taste, and touch. Some noises startle him, while others seem to soothe him. He closes his eyes on some sights and turns away from strong smells. When there is too much stimulation, the infant turns away, tunes out, or fusses to show displeasure. When there is not enough, the infant seeks it out by an ever-expanding repertoire of social abilities.

There is probably no better example of an infant's sociability than what occurs at feeding time. Even when he is hungry, a baby is not merely an empty cup waiting to be filled. It is the infant who sets the rhythm and tempo of the feeding, punctuating the process with pauses and active sucking. If Mother talks while he is nursing, the baby is likely to be distracted from the breast or bottle. Taking her cue from the baby, the mother limits her verbalizations to the baby's pauses, and synchronizes her actions to the baby's reactions. This rhythmic dialogue is not unlike a conversation between friends. One listens, one talks, then the listener becomes speaker again. Of course, between infant and parent, it is the parent who must interpret and respond. But the baby's reactions tell us if he is content or distressed, if we should continue rocking or try laying him on his stomach. Smiling and crying are two of the baby's major social tools.

During the first weeks of life a newborn's smile is often dismissed as "nothing but gas" or pure reflex action, but current research has shown us this is not always the case. At just six to eight weeks an infant will smile at the sight of a human face, and at three months he greets familiar faces with smiles, wiggles, and cooing sounds of pleasure. This purposeful smile is a landmark event in a baby's social development.

Crying is an infant's way of signaling distress. Babies don't cry without reason. Nor can infants control their crying. It is a reflexive response that is triggered by hunger, pain, tiredness, even loneliness. Crying is an infant's first form of communication, one side of a social dialogue that is programmed to bring results.

In the coming months, as the world becomes more familiar and the infant more physically able, he learns to use other signals and gestures to communicate what he needs. When a baby can point to what he wants, or creep after an out-of-reach object, or babble in a variety of interpretable ways, he is ready to exercise a whole new set of social skills.

CAN YOU SPOIL THEM?

Don't worry about spoiling the baby by responding to his distress signals or his cunning smiles, wiggles, or coos. What you want to do is encourage his ability to communicate with you. Research shows that babies can't be spoiled by too much attention and loving care during these early months. In fact, studies show that by the end of the first year infants who have been given prompt and loving attention tend to be less demanding and more independent.

WHAT TO EXPECT FROM THEM

Infancy is a time of rapid growth and dramatic changes. In a short time an infant develops

- *from* crying by reflex *to* specific crying that indicates she is hungry, or wants attention;
- *from* reflex smiling *to* using smiles to signal recognition and to get more attention;
- *from* reflex movements *to* a growing range of physical skills that enable her to move from aimless batting at dangling crib toys to purposeful reaching and grasping;
- *from* not knowing one person from another *to* a growing and significant attachment to specific people in his social circle;
- *from* not knowing where he begins or ends *to* a budding sense that the feet he sees are part of himself, and that he is a separate person.

As stated in the Foreword, children do not become social beings by accident. Let's take a look at the physical activities that support social development in infants.

Handling Your Baby

"Whenever they brought him to me in the hospital I stayed in the same position . . . for an hour or even longer. . . . I didn't dare move . . . even if I was sweating or my arm got a cramp . . . until they came to take him. . . . I just froze."

—Mother of a newborn

"I couldn't wait to hold the baby in my arms. But after forty-eight hours of rooming-in, I'd have given anything to send her back to the nursery or anywhere. The first week at home was no better. Every time she cried I tried to nurse her. She was nursing every hour on the hour, and I was beginning to wonder —what's wrong with her, or me? I guess it was a month before I felt confident about doing anything right."

—Mother of an infant

In their eagerness to do everything "right," many new parents suffer feelings of inadequacy and frustration. For many the tiny newborn may seem frighteningly fragile and an awesome responsibility. Yet as one pediatrician put it, "Relax, your baby isn't made of glass! She won't break."

It may also be some comfort to realize that not knowing what the baby wants is perfectly normal. Few of us are mind-readers. We can make educated guesses. If the baby is fretful after eating, he may have gas and need some gentle patting to burp. But what about Paul, who even after feeding, burping, and diapering, is still fussy? It could well be Paul's way of telling you that he wants more, or perhaps different, social contact. Keep in mind that what satisfies Paul doesn't always satisfy another. And even what works for your baby at 6:00 A.M. may not work at 9:00 P.M. What do you do, then? Have a variety of tricks in your repertoire, so if one doesn't work you can try another. Here are some practical ideas for you and your infant.

CUDDLING AND SNUGGLING

Some babies are natural cuddlers and snugglers. They thrive on the warmth of being held close to your body. Eye to eye, they study your face and respond to your voice and touch. Give these cuddlers plenty of physical contact. Remember, you won't be spoiling the baby. Rather you will be building a sense of security, confidence, and warm attachment that is the foundation of a child's social life.

Yet there are infants who are uncomfortable with too much physical closeness. This is probably an innate and individual preference. They may feel too restricted when they are held close, and unfortunately, parents of noncuddlers often interpret their child's squirming as a rejection of themselves. But cuddling is just one way to communicate love, warmth, and comfort to your baby. If it works, do it; if not, try other forms of contact. Noncuddlers are no less attached or dependent on their parents than cuddlers. They simply prefer visual and auditory contact to hugging. Without crowding his style, you can give such an infant a sense of belonging by bringing him into the social circle on his own terms. He may want less physical contact, but he still needs your physical presence and the contact that comes through the warm speaking, cooing, and singing voices of his primary caretakers.

HOLDING AND WALKING

Picking up a crying baby is probably the most reliable way to quiet him. It is also a great opportunity to extend his social world. Putting your baby up on your shoulder gives him a new and therefore interesting view of the world. After nine months in a dark womb, it's small wonder that he finds comfort in the familiar rhythm of being walked about, plus the added pleasure of now seeing this big new world as well.

For getting out in the world or even going about household chores, "wearing the baby" is an age-old solution.

FRONT-LOADERS. Most babies enjoy the familiar sound of your heartbeat, the warmth of your body, the motion of your footsteps; *and* you will still have both hands free. If your wiggler-squirmer seems unduly uncomfortable in such a confining space, don't force it on him. A lightweight carriage may be your best choice for mobility. But be aware that your baby still needs close and frequent contact with his primary caregiver.

BACKPACKS. These are for the older baby who can hold his head erect. For the curious child, traveling like a papoose opens new vistas—it's like going away from home without having to sacrifice the security and loving that home provides, since you are right there with him.

ROCKING AND ROLLING

A cradle that rocks or a bassinet that rolls is a great comfort when your baby is small. Research shows that infants generally respond best to rapid rocking, but you will probably be able to recognize your own child's preferred pace. Basically, it's the motion that soothes and comforts the otherwise immobile infant.

"Our four-month-old son seems to know exactly when our dinner is on the table. For him it's fussing time. Rather than eating in shifts, we found a better alternative. Instead of listening to him wail in his crib, we found a new use for the outgrown bassinet. It's perfect—I eat, with one foot rolling the bassinet back and forth. The only problem is one of my legs is getting thinner than the other."   —Mother of a four-month-old

If you have room for a carriage or access to a car, the constant motion of either can give both you and baby a change of pace and scenery.

As a long-term investment there's no piece of furniture more useful than a rocking chair. For the newborn or the teether or the lap-sitting, storybook tot, a rocker is a great place to get together.

FINDING WHAT'S RIGHT FOR YOUR BABY

For both parent and child there is a lot of trial and error (and plenty of room for the latter). Every bath will not run like a "no-more-tears" shampoo commercial. While young babies generally seem to find security and comfort in being swaddled, others seem happiest with minimal clothes to restrict them. Some sleep best on their tummies; others howl in that position. All of them have ways of letting you know.

- They can't turn themselves over, but they can let you know they're uncomfortable by kicking and fretting.
- They can't say it with words, but they can tell you through body language. An infant straining with his whole body while reaching toward a colorful crib toy is telling you, "I like that beautiful red thing. Help me touch it!"
- When they've had enough food or other stimulation, they can't say, "Gimme a break!" They can take a break by turning away or tuning out.

Gradually, parents begin to know what works best when baby is tired or gassy or fretful, or merely wants more human contact.

Although this new and exhausting business of being on call for twenty-four hours a day may seem endless, it is really a relatively short period in your child's life. After the first month or two, babies do settle down to more predictable routines and develop more readable signals.

READING BABY'S SIGNALS

Remember, too, that you're not the only one who's learning to read messages. Babies are keen detectives and pick up your attitudes of disgust or pleasure, disinterest or affection. Your manner of handling the baby is just as important as what you actually do. As you're changing diapers or playing peekaboo, your feelings are conveyed in your tone of voice, your facial expressions, and your gestures. If a parent is depressed, angry, or tense, it does not go unnoticed by the baby. In fact, researchers have found that babies become terribly upset if mothers handle them with deadpan faces. For your infant, the expression on your face speaks a thousand words. In remarkably little time an infant begins to mirror the smiles or frowns, the silence and cooing. This ability to read cues enables a baby to use your body language as a resource. Throughout infancy and the early years, you will remain a reliable reference to look to for a quick read-out on new sights, sounds, objects, or people.

Like all of us, babies get cold, hungry, achey, frightened, bored, and lonely. For an infant, the only solution to these discomforts comes by way of the people who handle him.

FEEDING TIMES

Endless as they may seem, changing diapers, rocking, bathing, and dressing the baby are short-term activities. In contrast, mealtime is an ongoing occasion that begins in infancy and continues through years. It is during infancy that fundamental attitudes about eating are served as part of every meal. Feeding is more than giving so many ounces of milk or so many spoonsful of fruit.

Right from the start, mealtime is a social situation, with a rhythm of its own. It is the infant who sets the pace and shows you when the pauses are needed. Rushing Paul or pushing in one more spoonful than he wants will generally come back to haunt you in the short or the long run. Your baby may spit up a feeding laced with tension; or you may be establishing the ground rules for small wars that are commonly called feeding problems later on.

At feeding time, the social quality of the meal is every bit as important as the quantity eaten. Even though Jackie may eat like a bird at some meals, she will usually make up for it at others. Given a well-balanced menu of choices each day, infants tend to select a nutritionally sound diet over the course of a week, without undue pressure. If your child is persistently a poor eater and does not seem to balance his diet over a period of time, talk it over with your pediatrician. Mealtime should be a relaxed, positive social occasion—not a battle of wills.

For some parents mealtime seems simple until their baby begins to try sticky-handed self-service. Messy as these meals may be, they are a positive sign of growing independence. It may help if you give your baby a spoon of her own. But finger food is more apt to find its correct destination than food that needs spooning. When you combine forces —you with a spoon, she with her fingers—mealtime evolves into a new kind of cooperative venture.

DIAPERING AND DRESSING

It may seem odd to think about diapering your baby as a social occasion. Yet it is one of those everyday activities in which you convey some very basic attitudes. If you send signals of disgust, your baby may get the idea that his body and its natural functions are repugnant or shameful. So changing time should be treated in a casual yet friendly fashion. This is a great time for tickling the tummy, or playing games, such as tweaking the baby's toes as you recite "This Little Piggy Went to Market."

Dressing the baby can also foster or foul up friendly relations. Clothing that requires too many over-the-head or arm-bending maneuvers can lead to ruffled feelings that erupt when it's time to dress. Stick to clothes that go on and off easily. Frills that rub and tiny buttons that test patience (yours and your baby's) put an unnecessary strain on everybody.

Choose clothing for ease of care and comfort in wear. That will free both you and your baby to enjoy each other. Making a big thing over staying clean may limit your laundry at the price of your baby's curiosity and independence. This is especially true as babies begin to feed themselves and become more mobile. Save the fussy dress or suit for a picture and save yourself a lot of unnecessary worrying.

BATHING

Bathtime is one of those everyday occasions when your baby has what he wants most—your undivided attention. For both of you it is an opportunity to make one-to-one contact without the usual distraction of phone calls, buzzers, and business as usual. Try to choose a normally quiet time, unplug the phone or ask someone to take messages, and insofar as possible, ensure that your baby's bathtime will not be interrupted.

If you think of baby's bath as a social activity, you can put cleanliness into proper perspective. Getting clean is merely an incidental benefit. A baby who is diapered regularly and sponged off with each change is not very dirty to begin with. He doesn't need to be overly scrubbed or rubbed. Stick to shampoos that won't sting the eyes, and if washing your baby's face makes him fret, do it later, maybe outside the tub. Remember, your baby's attitudes about soap and water last longer than the short-term benefits of any particular bath. What really counts is reading baby's signals of comfort or discomfort, and adjusting your actions accordingly.

Don't worry about buying elaborate equipment. Little babies are easier to handle on a waist-high counter in a plastic washpan, or in the kitchen sink. They don't need a tubful of warm water—a few inches is sufficient. To minimize your tension, just be sure to assemble the necessary towels, powder or lotion, and dry clothes before you begin. Test the water with your wrist or elbow. Talking and singing will help your baby relax and enjoy.

Although most babies enjoy their bath, there are some who cry no matter how, where, or when you bathe them. Parents of such babies find that the only happy solution is to get into the tub with them. The security of being in the water together does seem crucial for some babies. If this seems comfortable to you, try it. For safety's sake, put a rubber mat in the tub and a nonskid mat to step out on.

Bathtime is full of sensory experiences that are astonishing to your baby: the warmth and wetness of the water, the amazing sound and feel of splashing, the squish of a dripping sponge, the taste of a washcloth, the feeling of being wet and cold, then dry and warm, dusted and dressed—these and a game of patty-cake or a giggling round of tummy tickles are all part of the shared rituals of bathtime.

CRAWLING AND INDEPENDENCE

Once your infant starts crawling, a new world opens for exploration. No longer confined to staying where you put him, the crawler is on the way to a new kind of independence.

Now he can propel himself to things that attract his attention, but he can't tell what's safe or unsafe. So you'll need to check your home for potential dangers. While safety is the prime concern, child-proofing has a significant social dimension, too. By moving things ahead of time, you'll clear the way for curiosity and exploration, and limit the need for running negative interference.

A crawler needs more attention, and a different kind of attention, than his former less mobile self. Little Amy thrives on interested people who enjoy getting down on the floor, horsing around, and playing catch the crawler. She needs interesting objects that can be rolled, banged, lifted, and tasted. By providing space where a baby can roam safely, parents encourage the independence appropriate for the young explorer. Your baby still needs your watchful eye and a sense of your availability. In fact, babies tend to play more actively and independently when a familiar caregiver is in sight. It's as if knowing that you're nearby frees the baby from having to watch out for himself and allows him to make things happen—to dump and fill a plastic jar, creep after a rolling ball, scrunch up a piece of paper.

Obviously you can't give your child constant attention, and it wouldn't be good for him, anyway. But being within hearing or seeing range gives you a chance to recognize when direct contact is needed.

Baby Talk

From birth a baby can speak in two important and necessary ways: with her voice and her body language. Of course, these skills are not fully developed in an infant, but every day they can be improved.

CRYING AS SOCIAL COMMUNICATION

Responsible and loving parents can readily recall the shrill cries of their new offspring, accompanied by strong physical display—eyes shut tight, limbs moving or trembling, face flushed, or even purple.

The new parents' response is easy to predict: immediately rushing to the infant's side, picking her up, rocking and caressing her and murmuring softly, "There, there, honey! Daddy is here. What's the matter with Joanie? She has an old gas pain in her tummy? Or is my little sweetie hungry?"

If petting, rocking, and talking don't stop Joanie's cries, her parents can probably rely on milk to comfort her.

This event is so commonplace that we may not recognize its significance. This very new human being has sent out a strong demand, and that demand has been answered with reasonable effectiveness. That's pretty good social communication from a helpless newcomer!

Crying, then, is the first, most noticeable, and most effective pre-speech language in young babies. Experts have listed a variety of babies' cries that parents soon learn to interpret:

- the "I want company" cry
- the "I'm hungry" cry
- the "I'm thirsty" cry
- the "I'm tired or cranky" cry
- the "I'm nervous or frightened" cry
- the unexplainable cry

This last cry is the one that can be most frustrating and upsetting to new parents as they vainly try to answer it, and in the beginning there may be more "unexplainable cries" than any other kind. As time passes, a baby's cries indicate more specific needs to his caretakers. Before long the hunger cry begins to have a different sound from the "I want company" cry. The baby teaches his parents what he needs and what he wants them to do.

Whether or not you know what the cry means, *all* the baby's cries need attending. Some people still cling to the belief that it's okay to let a baby "cry it out" or that crying "will strengthen their lungs," but a brief commonsense examination of these two fallacies will show what happens if they're followed. First, a baby has no better means of communication. If his crying goes unattended, his first attempts at communication will be unanswered, setting up a barrier to any further attempts. Second, he will gradually come to mistrust his caregivers and consider them undependable and uncaring. Studies have shown that the baby whose cries go unanswered becomes the child who later seems "spoiled"—who clings to his caretaker, demands more attention, is easily distraught when things don't go smoothly. There is also evidence that such neglected children often become the adults who can never get enough attention and love, and who drive people away by unrealistic demands for affection.

Remember, you can't spoil a young baby. The more you attend to his cries, the sooner he will stop crying, and the sooner you both will be establishing real social communication.

BODY LANGUAGE AS SOCIAL COMMUNICATION

Babies' reactions evoke similar reactions from their parents. Your baby smiles and, almost invariably, you smile back. Smiling and cooing are social tools the baby uses to elicit attention and to obtain more pleasurable exchanges. It is interesting to note that although blind babies smile reflexively during the first months of life, their smiling decreases because they lack the visual reinforcement of a return smile. In contrast, babies who see learn quickly that smiles beget smiles and pleasurable attention.

Students of babies' body language have observed that the baby, not the parents, seems to set the pace and rhythm of this nonverbal give-and-take. When a baby gets tired, she usually turns her eyes or head away from the parental gaze or begins to wiggle or otherwise move. Though a father may not be conscious of this physical language from the baby, his responses change right away; he stops talking, smiling, or bouncing his daughter, though he still watches her intently. If the baby smiles again or shows other signs of wanting him to continue, he again begins the game of singing, cooing, or bouncing. Real social interchange is occuring, with the baby as the initiator. Most parents don't realize that they are learning from their baby; that they are changing their responses because of subtle signals from her; that, in fact, they are developing new parental techniques to enhance mutual social acceptance.

At other times the parent is the initiator of social intercourse, through body language or verbal language, as in this glimpse of Lynn Sutton and her eight-month-old son, Lance:

> Lynn is playing with Lance after she has finished diapering him. While she keeps up a singsong monologue, she is also using lots of body language. She smiles at Lance, widens her eyes, and

shakes her head. She makes clicking noises as she bends nearer to his smiling face. Then she buries her head in Lance's neck and blows into his folds of fat, while Lance squeals with delight. She rubs his round belly and tickles his legs.

They laugh together as Lynn surprises him with a game of peekaboo. She picks him up, holding him high, then zooms him down into her arms for a tight hug while she does a few dance steps.

Lance responds by wiggling, thrusting his arms and legs vigorously, smiling, rocking his own body back and forth, and gurgling.

Their physical communication obviously results in joyful feelings for both. But if Lynn keeps the fun going too long, Lance will let her know he's ready to quit, not only by ceasing to smile, but also by turning his head or straining away from her. Then Lynn will stop, almost as if Lance had spoken in words. A positive form of social give-and-take is already underway.

The Importance of Parent-Baby Play

Lynn Sutton's actions with Lance seem to be a spontaneous expression of her love. If she were asked why she plays with and talks to him, she'd probably answer, a little self-consciously, "Oh, I don't know. He's so cute, I just love to have fun with him."

Yet this kind of face-to-face fun, this voice-and-body engagement with the baby, is probably the most important initial step in developing a social child.

Why? Because this is the first social relationship in the baby's life. The establishment of later relationships largely depends on the quality of this one.

The baby's physical needs have been satisfied and will continue to be. Now he is experiencing the joy of shared human pleasures—the laughter, the pleasurable stimulation of the senses, the delight of surprise, the satisfaction of an interchange of human sounds—and all these happy feelings result from interaction between himself and someone else. The baby, though still self-centered, is forming a satisfying relationship with another person. He is learning the mutual feedback necessary to establish mature social relationships.

And all these important developments come from just "having fun with your baby."

Talking As Social Communication

Very soon babies and their caretakers are "talking together." This step, however, is based on the level of the previous communication in body language and sounds. Studies show that babies and parents who have already established such a dependable two-way response will start talking to each other sooner than those who haven't been as attentive to each other's signals.

Of course, the baby won't be using language for some six months or so after birth; but he will be cooing and making all kinds of verbal sounds, using most of the vowels and consonants. As parents respond eagerly and vocally to these burblings, they are setting the pattern for early verbal exchanges; replying to their babies' nonverbalizations is a natural response for most parents in our culture. Those who talk to their infants implant a kind of subliminal recognition of speech patterns, word sounds, and language rhythms, which encourages the baby's first attempts at "real" talk.

These crucial steps are accomplished in the easiest and most natural of ways. For most parents, regardless of their understanding of child psychology, talking to their baby is a routine matter, even if they sometimes feel a little foolish. One father said, "I find myself asking Joey's opinion of the league standings or the stock market, his views on the latest Oscar nominees. But I have to say that Joey seems to enjoy it; he keeps smiling and watching me, and gurgles back."

Sure, Joey enjoys this attention—one of his favorite people, pouring out a fascinating spate of sounds. He responds with pleasure, both physically and vocally. Babies are fascinated by and drawn to the sound of the human voice, and it's a good thing. For by being talked to, they learn to talk.

A sad event in the thirteenth century underlines the need for babies to be swathed in adult talk as well as in loving caresses. Emperor Frederick II wanted to discover which language newborn infants would speak if no one spoke to them first. So he conducted an experiment with a group of infants. The infants' nursemaids were ordered to provide food, warmth, and cleanliness, in complete silence. No one was to talk to, play with, smile at, or pet these unfortunate babes. Frederick's experiment ended in tragedy. Deprived of the language of loving care, none of these infants ever spoke, and all of them died. What Frederick had overlooked was the fact that from the start of life, an infant is a social being.

In more recent days, studies have shown that youngsters coming from homes where they were seldom talked to have more difficulty not only in academic skills but also in establishing early social relationships.

TALKING "MOTHERESE." Dr. Carol Tomlinson-Keasey calls the special way that parents talk to their infants "motherese." She notes that parents, especially mothers, talk in a much higher pitch than they customarily use; that they use shorter phrases, ask and answer their own questions, use baby talk, exaggerate their actions, and continually look at their child. Here's a typical example of motherese:

> *Mother:* "Want to go bye-bye, honey?" (Pause.) "Sure you do, my pitty, potty Patsy. You want to go bye-bye in Patsy's carriage—wa-a-y down to the store." (Mother puts on the baby's coat.) "Baby's arm goes in this sleeve—wa-ay, waay in." (Pause.) "Now baby's other arm in the other sleeve. In it goes, push, push, push." (Mother bends close to kiss her baby's frown.) "What's that big frown for? You don't like putting on your coat? Never mind, Mommy kiss it all away." (Buttoning coat.) "Here goes Patsy's buttons. Buttons, buttons, pop, pop, pop. Now where's Patsy's hat? Is this Patsy's hat?" (Mother holds up a shoe. Baby smiles, Mother laughs.) "No, no, this is Patsy's *shoe*. Here's Patsy's hat." (Mother puts hat on baby's head as baby frowns again, turning her head away.) "Patsy doesn't want her hat? Her pretty red hat?" (Pause.) "Sure you do. We'll put Patsy's pretty red hat right on Patsy's head." (Mother makes exaggerated facial expressions and baby laughs.)

There seems to be a natural development in the use of motherese. At first, mother—or whoever is the primary caregiver—imitates the baby's own sounds, as well as talking normally to the baby. A father reports that a favorite prespeech sound of his young son was a pretend cough—a kind of "uh-uh-uh" noise. When the father repeated this sound, his son grinned hugely. For a few weeks father and child played this game; sometimes Dad initiated it, at other times the baby began the game.

"We really had a lot of fun making this silly noise," the father said. "I know Danny enjoyed it; you should have seen his smile and the way his eyes sparkled."

This small incident also shows that motherese isn't limited to females or high-pitched voices.

How Babies and Adults Use Words. When talking to infants, most adults speak in short sentences or phrases, often just a noun and verb.

In this scene a mother is picking up her crying eight-month-old son:

> *Mother:* "Hungry? Timmy hungry? Don't cry, honey. Mommy get your bottle." (She carries son to kitchen, where she heats bottle with one hand, holding and jigging Timmy in her other arm. Timmy is still whimpering. She chants.)
>> "Pease porridge hot,
>> Pease porridge cold.
>> Pease porridge in the pot
>> Nine days old!
>
> "All done! Timmy's milk all ready." (Mother carries Timmy to chair, sits down, tests milk's temperature as she arranges Timmy on her lap.) "Ooh, milk too hot. A little too hot. A little too hot for Timmy!" (She rocks Timmy, humming and singing a nonsense song invented on the spot.)
>> "Shoo, shoo, my baby dear,
>> Milky, milky cooling now
>> Hungry baby shoo fly then
>> Almost ready now . . ."
>
> (Milk now ready, she arranges the bottle comfortably in Timmy's mouth, still rocking and humming gently as Timmy's tears cease.)

This little scene shows another important aspect of talking to your baby: reciting Mother Goose rhymes or your own. Babies respond to the lively rhythms and sounds that are reflected later in their own play with words. As Timmy grows older, he will begin to use words in a similar way; a baby's first real words are usually nouns, then he adds a verb or a word modifier.

At first, his devoted parents discern a word in his babblings. He may be burbling, "Goo-dah boo-dah, doo-dah-da-da," when his excited father yells, "Da-da! Timmy just said Da-da! He knows me! Say Da-da again, Timmy!"

Timmy usually doesn't. He still isn't linking his vocal play to specific objects. But sooner or later—perhaps stimulated by parental repetition—he will get the idea.

Similarly, he will begin to identify objects in his world—especially those objects that intrigue him: "ki-ki" (kitty), "muh" (milk), "tooey" (teddy bear). My own daughter's first and favorite word was "li" (light); just by flicking a wall switch she could plunge us into darkness or "let there be light"—great power for anyone.

First words also include verbs—usually used as commands. "Geya," Timmy would insist from his crib. "Geya"—"get up"—meant that he wanted to be taken from the crib at once. Sometimes one word serves as both noun and verb, as Timmy's "buh, buh"; translated, this meant both the noun "bath" and the verb phrase "want a bath."

As babies develop real words, as well as their own interpretations —still mostly understood only by their fond families—communication becomes more elaborate. Most parents unconsciously move to the next step and begin to talk to their baby in whole sentences, often elaborating on his one-word demand.

Sixteen-Month-Old Bobby (from his high chair, points to toy bear): "Toey. Boti toey."

Bobby's Father: "Oh, Bobby wants me to get his bear? Okay, Bobby, one bear coming up."

Bobby (throwing teddy bear on floor and grinning): "Up. Boti toey up."

Bobby's Father: "Now Bobby wants Daddy to pick up Bobby's bear, right? Okay, old man, just this once." (Father picks up bear and returns it.)

(Bobby, with a grin, tosses bear on floor again.)

Bobby's Father: "Okay, Boti, that's enough. You want your bear again, Boti-Bobby, you go get it yourself."

(Bobby's father lifts Bobby down to floor. Bobby creeps toward
bear, but flops down halfway and begins to pick up crumbs.)

Look at the social accomplishments in this short exchange. Bobby's
father translates Bobby's "toy words" (as they are called by one child
expert) into English—"toey" (teddy bear), "Boti" (Bobby)—and uses
them in sentences. Not only does he keep a two-way conversation
going, he also gives his son a lesson in social behavior. Through these
everyday, unrehearsed exchanges, parents subliminally teach social language and encourage social behavior in their offspring.

Manners in the Nursery

It's hard to make a case for manners in the nursery. Or is it? If you
think of manners as consideration, then your child's manners may start
here—with *your* manners.

There's every indication that infants' social reactions are shaped by
the way people treat them during the early months, even weeks, of life.
It follows that your own courtesy toward your child will be registered
in some way. It may be simply a matter of looking at your infant as a
person, with all the social rights that implies.

Take the matter of polite introductions, for example:

- You can't say to little Stan: "Stan, I'd like you to meet Casey,
  who'll be taking care of you while I'm away." But you can
  make sure that Stan and Casey have time to get to know each
  other before you go off to the office.
- You can't expect Paul to have a polite conversation with Aunt
  Fanny. But you can bring Paul and his relative together in a
  way that will bring out the best in both of them. You can
  protect Paul from anything that, to his little nervous system,
  is bad manners—faces too close, chucking, pinching, tickling,
  loud talk, or a smoke-filled room. If Aunt Fanny seems rude
  to you, she probably will seem so to him.
- You can't insist on table manners from tiny Awilda. But you
  can see to it that her dining table, whether it's her high chair
  or your lap, is neat, and that Awilda is clean and dry for
  mealtimes. She'll get the message that dinner and physical

comfort go together, and you'll be giving your little daughter the same courtesy you'd give any other dinner guest.

It's only polite to give baby some attention at mealtimes—even if she's the only one who's eating. If there's a family argument going on over her head while she's eating, even breast-feeding, she may get the idea that breakfast and brouhahas go together. You can't really teach babies manners, but they can learn. And infants do respond to social cues from the very earliest human contacts.

Your Baby's Expanding Social Circle

During the first year a baby's social circle centers on those who care for his daily (and nightly) needs. Although the first and most significant people in his life are his parents, they are not the only members of his social world. As the newest member of the family the newborn's arrival signals a whole new set of social relationships—as brother or sister, niece or nephew, cousin, and grandchild. All of his relatives play a part in socializing the youngest addition to the family.

SIBLINGS

"Tina was four when Jimmy was born. I worried so much about how she'd feel about not being the only one anymore. You know, would she be jealous or unhappy about having to share me? Well, I don't know why, but—so far, so good. Tina loves being the big sister. She really enjoys playing with Jimmy. To tell the truth, she's a terrific help, and Jimmy lights up when she's around."
                              —Mother of a four-year-old
                                and an eight-month-old

It's a safe bet that Tina's mom worried just enough to insure that Jimmy didn't turn Tina into a displaced person. By finding ways to encourage Tina's "help" and by allowing her to play with Jimmy, their mom enlarged the social learning for both children.

Of course, Jimmy is not a toy, and Tina doesn't always use good judgment. So it's up to Mom or Dad to protect them both. But what do we mean by protecting? In part, it means supervising and steering the way for positive encounters. Tina can't give Jimmy a bath. She can bring Mom the diapers and help pat him dry. The fact that Mom can do the whole job faster and more easily by herself is beside the point. By involving Tina, Mom is opening a door rather than shutting Tina out.

Though there is great concern about sibling rivalry and jealousy, the potential for sibling affection and exchange is often overlooked. These early months offer a rich opportunity for parents to encourage the budding relationships that siblings build through play. From Jimmy's point of view, Tina has a lot to offer by way of companionship and stimulation. She walks, talks, picks up his rattle, rolls a ball, teases, laughs, and delights in "teaching" him how to "do it right." To Tina, Jimmy is a novelty, a new "plaything" who responds to her lead.

Since they are so unequal, Tina serves as an inspiring model of competence rather than one of competition. That doesn't mean that Tina is a baby-sitter whom her parents should rely on or expect to entertain Jimmy. Tina has her own needs. Unlike Jimmy, she enjoys playing with children her own age. Like Jimmy, she needs time with Mom and Dad all to herself. And she needs time to play alone.

So Tina's and Jimmy's parents have to juggle the children's separate needs. For instance, when Tina complains about Mother's prolonged nursing time with Jimmy, there are several ways for Mother to reassure Tina:

- Telling her a story, with Tina as the heroine, while continuing to nurse Jimmy.
- Asking Tina to tell Mother a story.
- Asking Tina to draw a picture for Mother or Jimmy.
- Playing Tina's favorite records for all of them.
- Having Tina's dad do something special with her while Jimmy is nursing.

What Tina's mother should not do is to send Tina away or scold her. Parents teach more about love by their example than by long lists of dos and don'ts. If you want to see a replay of your own behavior, just watch your preschooler playing with the baby.

THE EXTENDED FAMILY

Fifty years ago a baby was likely to live with or near a good many cousins and grandparents. New parents could rely upon the extra hands and practical know-how of aunts or grandmothers. The day-to-day business of child rearing was shared, and new parents could count on the extended family for physical as well as emotional support. For the baby, these familiar faces were a first introduction to the wider world of friendly "others." They allowed him, at an early age, to learn to adjust to different expectations from different caregivers. A child's ability to accommodate to different styles was a real step up the social ladder.

Large extended families also provided a social circle of children of mixed ages. Often the slightly older child acted as an intermediary between the adult and the infant. The four-year-old, for example, might be in better contact with the preverbal messages of the baby than the adult, and thus might be able to act as an interpreter for the infant.

Today's nuclear family may have to cross a continent to make the kind of contact that our mothers and grandmothers took for granted. Even if grandparents and cousins live nearby, they're apt to have a busy schedule that does not allow for more than an occasional visit. Babies and parents still need a support system of "others," but it usually takes more effort now to establish one. Whether both parents work outside the house or one does the full-time-at-home job, parents and babies need friends who are going through similar experiences, and competent helpers who can be called on to share the care. In learning to know "others," your baby will begin to understand that there are others who can be trusted to care for him and read his signals. This knowledge does not diminish the importance of that special relationship between you and your child. Rather, it extends the child's view of people and himself.

SITTERS AND OTHER STRANGERS

"Mindy was so friendly. Until a few weeks ago she'd go to anyone who held out his arms. . . . She smiled at strangers in the grocery store and anyone who came visiting. Only now, it's

odd. She's so shy and clingy. Even people she's known, like my mother or sister, seem to worry her. It's so strange."
                                        —Mother of an eight-month-old

Actually, Mindy's behavior isn't strange at all. Babies between six and eight months old frequently become less outgoing than they were just weeks before. Even the sight of a semifamiliar person can set the chin aquiver. A total stranger can start a storm. Mindy has reached a developmental landmark. Now she knows one person from another, and she has very definite preferences. People are no longer interchangeable. Her attachment to Mom or Dad is the outgrowth of a process that has evolved slowly through the first half-year, a day-to-day dialogue that they have learned together. Mindy is not just "used" to Mom, she depends on Mom as a reference point to understand the world. At three months, if Mom was out of sight, she was also out of mind. Now, although Mom may be out of sight she is remembered. When Mindy cries for attention, she cries for the attention of this very special person who is her protector, playmate, provider of life's pleasures. Whereas the newborn Mindy cried and sucked and cried again until food magically filled the void, now she anticipates both the food and the special magician who feeds, holds, and talks to her. Mother is no longer merely an extension of Mindy's own body, but a separate being. It is at this stage that Mindy begins to develop a sense of herself and others. Indeed, her own identity grows out of this first and significant loving relationship. Small wonder, then, that this special bond between Mindy and her mom now overshadows all others.

Yet child experts are beginning to recognize that this attachment behavior is not exclusively reserved for Mom. Increasingly, fathers are taking a more active role as infant caregivers. Although nursing an infant falls within its mother's province, fathers can nourish the newborn's hunger for tender loving care. Holding, rocking, talking, massaging, bathing, singing, and playing are just a few ways a father can interact with his baby right from the start. In part, the possibilities for building the father-child relationship are based on a willingness of both parents. Not only does Dad need to make and take the time, but Mom needs to support his involvement. Too often there's a hiatus between the togetherness in the delivery room and the new father's hands-on experience with the newborn. Even if Mom is the primary caregiver, Dad needs opportunities to handle the baby with confidence.

With the growing bonds of trust and attachment there are moments when Mindy may prefer one parent over another. Sometimes it may be Mother, other times Dad. It's not a question of one person's being more competent than another, but rather both parents' reading baby's cues and responding as caring adults. Infants who have consistent and ongoing relationships with others form meaningful attachments to more than one caring adult. Fathers, older brothers or sisters, a grandparent or next-door neighbor are among those with whom the infant may develop a special, trusting relationship. They can develop an intimate dialogue of sending and reading signals.

It is the arrival of an occasional visitor or a new babysitter that often represents a real threat to eight-month-old Mindy. This is especially true of those well-meaning people who rush in oohing and aahing. Like all of us, infants don't like being crowded or having their own personal space invaded—no matter what the intentions of the invader. Grownups don't generally do this to other grownups, but they may think nothing of rushing in on an infant's territory.

Parents can avoid crises or make them manageable by respecting the infant's inexperience and introducing new faces gradually. Invite a new sitter to arrive an extra hour or two before you're planning to leave—give the baby a chance to get acquainted instead of hysterical.

If you're planning to go back to work either full or part time, it might be better to do so somewhat before or after this period of intense attachment behavior. What seems to matter most is finding an arrangement that is warm, comfortable, and consistent. Whether you have a sitter in your home or take your baby to a daycare center, the most significant ingredient will be consistency. Babies just don't thrive when they're faced with a constantly changing cast of people in their social circle. (For a fuller discussion of daycare for infants and toddlers see Chapter 4.)

Getting Out in the World

LITTLE TRIPS

Getting out together is beneficial for both you and your baby. You might call it preventive medicine against cabin fever. Like all of us, babies get bored and fretful in the confines and isolation of home. Trips to the grocery store, the mailbox, the park, or a friend's house all fall under the heading of little trips with big pay-offs.

With its new sights, sounds, and faces, the world outside is full of fascination for your curious baby. She can't name the truck, bus, or dog that she points to, but you can. Sharing these adventures enlarges the dialogue you're building. Long before your baby talks she understands a great deal. It is from such understanding and experiences that words and new ideas flow. And your active style represents a model for living. If you don't want a preschooler glued to the television set, this is the time for turning your infant's interests toward a more active life style.

Big Trips

Out of necessity or by choice a long-distance trip may be on your agenda. Sometimes you don't have the option of bringing along an infant. You may need to hire someone to stay with your baby, or you may have to leave her with an aunt or grandmother. But when there is a choice, what then? Should you take your infant on a big trip, or is she better off at home?

In most cases the answer is simple. To your baby, *you* are home. Your prolonged absence may represent a true loss and anxiety to her. On an infant's timetable a few days is a long time. If you're going on vacation, you may be more relaxed with the baby than worrying about her at long distance.

In many ways traveling with an infant is easier than most people think. Unlike older kids they can't take off in opposite directions or keep asking, "Are we there yet?" Although their everyday routine may be disrupted, infants are pretty flexible and are hardy travelers. Given the probability of waits at the airport, missed connections, and other minor discomforts, the first thing to do is try to control your own anxiety. If you start to worry, little Sarah's going to see it on your face and hear it in your tone. It's through you that she interprets what's going on.

Taking trips with infants demands a certain amount of planning and discipline. If your baby still has to be carried, you are, by definition, no longer "traveling light." But you can limit the other things you carry to the real necessities. Unless you're going to a remote retreat, you'll be able to replace supplies as you go, instead of carrying surplus weight. Forget about economy-size packages—you don't want to carry them. On the other hand, if your baby is attached to a particular blanket or toy, don't leave home without it. It may make a wait at the airport or a strange crib a lot cozier. You'll also need some small snacks, damp clean-up towels, and enough diapers for a little more than normal consumption. That way you're covered for all emergencies.

Freed from your daily routine at home, you'll probably be spending more time together than usual. Family vacations give working parents and their children unique opportunities to share some special hours and experiences. It doesn't mean you have to do everything together all the time. In fact, it might be an ideal chance for some one-to-one outings with the infant, when one parent takes over and gives the other a bit of time alone. Splitting up during the day can be refreshing for everyone on a family holiday. Don't overlook the possibility, too, of an evening out just for grownups. Most resorts have bonded babysitters, who will cover you while you spend a few hours of free time without your young traveling companion.

Traveling as a family may limit where you can go and the kinds of things you can do. Having your baby along may make it different, but it needn't curtail your fun.

Toys

To your baby there is nothing more interesting than people. Indeed, you are your baby's first and favorite plaything and it is also you who will introduce him to the world of things.

Long before infants can reach out and take hold of playthings, they are ready for the sights and sounds that toys provide. Naturally you will have to activate the rattle, music box, and fuzzy bear. Such toys bring a new dimension to your shared games.

Studies show that infants' interest in objects is rather short-lived. What attracts them is the novelty of sounds, sights, and textures. Bright colors and interesting sounds give the baby something stimulating to focus on and eventually to reach out and touch. For babies who are usually confined to the horizontal position, a change of crib toys adds new interest to a limited view of the world.

As your infant's physical skills grow, so will his interest in playthings that he can activate, chomp on, and bang. Dolls that squeak, balls that roll and chime, mirrors that smile back, all add elements of surprise and interest. Some of the best playthings are not toy-store items at all. A spoon and an unbreakable bowl, a set of measuring cups, little boxes that open and close, paper bags and old magazines, or a box of facial tissues can be almost endlessly fascinating to a baby. For bathtime there are all sorts of playthings that make it fun. A sponge, washcloth, cups for filling and spilling, a funnel or rubber duck, will help your child look forward to baths.

With a baby's growing ability to play with toys and other objects comes a new pleasure in playing alone. Playing independently should not be overlooked as one of many important social skills that your baby is learning. It doesn't mean you should expect him to amuse himself for long. But you can encourage limited solo play by choosing toys that are easily activated and rewarding.

Try to avoid leaving all the toys out at once. Too many choices may actually clog up the baby's active play. Better to keep some toys out of sight and change the available items from time to time. Try mixing a few new items with some familiar ones. That will extend the novelty and appeal of your baby's playthings without disorienting him.

Take the time to introduce new toys by playing a little game together. A baby may taste, turn, or bang a toy and then ignore it. Give the baby time to investigate, and use a new toy for a while. Take your cue from there. You don't have to give "right and wrong" lessons, but you can spark babies' interest by building a tower and knocking it down, or filling a box and dumping it out. Showing your baby some of the things that he can do with the toy may enlarge the potential for both independent and social play.

Many babies have more toys than they need. Don't lose your baby in an overcrowded crib. The best-stocked nursery is no substitute for people. Toys alone do not lead automatically to play. Toys are merely the tools that can enrich your infant's social life. During these early months you remain the favorite and most essential ingredient of play.

The First Birthday

Your baby's first birthday is a time to celebrate. In just twelve months you've probably celebrated many first and significant events—the first smile, tooth, the first time your baby sat up alone, his first word, and maybe even his first steps!

Looking back, you can sense how far you've come together—creating a loving dialogue that grows fuller and richer each day. By now your one-year-old is very much a member of the family. Indeed, if he is your first, he has changed a couple into a family. So make this birthday an intimate family affair—no need for a crowd, which could distract rather than delight a baby. If neighbors or a few relatives want to share the occasion, however, you could invite them in for a friendly cup of tea. If they're bringing along tots of their own, don't expect too much in the way of social interaction. Babies of this age are more apt to watch or reach out to investigate each other rather than play together. Keeping the party short and small cuts down on the need for restrictions and rescue missions between small grabbers and jabbers.

Most often the birthday is celebrated as an intimate family supper. Keep the menu simple; a family feast of finger foods gives the nod to independence and gives everyone an equal hand on things. Get out the camera for that traditional hands-in-the-frosting shapshot. Today's pictures are a piece of your child's social history, a memento of a day your child may not remember, but one you'll all enjoy looking back on in years to come.

As your baby moves toward toddlerhood, he has developed from a small being who didn't even know himself as a separate entity, to an increasingly competent person with effective methods of communication. And how did this seemingly miraculous change occur? Partly from his enormous physical and mental growth; partly from his increasing exploration and knowledge of objects and beings in the environment; and partly—perhaps most of all—from mutual communication with his primary caregivers. The first two methods alone don't seem to help the baby develop to his or her fullest potential; it is the loving care and communication between baby and parent that are essential in establishing the best foundation for raising a social child.

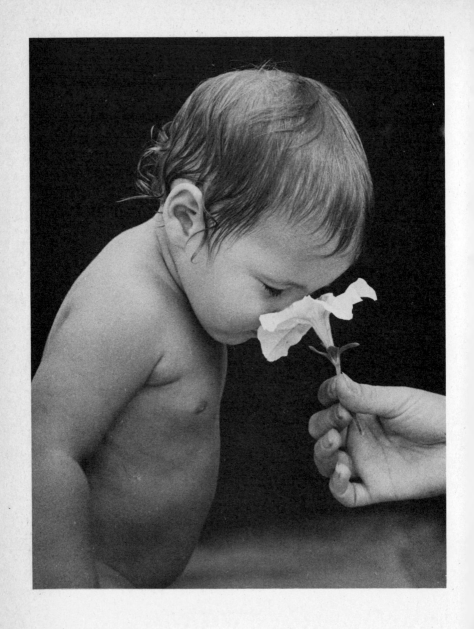

3

Toddlers

EIGHTEEN MONTHS TO THREE YEARS OLD

What They're Like

MOTORS RUNNING

Upright and eager, toddlers have a heady view of themselves and the world. They're no longer totally dependent on other people for getting around, and so they sometimes seem almost drunk with power and love of motion.

Small children take frequent tumbles, which usually do little damage. But in spite of spills, they'll persist in getting on top of, underneath, and into everything. Call them and they run in the opposite direction. It's not that they don't hear you, but rather that they can't yet fully relate what you're saying to what they're doing. They simply expect obstacles to move out of their way, and they're sometimes not quite sure how to turn off their own motors.

This lack of understanding of cause and effect shows itself in other ways, too. That lovely piece of china is in jeopardy if it's within reach, because toddling Harry does not know that china breaks, even though his ball bounces. It will be a while before he understands, even if you tell him over and over again. That's why child-proofing the house works better with this age group than saying "no" or "don't touch."

EXPECT THEM TO BE SASSY

Along with the power of locomotion, your toddler may acquire more mouth power—that is, she may be slightly sassy in asserting her new-found, separate self. Though her command of language is limited, she seems to learn "no" long before she learns "yes." In fact, she often says no when she means yes. That can test the limits of a parent's patience and will, and that's the basis for the name "terrible twos." Some of the impatience, though, may evaporate if Mom and Dad can focus on the positives.

Along with his sassiness, the toddler often tends to be less cuddly and demonstrative. It's almost as if there's no time now for mushy stuff. A quick hug and kiss may be tolerated, but a game of chase and catch is much preferred. Grandma and Grandpa will just have to understand that it isn't a breach of manners on Greg's part if he sometimes squirms out of their tender embraces. For a time, long lap sessions may be too restrictive, but this will change. Greg will be back for hugs; meanwhile he's learning that he has some choice about when to have them and with whom.

They Love Ritual and Instant Gratification

What your toddler wants, he wants now, and waiting seems unreasonable to him. This is clear when he gets dressed, takes a bath, goes to bed, and in almost every other activity. Transitions seem to be the worst. Any shift from one activity or place to another can give rise to loud protests and attempts to escape. It's almost as if the toddler is saying, "Hey, give me a break. I just got used to this routine and now you want me to do something else."

Preparing the child with a short announcement of what comes next often softens the way. You might say, "When you hear the water running, it will be bathtime." This gives the toddler a brief time to adjust to a new activity and smooths the transition. Sometimes this works. At other times, firm picking up and carrying is the only solution. At this age a youngster is still not ready to learn to go gracefully from one daily activity to another. This part of becoming social involves *timing*. And the toddler's timing is still off.

But there are advantages to the two-year-old's new habits. Repetition of routine is what the toddler loves. You can sing the same song before bedtime for weeks or go through the same bedtime ritual and only you will be bored. Tots thrive on the predictability of small daytime events and, in the absence of ritual, will establish some of their own. Lining up dolls in precise order, the same sequence of events at bedtime and bathtime—these are things that toddlers crave. What is the reason for this insistence on order? It's the way that toddlers begin to piece together the who, where, what, how, and why of their lives. Repetition helps them make social order out of a big, confusing world.

WHAT THEY CAN DO VS. WHAT THEY WANT TO DO

Again and again in the course of a day, the toddler runs head-on into things he can't quite do. He can take his clothes off, but getting them on is too hard. He can see what he wants, but he doesn't know the word for it. He can take a puzzle apart, but he can't put it back together. Faced with two choices, he can't make up his mind which one he wants. One minute he's full of bravado, the next he's a clinging vine. Being small and young can be both infuriating and frustrating. A toddler is just old enough to sense how many things he doesn't know and can't do. That's why temper tantrums are so common in this age group.

The bright side is that many of the tantrums will pass when the child's ability to communicate with words begins to match her ability to understand, and when she can do more of the things she wants to do. For now what the toddler needs most are caring adults who can help her complete a task and can make educated guesses about her needs and desires. We'll try to help you do that.

How They Learn

Looking, listening, touching, tasting, sniffing, banging, turning things over—this is what toddlers do. They use every sense they have to help them understand the world. It is how toddlers learn, and they are willing to practice their skills over and over again. This is what Piaget refers to as the Sensory-Motor Period, and it is an extension of behavior that began in infancy. In the early part of toddlerhood everything must still pass the mouth test. Because of this, toddlers need supervision as well as an atmosphere that's conducive to safe exploration. They need adults who are attentive without hovering, and ready to share a child's enthusiasm and discoveries. But they also need moms and dads who, at the same time that they're preventing inappropriate behavior, can instruct. If you say, "Sand is not for eating. Sand is for playing," you are giving a sound piece of information as well as cautioning them. You are also avoiding the repetitive "No, no," which often becomes ineffective.

As a toddler approaches the age of three (sometimes earlier, sometimes later) his random exploration and his direct action with objects become increasingly modified. He develops some simple skills, especially in the area of eye-hand coordination. He puts the blocks one on top of another. He puts the simple puzzle together. He is taking another step—what psychologist Burton White calls "learning to learn."

WORD POWER

Once most toddlers get the hang of walking, they're ready for more talking. At fourteen months Sally may have had a vocabulary of four or five words. But by twenty-one months she'll probably be asking, "What dat?" and by thirty-six months she'll be talking up a storm.

To a child of two and even three, words are not used solely for communication with other people. Toddlers often *play* with them:

> Stevie toddles over to the stove and reaches up as if to touch it. "No, no. Stevie no touch. Never. Never," he tells himself.

But a characteristic of this monologue is that the toddler may not obey his own words. Parents can help toddlers with this difficult task of following verbal instruction by reinforcing what a child is saying and adding to it when it helps make the action clearer:

> "That's right. Never, never on the stove. No hands. Hot stove." You might even help the child understand by holding his hands away. "Let's take the hands away. Far, far away from the hot, hot stove."

Action helps make language more meaningful to a young child. And even though action may not always coordinate with words at first, it's a promising sign that another form of socialization (with lots of help from you) is sliding into place.

There is a rich variation in the style of learning language among any group of two-year-olds. For example:

- Melanie understands everything, but she doesn't talk.
- Greg spoke his first word at a year and is now speaking in full sentences.

- Danny says a few words and babbles a lot.
- Gerri not only speaks clearly but also sings and recites simple rhymes.
- Alan never stopped talking from the moment he learned his first word!

What do these examples tell us? Simply that all these children are learning to talk but not in the same way or at the same rate.

Some children seem to need to listen for a longer time before they actually start using language in a more than tentative way. Other children readily make the switch from grunting and pointing to indicating their wants clearly in speech. But regardless of their style, all children seem to recognize the power of this particular social skill.

Encouraging Language as a Social Tool

Parents and caregivers who engage in wordplay with toddlers provide a big helping hand in the complex game of sorting out the thousands of parts of language that we use automatically but may not even know the names of.

For example, listen to this father sitting on the bus with his almost three-year-old:

Bruce (pointing to a bus sign): "That lady drinking."
Dad: "Yes, the lady is drinking. What's she drinking from?"
Bruce: "Cup."
Dad: "That's right, the lady's drinking from a cup. Maybe she's drinking coffee."
Bruce: "I don't like coffee."
Dad: "I know you don't like coffee. Who likes coffee? Does the baby like coffee?"
Bruce (clearly enjoying the joke): "Nooooo! Baby not like coffee."
Dad: "What do babies like?"
Bruce: "Babies like milk." (Ponders for a minute.) "Baby don't drink from cup. Noooo!"
Dad: "Nooo!" (Both shake their heads.)
Bruce: "Coffee-offee coffee-offee." (Then, getting restless): "Brucie down." (As Dad releases him): "I down."

Just think what this conversation contains: a bit of verb conjugation (I like, you like, she likes); a little question-and-answer practice (Who likes coffee? What do babies like?); even a little nonsense (Does a baby like coffee?). Though this may seem like a low-level conference between Bruce and Dad, it really isn't. Dad and son are passing back and forth some models of language that will be stored in Bruce's memory bank. It's not so much that this particular conversation is memorable, but that the concepts that are being practiced are vital. Within the framework of these seemingly trivial exchanges some of the bases of social intercourse—conversation, exchange of ideas—start to grow. When looked at this way, they're extremely important.

You can help the process along in many ways. And it's not necessary with toddlers to keep your own language as simple as theirs. For instance, when Debby says, "Want shoes," Mom can say, "Yes, you want me to get your shoes." That way she models a whole sentence for Debby. It doesn't mean that everything has to become a lesson, or that children should be harassed or embarrassed because they say "he" for "she" or call spaghetti "pisketti." Too much correction may actually impede the learning of grammar, which is built on a certain amount of trial and error.

PLAYING WITH WORDS

Part of learning language also involves playing with words. Noisy shouting of words, silliness, is all part of the game. Youngsters will often mimic one another in what may seem to adults like nonsensical or annoying ways. A little tolerance may be in order and may prove easier to acquire if you realize that this playing with words is part of learning too.

At the toddler stage, talk gradually takes the place of some body language. The pointing and grunting that were so common in babyhood give way to asking for "apple"; which at some point is replaced by "Stevie wants a apple"; then, "I want a apple"; followed by "I want an apple, please"; and finally, "Thank you."

Playing simple word games with your toddler can enhance his word power. Remember that the strongest appeal to him is repetition. So choose some of the well-known fairy or folk tales that have recurring refrains that the toddler can repeat. "The Little Red Hen" is a favorite, with its short, constantly repeated, "Not I!" phrase that all the animals shout when the Little Red Hen asks them to help. Toddlers will also love the hen's final remark about who shall eat the bread, and with the slightest encouragement, they will enthusiastically supply the line "All by myself!"

A favorite phrase such as "all by myself" can then become the springboard for a word game in which both parent and child participate. Try naming the things your toddler can do "all by himself." For instance:

> *Parent:* "Tom can put on his cap."
> *Child:* "All by myself."
> *Parent:* "Tom can ride his toy car."
> *Child:* "All by myself."
> *Parent:* "Tom can throw his ball."
> *Child:* "All by myself."

The same kind of participatory interplay can also be used with nursery rhymes that your toddler has heard since babyhood. Pause at the end of "This Little Piggy Went to Market," and encourage the toddler to finish the rhyme with "... wee! wee! wee! all the way home."

THE LANGUAGE OF MANNERS

What about the language of manners? While we said earlier that consideration is not in the toddler's province, there's no harm in encouraging good manners. If your toddler's talk interrupts a conversation, you might say, "Just a minute, please. Someone else is talking." If he accidentally walks into someone, try, "If you bump into someone, you need to say, 'Excuse me.' "

It's hard to make specific prescriptions for developing good verbal manners in toddlers, because much depends on what your own family's customs are. Chances are if you verbalize good manners in your household, your child will mimic you. If it becomes a habit, all the better. And although you can't make a big issue of polite phrases at this age, you certainly can begin to implant a vocabulary of respect. The deeper social feelings will "set" in later years.

One thing you are sure to realize is that out of the mouths of babes can come both wisdom and embarrassment. Sometimes it's simply a matter of a tot hearing something not intended for his ears. He'll pick it up and shout it out. He figures all words are there to be spoken, and will be totally surprised if told otherwise. In fact, a toddler's use of four-letter words is quite innocent and even sometimes amusing. What probably captivates us is the absurdity of a small person using such a "grown-up" word. But it's a mistake to give young Betsy or Bill the idea that it's cute. If you do, you may be embarrassed in the shopping mall or humiliated at the next family party. At the same time, you have to remember that no toddler will understand that he's not to say what he hears Mom say every time she can't find her keys.

Sometimes toddlers pick up nasty words from an older sibling. They will try "talking tough." Sometimes they even learn these harsh or scolding phrases from their parents. Every family has to have its own standards about where word-freedom ends, and those standards have to be applied to everyone.

What about embarrassing truths? What do you do if what your child says makes your toes curl?

"That man has a big nose."

"Grandma, I don't like you."

Conversations of this kind are par for the course among two- and three-year-olds. They're socially unnerving for parents, but they don't mean that your child is rude so much as young. The best way to deal with inappropriate remarks at this age is to try to anticipate them, if you can. Head off the conversation if possible. Take the case of Joan Stein:

> Joan was in a bus with her toddler, Ronny, when a crippled man boarded it. Joan's heart sank, for she knew Ronny's propensity for loudly blurting out comments on any unusual-looking person. Quickly she said, "Look out the window, Ronny! Is there anything in that toy store you really like?" Ronny's attention was momentarily diverted while the man found a seat.

Joan could also have called his attention to anything else outside the bus that would have interested Ronny.

She might also have considered being straight with him: "There's a crippled man getting on the bus, Ronny, but I don't want you to say anything out loud about him right now—it might hurt his feelings. Later we can talk if you want to."

If this doesn't work, you can apologize for your toddler:

Small Marietta and her father stopped as usual to buy the morning paper at Mrs. Barnard's newsstand. As they left, Mrs. Barnard called, "Good-bye, now, Mr. C. Good-bye, Marietta, darling!" To which Marietta replied, "Good-bye, Fatso!" Mrs. Barnard gasped and stopped smiling.

Marietta's father said, "Please don't be offended, Mrs. B. That's Marietta's favorite word lately, but she doesn't know what it means. She sure didn't mean to be impolite, because she really likes you."

When toddlers get a bit older, you can explain more to them about how certain words hurt people's feelings. Keep in mind Margaret Mead's comforting statement "All children are immigrants. They must learn the customs of the tribe."

PATTERNS OF COMMUNICATION

Children who are talked to frequently learn to talk at an earlier age than children who aren't.

Children whose parents communicate richly tend to communicate that way themselves.

Children who are introduced to books early acquire a love of stories and the spoken word and often learn to read more easily than children who aren't exposed to books.

And children seem to learn better in a fairly quiet environment. Communication is not as effective when shouted over the sound of the TV or stereo, or in a hectic and noisy room.

As toddlers gain command of a vocabulary, they can be more at ease socially. Studies show that children start learning and imitating language in infancy. By the time they are toddlers, they understand many more words than they can say. The more they can command words, the less hitting and biting you can expect. They are less likely to be frustrated into temper tantrums because of an inability to say what's bothering them or what they want. Nor is this new-found facility with words a one-way street. With it comes a broader understanding of their parents' language, an increased ability to comprehend what other people say.

The acquisition of language is probably the most significant milestone in the socialization process. Parents instinctively understand its importance, which may be why a child's first words are always remembered and sometimes even recorded formally in a family album or diary. We recognize that with language the toddler opens up a totally new avenue of social interaction between himself and the world.

How They Play

When Janie was a baby, she learned how to play. Her first playmates were her parents and caregivers (peek-a-boo, "This Little Piggy Went to Market"). She also learned to play by herself (shake that rattle, roll that ball). Later she learned to play alone for longer periods of time, and played more complicated games with parents, siblings, and caregivers. At eighteen months she played fetch-and-drop, dragged a pull toy, and could manage some very simple play with blocks. Now, at two, she's getting out more. What's happening to Janie's play habits now?

SIDE-BY-SIDE PLAY

In the park or at the beach the less-than-three-year-old spends a good deal of time watching other children. When she's at ease with the kids around her, she may do some of what we call "lateral play." She'll play side by side with someone without actually playing *with* him. Playing side by side represents the threshold of becoming socialized. Toddlers need to go through this preliminary step before learning to share, take turns, and play cooperatively. Tots in the same room are more likely to poke, grab, or ignore each other than to play together. They tend to treat others more like objects than like people, so adults should monitor the scene. Snatched toys must be returned, and biting must be forbidden. But when rules are broken, don't try to teach your child by delivering a long lecture. Toddlers respond better to actions. Say, "David, Mack needs his truck. Thank you," and deliver the vehicle to its owner. You want to interrupt the play as little as possible.

BEYOND SOLITARY PLAY

In their play, toddlers often seem to be imitating social skills, as if their play were practice for life. And so it is.

Some of their games advance the cause of sociability quite directly. For example, a two- or three-year-old may invent a typical game of rough-and-tumble. It may have been first modeled by a parent—tossing her in the air, swinging her, and romping on the floor with her at an earlier time. Now in toddlerhood she may initiate a similar tussling roughhouse play with Mom and Dad, with a tolerant older sibling or sitter, or even with a good-natured family dog. Later she may take her rough-and-tumble play to the playground or to the daycare center, where, in many versions of games of roughhouse, toddlers discover the limits of one another's tolerance.

Chase-and-catch, too, is often first modeled by a parent. "I'm gonna ... get you!" says Dad, laughing and feigning a lunge as his baby scoots across the floor. Later, when the toddler is upright, she may play the same game. This sometimes aimless running away is channeled, fine-tuned, and brought under control through games of chase-and-catch. In this kind of play, encouraged by thoughtful caregivers, toddlers learn how to make their bodies do what they want them to. They practice how to unleash their physical energies and how to control them.

Simple games of hide-and-seek seem to be invented by parents and children in every culture, perhaps as another way of exploring certain social concepts. What started with peekaboo in infancy now takes a more elaborate form in toddlerhood. Two-year-old Josh hides from Grandpa by burying his head in the sofa cushion. Never mind that the rest of Josh is showing. He still doesn't know that just because he can't see Grandpa, it doesn't mean that Grandpa can't see him. By three he'll be hiding his whole body behind the curtain or in the shower, and by five or six he'll be a veteran hide-and-seek player.

The importance of game-playing is that it is a giant step beyond solitary play. Young Josh is either hiding from or finding someone else. He is learning about interaction.

In the spontaneous games of follow-the-leader that spring up in the playground or at the daycare center, toddlers begin to copy their peers as well as their parents. In the process they learn a great deal—how to observe and mimic an action, as well as how to invent and control one.

The playground and the sandbox are the social testing grounds for toddlers. It's here that they use their newly acquired physical and verbal skills to play games and to deal with their peers on a social level that involves a certain amount of give-and-take.

A supervising adult can encourage these sociable games and, if they get out of hand, act as gentle referee or steer the activity in another direction. For example:

> Two toddlers, Barry and Rose, are about to get into a fight over a dump truck. Rose's dad, seeing the fight coming, says, "I think there are two swings over there waiting for Barry and Rose. Let's go!"

Or, should the dump-truck fracas escalate too much, the following scenario might be useful:

> Rose's dad says, "Barry, that truck belongs to Rose. She *needs* it. You'll have to give it back to her."

If Barry doesn't return the truck, Rose's dad gently takes it from him, providing a little social lesson in property rights.

EARLY MAKE-BELIEVE

As they approach three, toddlers begin to act out little scenes of make-believe. They play by themselves, with a sibling, or with a pet. The simplest objects will often serve as props; what the child invests them with is what makes the play so creative and invaluable for her growth.

- Here's Althea, pretending she's a fierce crocodile.
- There's Jason, giving the patient Labrador a bottle.
- There's David, tenderly fixing his big brother's imaginary scrape with a Band-Aid.
- Here's Betty, flying with wings made from a towel.

There seems no end to this magical make-believe, and the presence of other children or pets enriches it. Even though the decibel level may not be pleasing at times, and even though there may be incidents that require intervention, the value of imaginative play with peers far outweighs its negatives.

As tots pretend to shave, drive a car, cook dinner, or read a magazine, parents can see themselves and their actions from a toddler's-eye view. Through imitation toddlers try out their understanding of the world, and practice their interactions with others. You can encourage your child's exploration of the adult world by buying a child-sized vacuum cleaner or a tiny tea set. You can also involve your toddler in the real household activities. Much is learned through helping Daddy set the table or handing Mommy the measuring spoons and pans. It gives the toddler a sense of being part of the family and of doing real things. And encouragement is vital.

There's much more likelihood that this type of play will take place if the tools are at hand. So wise parents will make them available whenever possible. They don't have to be expensive or complicated. How about a kitchen drawer that contains Sarah's or Sam's own set of measuring spoons, nesting cups, and unbreakable mini bowls? Or a corner of the broom closet with a mini set of clean-up implements?

Providing the wherewithal is only part of the story. The other part is patience; being sanguine when most of the cooking goes on the floor, and being reassuring while your "helper" does the sweep up "all by myself." Don't expect too much from your toddler who's exploring the play of housework. Just because Todd is willing to help you dust a table doesn't mean that he's ready to have the sole responsibility for putting away his toys. This is the time, though, to begin to play cleaning-up-the-toys with him, both in his room and when he's visiting, thus setting another piece of social behavior in motion.

Dressing and Undressing

Dressing independently is another great social step in a child's life, but keep in mind that undressing usually comes first, and that your child probably won't have perfected the art until he's five. Amy, an eighteen-month-old, worked and worked until she got her socks off. Stan, a two-year-old, startled the sitter by stripping right down to his diaper within ten minutes of the time he was put to bed. Bette, a two-and-a-half-year old, proudly put her shoes on—but couldn't tie the laces, so she kicked them off again and cried.

Different children, different rates of growth in the dressing area. At a year and a half, the beginning of our toddler frame, a child usually cannot control his movements enough to dress independently. A two-year-old may be able to take simple items of clothing off. Another child, six months older, may abandon all attempts to dress or undress and then return to them at a later date.

The question is, how can parents work with these and other normal growth patterns to facilitate dexterity in dressing?

- By showing how to do it. If your youngster wants to try pulling on his trousers, give him some help and maybe even a short explanation: "First we sit down; then put one leg in like this; then the other leg like this; then stand up and *pull*."
- By buying clothes that are simple to put on and take off. Elastic-top pants, slip-on shoes, and zipper-neck shirts make it easy for a toddler to begin to dress on his own. You might also want to buy one of those play boards that have zippers that open and close, buttons to button and shoes to tie. Or you can let your toddler practice on his own clothes.
- By allowing your toddler to try. If you rush in with help right away, you may turn off his urge to do it himself.
- By making allowances. The shirt may go on backwards. The zipper may get stuck. The shoes may be on the wrong feet. Don't laugh or ridicule. It's better to praise what was done right.

Appreciate the fact that your toddler (and later your three- and four-year-old) is trying his best, and that it's most important that he continue to want to try.

Toileting

Using the toilet is one way in which a child leaves babyhood behind, taking on another of civilization's social conventions. The toddler who gains this control over bodily functions enjoys her mastery.

How does the parent benefit? Liberation from diapers and disposal duty; pleasure in the fact that young Matthew or Michel looks better, smells better, and is much more welcome on anyone's lap.

Maybe it's the anticipation of that liberation that sometimes makes parents try to speed the process up a bit. And maybe that's why some children may feel too much pressure to perform on the potty, pressure that can get in the way of their normal mastery of bladder and bowel.

Dr. Berry Brazelton, chief of the Child Development unit at Boston Children's Hospital Medical Center, finds that children train themselves at an average age of twenty-eight months. This doesn't mean that toilet training can't happen earlier or later, but just that it's *around* this time that most children become trained.

In fact, there seems to be an optimum time for starting toilet training. Before the big social step come some smaller ones. Does your toddler know how to wash her hands and brush her teeth? Does she know what bathrooms are for? Has she seen other people performing bathroom functions, and has she tried to imitate them? If you've answered yes to these questions, your toddler is probably ready for a potty seat.

This is the time to make one available and to encourage her to sit on it at least once a day, first with clothes on, later without. Cheer if something comes of the sit-down; don't pout if it doesn't. After she gets used to the once-a-day routine, you might try the same thing a few times a day. One way to increase your chances of success, and hers, is to have the sittings coincide with her usual elimination time. Try to pay attention to her schedule in the weeks before you start the toilet training.

If the child has used the potty seat successfully for a few weeks, training pants are the next step. But don't try to put them on your toddler too soon or young Debby or Dan may have an accident and be so mortified or uncomfortable that further progress will be hampered. Be cheerful about mistakes and steps backwards. Remember that urine control usually comes before bowel control, and that daytime training is accomplished sooner than nighttime. Don't be afraid to leave diapers on at naptime and at night for a while. On the other hand, don't let the convenience of disposable diapers lull you into using them after their time has passed, or you may unwittingly prolong the training period.

Sooner or later everything will occur in the proper place. Most kids acquire this elegant piece of social behavior around the beginning of the third year. It usually takes boys longer than girls, and there may be a temporary setback for either one if a new baby or other big event occurs in the household. You can help your child over temporary loss of bladder or bowel control best by neither over- nor underreacting to it. Once a child gets used to being toilet trained, wet or soiled garments are both humiliating and uncomfortable. Help him get clean and dry as quickly as possible. Show sympathy and interest: "You must be uncomfortable, poor fellow." If he cries about it, soothe him. Treat it as an unfortunate happening, but not a tragedy.

Sometimes offering a specific remedy helps overcome embarrassment, such as, "How about if you try not drinking water or juice before bedtime?" Sometimes eliminating a last glass of water or a nighttime bottle does the trick.

One more caution: don't wake your child for a trip to the toilet. The less pressured children feel, the more easily they learn this new skill. Waking them up tends to make them more anxious than they need to be.

Temper Tantrums

"She goes to pieces so completely!"

How well all parents know this feeling. Mom suspects it's a plot against her. Tommy always carries on just when she's trying to get dinner, feed the baby, or put away the groceries. Dad can't understand why Jeannie always acts up when he's in the supermarket doing the weekend shopping or trying to get the yardwork done.

There's no foolproof way to predict when a toddler will "go to pieces." And there are very few children in this age group who don't occasionally fall apart. Every parent knows the scenario—screaming, red face, kicking, rolling on the floor: a temper tantrum. What makes your toddler turn on this kind of behavior? Will he ever learn control?

It's always good to understand *why* a specific behavior is occurring. It somehow makes it easier to deal with. In the case of a toddler, temper tantrums arise from that childhood frustration we spoke about earlier. Here's a small person who has been around for a very short time and has had to learn a great many things: how to make his wishes known; whom he can trust in his world; when to sleep and when to be awake; what a spoon is for; why he can't run into the street. It's a long list that we take for granted and that for him is an entirely new set of lessons to be learned. Some things are easier than others. Hardest are the social lessons, and one of these is learning to control your temper.

Most toddlers have a chronic problem with what can best be described as overload. It happens when the child is subjected to too much excitement, or too many adjustment tests, or too many new experiences at one time. You may see overload at the end of a particularly active weekend, of if you're moving, or during the first week at the new day nursery. Overload is one of the prime causes of temper tantrums, so it pays to be aware of the things that seem to upset your toddler the most. Then you can anticipate, or even avoid, his outbursts.

Frustration is another cause of temper, and it's very easy for a toddler to get frustrated. Frustration leads to anger; anger often leads to temper. Someday young Pat and Priscilla will learn to express coherently what's bothering them. They will be able to tolerate being tired without crying, or being hungry without going to pieces, or being in a new situation without getting anxious and ornery. It probably won't be until around age five. In the meantime, there are things you can do to encourage this aspect of social development.

What Can a Parent Do?

The best thing to do is try to anticipate tantrum time. Ask yourself if Tony's tantrums follow a pattern. Do they happen when he's tired, when he's hungry, or when he's trying to cope with a new social situation? If you clue in to when the frustrating times occur, maybe you can help to smooth them out. Maybe Tony needs a snack in the middle of the afternoon. A glass of milk and a graham cracker may get him through the most vulnerable hours. Maybe it's lack of sleep that triggers temper in your house. One parent told us:

> "Jim always comes apart at the seams when he's tired. Even now that he's a teenager we can still predict when he's going to be surly—it's when he has been up too late for a number of nights."

If it's lack of food or sleep that ticks your toddler off, then try to plan a schedule that provides for regular meals and rest.

You can only do so much, however. You can't run your life so that your child is never frustrated. Along with being reasonable and considerate yourself, you have to show your toddler that blowing off steam in the form of a temper tantrum is not appropriate behavior:

You're in the shoe store and suddenly Steve starts to lose his temper. It's sometimes difficult for an adult to keep from reacting with anger to what is clearly unreasonable and unthinking behavior. But a calm as well as firm approach will provide better results. The first thing to do is get things under control. "Let's go, buddy," you can say with gentle authority. Then pick Steve up and get him out of there. Show him that he must not behave that way in a public place (social lesson number one) and that you, his parent, will help keep him from going out of control (social lesson number two).

Sometimes it's a matter of being sensitive to what's going on with your child:

Edie is tying her shoelace, or trying to. After a good five minutes her lower lip is beginning to quiver. At this point, it would be appropriate to offer some immediate help.

Sometimes the best thing to do is ignore the whole thing and walk away:

You're a dad, you're home for the day, and it's time to go to the station to pick up Mom. All of a sudden, Jennifer goes limp and has a screaming fit on the floor. Best thing to do, perhaps, is walk out of the room. Leave Jennifer to get over this bit of business without giving her an audience. When she's finished, pick her up, wipe her face gently, give her a kiss, and be on your way. "Better late than never," tell Mom.

If you think the temper stems from budding independence, you might try another tack:

It's time for Juan to get dressed for the day. You can feel a battle shaping up for a particular T-shirt or a pair of sneakers. Sometimes you can prevent or block the battle by saying simply, "Juan, which shirt do you want to wear, the green or the yellow?"

Most toddlers have at least a few temper tantrums. Some start just about the time they run up against that famous word "no." Others can tolerate being told "no," but can't handle lack of sleep. Part of what creates a testy toddler may be in your child's make-up. But the other part you can shape.

A good way to start is by recognizing where your toddler's tension areas lie and trying to avoid them. For example, if Ginny's temper always flares up when her dinner is postponed, it's wise to adjust dinner time. Feed her earlier. Don't think of it as catering to Ginny so much as helping her toward a pattern of sociability at mealtime. Somewhat later in her development, she will be able to tolerate delayed meals, and the whole family can eat together. Until then, it's better to adjust to her needs. Avoiding areas of confrontation is one way of keeping mealtimes sociable.

Parents and caregivers can also play a part in shaping a toddler's good disposition through example. A child who sees adults around him handling day-to-day frustrations with calmness and patience is less apt to continue temper tantrums than one who sees short tempers and crankiness in adult members of the household.

Neither of these two approaches—avoidance or modeling—rules out the third, which is to show a toddler clearly that temper tantrums are not acceptable behavior.

Martha is visiting a friend with Ben, her two-and-a-half-year-old. Suddenly, without warning, Ben has a screaming tantrum. Martha could:

- lose her own temper and spank him;
- placate him with a toy or sweet treat;
- ignore his behavior;
- remove him from the scene or end the visit.

Ending the visit is by far the best option. If leaving isn't possible, Martha might pick Ben up, restrain him so he doesn't hit or kick her, and say firmly, "I don't understand when you scream. You need to tell me what you want." And if this doesn't work, "Ben, I think you will have to be by yourself for a while until you can talk more quietly." Martha might then put Ben in another room (if possible) and tell him he can come out when he is calmer. A time to think and be alone is sometimes essential for a toddler.

Some displays of a toddler's temper are to be expected. That doesn't mean it shouldn't be controlled. Temper tantrums are one of the great manifestations of toddlerhood. But too many of them can sour a family's social life. If your toddler is having tantrums frequently, if these tantrums last more than a few minutes, and you see no cause for them, you should talk to your doctor about it.

Manners for Toddlers

There's good reason to introduce some manners at the toddler stage. It's not that we can expect miniature ladies and gentlemen overnight. It's more a matter of laying the foundations in early language and thought for the behavior that we all rely on and accept for pleasant, considerate relations.

PRETTY PLEASE

The best way to instill manners in the toddler is by example:

- "Thank you, Tina," says Dad, as he accepts the grungy piece of zwieback she offers him.
- "Please hand me that can," says Mom to an older child, as a younger one watches and absorbs.
- "Oh, I'm sorry," says the sitter, accidentally pulling a toddler's boot on a bit too vigorously.

The point is for the toddler to hear words that stem from genuine concern and to begin to understand why they're used. "Thank you" is an easy place to start. You can say "thank you" appropriately for everything from taking an undesirable object out of your toddler's hand to showing your gratitude for help at clean-up time.

When the occasion arises, a little direct instruction is appropriate, even for children as young as two:

- "We wait our turn to get on the bus."
- "If you bump into someone, be sure to say 'Excuse me.' "

- "If you pinch Betty, you hurt her. You mustn't hurt people."
- "Wait until Sara has finished talking, Danny. Then you can have your turn."

And rest assured that manners do rub off. You'll hear them coming back to you—another signal that a social lesson has been learned.

TABLE MANNERS

Table manners are tricky at this age. The most you can hope for is that by three your youngster can feed himself and keep most of the food off the floor. Small portions should be the rule (he can always have more). A spoon is the most useful utensil. Forget forks for a while; fingers are still fine for pieces of meat and cut-up vegetables. Knives are out of the question.

Most toddlers can drink well from a cup by the age of two. But save yourself irritation by making the drinking vessel paper or plastic, and try to remove it from the table promptly after the liquid is "all gone." Otherwise, the cup will turn into a toy.

Most toddlers can't spend a long time at the table or in a highchair or a chair seat. When the meal is over, it's time to leave the table. Be sure to excuse the toddler of the family from the table when you see restlessness setting in. That's when things get spilled and tempers flare. Your goal is to have as smooth a meal as possible, so that neither you nor your child associates mealtime with crisis.

You may even get little Emily used to asking to be excused. She may not know what "Be excused?" or "excuse, please?" means, but it sets the form in place, and later, when she says, "May I be excused, please?" she will understand the words. It will be one of those small courtesies that grace a family meal.

POLITENESS

Can you expect real politeness from a toddler? No. Remembering not to interrupt, greeting strangers politely, waiting until another person has finished speaking, shaking hands—all this will have to wait. You must be able to train it in by insistence, but for the child of this age group, politeness doesn't have the meaning behind it to make it stick.

It will in a few more years. In the meantime, you can be the model for the polite behavior you'd like to see later.

Parents often forget that small children are small people. Here's an interesting quiz on Parents' Politeness to Toddlers:

- When your child is talking with a friend and you interrupt, do you say, "Excuse me"?
- If you're standing with your child and someone you know comes along, do you introduce your child?
- Do you frequently scold, spank, or yell at your child in public?
- Do you take the time to listen when your child talks to you?

These little courtesies may not seem important, but they are precisely the courtesies you'll want to see in your child. The way to set them in place is to follow them yourself. Say to your youngster that in your family, and his, people respect one another.

TAKING TODDLERS TO DINNER

Can you take a toddler to dinner? *Not* at a four-star restaurant, unless you like aggravation. What you can do is take your child on casual outings. Fast-food restaurants and pizza parlors, places where the service is quick and the dishes are unbreakable, are really easier on you and on your toddler. These outings accomplish two things: First, they accustom your two- or three-year-old to restaurants and to the experience of eating in public. Second, they give you a welcome break.

If you have a fairly placid child, you may occasionally want to try a more formal eating-out experience. If you do, be sure to bring along a chair seat or other device for placing him at the table, in case the restaurant doesn't have one. Also bring a plastic bib and some toys or a book or two, so that if the service is slow, your child won't run out of patience.

Some public places are more attuned to the needs of young children than others. Many restaurants keep highchairs and infant seats on hand, but some do not—they discourage the patronage of family groups. If you go to such a restaurant with your toddler, you may be ill at ease; and your attitude will inevitably lead to your child's being uncomfortable, which could lead to a disastrous evening all around.

A phone call beforehand is often the easiest way to insure a relaxed evening. You can ask straight out, "Do you welcome families with young children?" "Do you have a highchair?" It may also be a good time to talk about seating position. Ask to be seated in an alcove or near the exit, so one of you can take the toddler outside for a break during the meal.

It's also a good idea to time restaurant outings to coincide with regular eating schedules, or even plan them a little earlier, to allow for waiting. Don't stretch a toddler's tolerance by deciding to have a sophisticated eight-o'clock dinner. And if there's any question about it, hedge against hungry temper tantrums by bringing along a bag of fruit or crackers.

Some of these rules may be harder to follow if you're going to a dinner party with family or friends. Often it pays to ask beforehand what the program is going to be. If you find that lunch or dinner is going to be late and leisurely, it may be wise to feed your toddler beforehand. You can't really expect the rest of the guests to conform to your two-year-old's needs. If you're visiting close relatives, you may be able to rummage in the refrigerator and put together a meal for him. But if not, it is considerate to bring your own food. Feed your child beforehand in the kitchen. Then settle him in a place where he can play quietly, and where he and your host's property will be safe.

You may have to toddlerproof a room or improvise a gate or barrier of some kind. But it's worth doing; otherwise, you won't enjoy your meal or have a chance to be sociable yourself. And your toddler will associate such outings with impatient scolding from you, and no freedom to explore on his own.

Traveling with Toddlers

Anticipating problems and planning for their solution can make things easier for you when you travel with your toddler. Some parents keep a kit of travel totes. Here's a list that you can tailor to meet the needs of a bus trip to the beach or a cross-country trip in a car:

- a car seat that doubles as a chair seat
- a plastic bib
- disposable diapers

- a bottle or plastic cup, and small cans of juice
- a waterproof bed cover
- snacks (boxed raisins, crackers, simple cookies)
- a box of distractions—a few simple toys, some books, a hand puppet
- a security object

Use your judgment about this list. Some things will come in handy for one occasion, some for the other. But under no circumstances should you overlook the last item—the security object. It could be the most important contribution to the success of any social outing. Whether it's a blanket, a doll, or a tattered furry animal, it's a must, and it will forestall many a temper tantrum. Be assured that to make sure "blankie" is remembered isn't giving in to a quirk; it's providing your very young person with the same sort of social bolstering that you may get in company from wearing a becoming outfit or knowing that you look fit. Don't assume that what Donna needs is her fancy stuffed elephant when it's really that dirty old duck she wants.

The Brent family always vacationed with their small children. They traveled by car—adults, children, dogs and gear—and they often went long distances. With toddler-age children they had several strategies for making the time pass socially. One was to play simple games, such as "I spy." The Brents tailored the game to fit the particular landscape: "Keep your eyes open for cows. The first one to spy a cow wins!" The Brents never tried to drive long distances without stopping to stretch their legs. They found that it was worth losing a little time to avoid taxing their toddlers' patience. They also found that frequent side outings helped make traveling more pleasant. Stopping to watch ducks on a pond, or a giant steam shovel dig into a mountain, helped rid both parents and toddlers of pent-up energy and the monotony of continuous travel.

What about staying overnight? Some families with toddlers go camping or rent a trailer. In this setting less is expected of the toddler than in a hotel or motel. If he cries before going to sleep, no one will be disturbed. If he wets the bed, it's *your* bed, not the hotel's.

If you don't like camping or being confined in a trailer, however, you can find motels and hotels where you and your children (even toddlers) will be comfortable. The Automobile Club of America (AAA) and several other automobile organizations offer guidebooks to various regions of the United States and Canada that tell you which motels and hotels have special facilities for children.

If you're going to a resort with your toddler, you'll surely want to know beforehand what kinds of facilities and activities are available for children. Whatever is offered will be mentioned in the brochure. If nothing is said, don't take a toddler there.

Some motels and hotels offer a babysitting service to their patrons. This may work well for you if you want to have some time for an activity without young Jennie. But if Jennie is the type of toddler who warms up to people slowly, you'll have to resign yourself to doing things with the whole family. Jennie may simply not be socially sophisticated enough to tolerate a strange sitter in a strange place. You may ruin your vacation if you try to press the point. Some parents of toddlers find that taking the babysitter along on the trip works out even better.

Some toddlers travel better than others. We don't know exactly why one child waits for his dinner with equanimity, naps anywhere, and occupies himself quietly while his parents chat with friends, while another gives Mom and Dad grief, on the road or in the diner. You know your toddler better than anyone else does. If you find, through experimenting, that Michael is nothing but trouble on outings, then maybe you should postpone all but necessary eating out until he has mastered this piece of socializing. If Michael takes to restaurants and likes visiting relatives, give him the chance to explore the social experiences he's clearly ready to enjoy.

New Experiences

The love of new experiences has a great name—it's called *neophilia*. *Neophobia*, it's opposite, is an extreme fear of new experiences.

As children grow, parents would like them to accept new situations with a certain amount of verve and enthusiasm. But this isn't easy for toddlers. Sometimes they seem ready for anything. At other times they'll cling or become stubborn. They'll suddenly turn fearful and you'll wonder, Why isn't Sandy adjusting to his daycare group? Why isn't he excited about going to the beach? The other kids seem to be.

One good way to assess the reasons might be to take a closer look at a toddler in one situation:

Twenty-two-month-old Jill is starting to go to a daycare center. Her mother was considerate enough to introduce her both to the setting and to the teachers. But now it't time for the big parting. Jill cries when her mother leaves. Jill's mother goes off to work feeling guilty. She's slightly embarrassed, too. None of the other toddlers cried.

Jill is obviously having trouble making the switch to daycare that Mom's new job requires. If it's at all possible, her mother should arrange to spend some extra time at the center with Jill, so as to make her leave-taking a little more gradual. Jill is quite young to be away from home all day, and this new experience may be something she has to work into. Jill's social skills are not up to it just yet; she needs the help of a gradual transition.

Here's another kind of new experience:

Jane's dad was stunned that she simply wouldn't dip into the community wading pool with the other kids. Then he figured out why. The children were wading in their underwear. Jane had just learned from her parents not to get undressed down to her underpants in public. She couldn't forget that rule in favor of a new social situation where it was okay to strip. As soon as wise Dad went home and helped her change to a bathing suit, she was fine.

What's true of Jane is true of many toddlers. It's often easier for a toddler to face new experiences when everything isn't new. Don't introduce your child to a new housekeeper and then leave for the weekend. Don't put Jan into a big bed and take away the night light, too. One new thing at a time is enough.

One other thing that you can do is try to prepare children for new experiences. A sentence or two may do it for a toddler:

- "As soon as we finish breakfast, we're going to get in the car and go to Grandma's."
- "We need to go to the store now, and you can take Teddy Bear with you."
- "There will be two cats at the house we're visiting today. Two cats and three children."

Another good route might be to play out the new experience:

- "Let's play that the rabbit is going to Grandma's. First we give him lunch. Now we put him in the car with his blanket and a snack. Now here we go—zoom, zoom up over the hills and onto the highway . . ."

Acting out gives children a notion of what to expect and makes a new experience easier.

BIRTHDAYS AND HOLIDAYS

A mother has terrible trouble getting Adam, her two-and-a-half-year-old, to go to any sort of children's party. When he is finally there, instead of enjoying himself as the other children do, he clings to his mother, to her embarrassment. Adam seems to warm up when the party has cooled down and there are only a few guests left.

Perhaps what Adam can't handle yet is all those new faces. But obviously he can handle a few. So the answer might be to keep Adam's partying to intimate groups rather than to big bashes. That way he'll gradually get more used to being around new people.

A common thread in all of these ministories is the message that parents can make new experiences much easier for a toddler by taking clues from the child's behavior. This doesn't mean giving in, so much as it means working with your child's strengths, and trying to figure out *why* a particular experience isn't working.

It's often tempting to compare your shy child to someone else's seemingly fearless one, but those youngsters may show their social immaturity in another way. Maybe they're older. Don't worry about

it. Next year it may be your child who handles new experiences with
aplomb. It's always good to keep in mind that children's social growth
is a jagged process. Sometimes they may seem to be stuck in one stage
or even to move backwards. Two steps forward, one step back is normal too.

PARTY-GOING. Whether it's Thanksgiving for the whole family or Cousin Jenny's third-birthday celebration, party-going is a big social occasion for toddlers. Your child may thrive on being the center of attention
or be totally overwhelmed by so many new faces. Either way, it's your
job to smooth the way to help her get into action. For openers, stay
close at hand, and don't feel you've got a social misfit on your hands if
your toddler is clingy. Give her time to watch the action from the safety
of your lap, arms, or kneeside. You may need to be the buffer against
those who can't resist rushing in before she has taken stock of this
lively situation. No need to be abrupt with the oversolicitous; just carry
on the conversation and let your little one watch. If you're friendly
yourself, that's a message she can read. If you're stiff and defensive,
she'll pick up on that, too.

Even the best gathering of the clan may go on too long for sustained
contentment. The family feast may not coincide with your toddler's
lunch or nap needs. Go prepared with familiar finger food and snuggly
quilt or toy, and take time out. If you anticipate when hunger and sleep
are apt to set in, you and your toddler might find a quiet corner and
take a pause that refreshes.

GIVING A BIRTHDAY PARTY. Tempting as a big celebration may be,
keep a toddler's party simple. Two or three friends are best, five is the
absolute limit. Plan a lunchtime or postnap celebration and limit the
party to an hour, at the most.

Your guests' mom or dad should definitely plan to stay. This is not
the year for dropping kids off and saying, "Have fun!" Offer some
coffee or tea and cake for adult guests, and keep the menu simple for
the little ones.

If you're planning lunch, serve familiar finger food. Sandwiches cut
in quarters, with a festive touch of carrot curls or crunchy celery, are
fine. Naturally, the big moment arrives with the birthday cake and
candles. Toddlers can actually handle cupcakes more easily, so why not

present a lit-up platterful? Light up the candles, let the birthday child wish and blow, and get on with the treats. Don't forget to have one of the parents standing by to take a picture of the big event. For a midafternoon party, limit the menu to dessert and milk. If ice cream is a birthday must, give the children individual paper cups, with slightly soft ice cream for easy self-feasting.

Formal games are a bit demanding for two-year-olds. After their feast a short sit-down story might be appreciated; or you could lead a finger game like "Where Is Thumbkin?" or "The Eensy Weensy Spider." If you can't resist some group games, try a short round of Ring-around-the-Rosie or a slow-paced game of Simon says. Basically toddlers will have a better time if they can play near each other without too much hovering.

Define the room you plan to use for the big day, and be sure to select some toys that everyone can use. With your toddler's assistance, put away special toys that he the birthday child just "can't" share, and avoid midparty tears. If the weather is good, a little time in the sandbox or with wheel toys may be just right for warming up the party.

Indoors, set up some Play-Doh at a low table for pounding and poking. Small wheel toys, dolls, puzzles, and balls all invite young guests to do what children do best—play.

As for presents, it's pretty hard for toddlers to postpone looking inside. They may also forget the required "Thank you" and "I love it." Here's where you can fill in the dialogue and play the next move by ear. A new toy will probably get put right to use. If it's something that can't be shared, give the birthday child a few moments and then explain that you'll put it away for later. Remember, only toys that can be used by everyone should be left out.

Toddlers don't need lots of horns, hats, and favors to celebrate. Save the doodads for future events, and keep this one short and simple. A going-home treat is nice but not an absolute must. A toy wrist watch, a boat for the tub, a small car, or a bag of potato chips makes an inexpensive going-home favor.

If home space is tight and the weather is right, you might even consider a picnic in the park. Buy a pail and shovel for every child, and pack lunch and treats. Bring along a thermos of juice and throw-away cups for all. After feasting, the sandbox and play equipment are ready made for a lively afternoon.

Whatever you plan, keep in mind that less is more when a toddler's birthday rolls around.

DOCTOR AND DENTIST

Of course the hardest test of social ease is being able to tolerate a less-than-pleasant experience.

With a toddler, new experiences that may be unpleasant require advance preparation. If, for instance, a child is making a first visit to the dentist, there are several things you can do to minimize the likelihood of a scene.

If you have time, it's often very helpful to take your toddler along when another member of the family has a dental appointment. Introduce him to the dentist and the nurse or technician. Let him sit in the chair and touch the instruments. Help him familiarize himself with the place so that when it's his turn, the office won't be totally strange. If possible, let him watch the dentist at work—but not if you think that the patient may be in pain or unconscious, or in any situation that might seem frightening. Try to have your child leave the dental office feeling that it's a pleasant place and that the people there are friends who won't hurt him.

If there's no way that you can arrange a dry run, give your child a preview at home. A good way is by reading and looking at pictures in a book, like Harlow Rockwell's *My Dentist* (Greenwillow). It will be comforting for your child to go to the dentist along with the young narrator of this reassuring book. Or play a "dentist game." Let your child look at your teeth to see if he can spot a cavity. Let him pretend to clean them.

Visits to the doctor will go more smoothly if you prepare for them the same way. Use Rockwell's *My Doctor* (Macmillan). The only difference is that a visit to the doctor is probably not a new experience, and there may be a reservoir of memories of discomfort that color your son's or daughter's attitude about the family physician. You can't take away the memories, but you can relieve anxiety. Now that your child is more aware, reassure her that this time there will be no shots, or that this time the doctor just wants to weigh and measure her and listen to her heart. Let her know as much as you can about what will happen. And never make promises that aren't true.

Haircuts

For many youngsters in this age group, getting a haircut is even worse than going to the doctor. It has some of the same scary elements. There's the big chair, terrifyingly restrictive to a toddler. There's the frightening machine that buzzes, and the business of losing some of yourself, whether it be hair or, in the case of the doctor, a blood sample. Toddlers are newly conscious of the parts of themselves that make up their wholeness, and anything that impinges on this new concept of self is upsetting.

Many toddlers simply cannot adjust to the barbershop. Since it's not an essential the way going to the doctor may be, perhaps it's best to skip it for a while. Give your child a haircut at home, or at least make your visits to the barber as infrequent as possible.

One good way to soften the trauma of a haircut is to have the child go with a parent or older sibling to get one. A toddler who watches Mom or Dad having a haircut may be more willing to submit to having one himself later. He may also be reassured by sitting on Mom's or Dad's lap in the barber chair during his first haircut.

A Toddler's Sense of Time

Patience is a social concept a toddler is not prepared to handle, but he needs to learn it as he grows, and you can help.

At one and a half, for instance, his attention span is short, and he won't sit still for very long, anywhere. On the other hand, he's easy to distract. You can help him pass the time in the doctor's office or in the car with the simplest diversions. That's why it's a good idea to carry a bag of "distractions" when you travel. Almost anything that's safe, interesting, and lightweight—a bunch of plastic keys, a magazine or book, things that fit into each other or can be taken apart, like wooden nesting boxes, a small hand puppet that you and he can play with—will help a toddler endure a wait. Just don't expect too much from him for too long.

You'll see impatience surface when you get on the phone or when a toy needs fixing. With a two-year-old, you can gradually introduce the concept that for some things there may have to be a short wait. You can say, "I can't do that right now, Debby," or, "I'm talking on the telephone now, but I will help you very soon." It's not too early to help your toddler start to understand, and accept, the important social concept of delayed gratification.

Remember that toddlers have almost no conception of time. It's a very vague notion unless it is linked to something that has meaning to them. "After we eat lunch" or "right after Daddy comes home" makes it concrete because it is part of a daily routine. Talking about "next week" or "Monday" is meaningless to them. The most they can manage is "soon." Try discussing events with your toddler in terms that she understands and in a time frame that she can encompass:

- "As soon as we wash our hands, we'll eat lunch."
- "Up this hill and slide down one more time, then we have to go inside."
- "First we'll stop and say good-bye to Grandma, *then* we'll go to the zoo."

Sex and the Toddler

Sex plays a central role in the lives of all humans. Whether we accept the Freudian view that sex is the predominant driving force, or the behaviorist view that it is among the powerful stimuli to which we respond, we acknowledge its importance.

It is a social force in several ways. One is the gender context. Whether a child is born male or female has powerful social consequences in all cultures, which begin to show themselves clearly from the time of his birth. There's much evidence that male and female infants are treated and perceived differently. In many families, male offspring are favored. On the other hand, females in our culture are often treated more tenderly from the time they are born. They may be more apt to be regarded as "good" and "sweet," or expected to be docile and "easygoing." Boys may be expected to be boisterous and naughty, even in the bassinet. Are these assigned traits accurate, or are they in some cases self-fulfilling prophecies? There is some evidence that girls are generally more placid, more adaptable, and less prone to certain types of emotional upsets than boys. But whether this behavior is biologically or culturally determined has never been answered satisfactorily.

For parents the important point is that gender identification and gender-related expectations are a crucial part of the social development of all children. It's in toddlerhood that we begin to see clearly a child's first awareness of which sex he or she belongs to, the roles that the identification brings with it, and some of the gender expression of that role.

Many of these gender-identification lessons are learned by modeling. Girls begin to understand that they are more like their mothers, boys more like their fathers. Every family has its own definition of these roles, which obviously will affect how the children view themselves.

Some of the traditional roles are changing, and your child cannot help but notice them. If Mom has a career, if Dad participates in the cooking and housework, if girls and boys are seen by the family in less stereotypical ways, these values will be picked up by your toddler, and both boys and girls will be enriched by a broader social view of the roles of men and women. It's important for boy toddlers to know that they can be tender, compassionate, and gentle—as well as assertive, energetic, and physical—and still be manly; and for girls to realize that being energetic, even boisterous, will not conflict with their femininity.

Sometimes less restrictive gender assignments need to be talked about with toddlers. In the daycare center, for instance, a boy and girl were playing in the doll corner:

Boy: "The baby is sick. Now I must be the doctor and you bring the baby to me. I'm the doctor."
Girl: "I want to be the doctor."
Boy: "Girls can't be doctors."
Teacher: "Todd, Mara's mother is a doctor, did you know that?"

Toddlers of both sexes need to feel that whichever sex they are, it is worthy. Girls shouldn't be petted and pampered or boys deemed special simply because of their gender. Both girls who are rascally and boys who are placid need to feel that they are accepted for what they are, rather than be pushed into a mold determined more by stereotype than by personality. Toys should be selected that give full range to all capabilities of both sexes. So give your male toddler dolls as well as trucks, and your female toddler building blocks as well as tea sets.

SEX PLAY

All children indulge in sex play during childhood. Boys tend to discover their genitals earlier (probably because they're more accessible), and therefore to engage in erotic play earlier. But parents of both boys and girls should be prepared to find their toddlers masturbating. For the child, masturbation is one of many ways to discover what his body is like and what he feels. For a parent, however, sex play is often a social question, and a difficult one to deal with.

One mother of a toddler expressed her dilemma:

> "There was Jessica, rubbing this stuffed animal between her legs. She didn't even stop when we came into the room. My parents were with me and they were horrified. I didn't know what to do."

This two-and-a-half-year-old is not yet tuned in to the social message that sex play is a private matter. And at this age, delivering the message in a rebuking way—"Don't do that!"—may give your child the idea that those good feelings are taboo. If you, as a parent, show discomfort or disgust at your toddler's normal urges, it may lead her to suppress them or act them out in destructive ways. You can channel your toddler's normal questions and urges into more acceptable social modes by using strategies appropriate to the age.

SOCIALIZING SEX

One of the things you can do is to answer questions frankly and briefly. This is the age when your child will be puzzling over body parts:

- "Why doesn't the baby have a penis like me?"
- "Why do you have hair down there?"

These questions need to be answered briefly—and simply:

- "Girl babies don't have penises. They have vaginas."
- "Because I'm a grownup. You'll have hair there, too, when you get to be a grown woman."

There's no need to get technical with a two- or three-year-old who wants the answer to a simple question. On the other hand, as long as your child is learning a new word, it may as well be the proper one. Buttocks, penis, vagina are all respectable words, and they're much less apt to provoke suggestive snickers than "wee-wee," "mekkie," "tinkle," and the other euphemisms that children learn and then have to unlearn. We feel strongly that in an area so fraught with social taboos, the child who is equipped with a serious, and correct, vocabulary is a lot more comfortable.

Siblings talk about sex with one another. Sometimes the children may be able to speak more frankly to one another than to a parent. Once in a while, however, an older child can pass on serious bits of misinformation. It's better not to assign your ten-year-old as your toddler's sex-education teacher.

If a toddler gets straight answers to questions, she's much less likely to focus obsessively on sexual subjects. What do you do if your two- or two-and-a-half-year-old announces her new-found knowledge in public? First, be relaxed about it. Later, you might want to explain that "body talk" is to be discussed only at home.

Help your toddler deal with awakening curiosity and sexual feelings in private and appropriate ways. You can often distract a child engaged in sex play or sex talk in public. After a while, he will get the idea that the activity isn't appropriate for that time and place, without feeling that it's forbidden or disgusting.

Certain situations related to sex may bring you into conflict with others in your neighborhood. You may feel that young children should be comfortable with their own bodies. Your neighbor may complain that you're "letting your kid run around naked." In this case, you have to decide what's important for your family and continue to reinforce those values, while at the same time giving some respect to the feelings of your neighborhood.

Friendship

Are toddlers capable of true friendship? Most child psychologists feel that friendship in the deepest sense is beyond the toddler's scope. Relating to other people in meaningful ways is more a feature of older age groups, as is playing with another child for an extended period.

What is more typical of toddlers is the side-by-side play described in "How They Play." Most toddlers go through this stage—playing next to or near peers, but not really engaged in play *with* them. Isn't it comforting to know that two-year-old Jesse, who ignores the other occupant of the sandbox, is not being antisocial; he's simply acting his age.

FRIENDSHIP WITH PEERS

What can you expect from your toddler who is spending the afternoon with another small person or persons of about the same age?

- You can expect some swatting, pushing, shoving, and swiping of toys.
- You can expect some behavior problems at the birthday party.
- You can expect some shyness and fear of strangers.

What can you do about it?

Because they're so unpredictable, it may be hard to prepare toddlers for day-to-day social encounters. In fact, if you say, "Now, don't fight with Melissa today," it may be tantamount to saying, "Don't put beans up your nose." You're planting the idea. The best course of action may be to reinforce positive ideas and recall positive experiences.

- "Oh, there's Eric. Maybe you and Eric could build another sand castle today."
- "I wonder who will be at the center today. Do you think Tom will be there? What about Marsha?"

But recognize that toddlers are fickle. Susan may not want to play with Eric today. Eric may not want to play with Susan. You'll have to take your cue from the toddler.

Nonintervention is a good policy when it comes to putting children together. It has its limits, though. Do intervene when antisocial behavior surfaces. Return the purloined pail to its owner. Separate the combatants. Hold the hand that's about to hit. There's no sense in allowing a couple of two-year-olds to "fight it out." Put a stop to it. Every time you do, your child is learning a social lesson. But don't deliver the lesson by hitting the child. She won't be able to sort out the idea that she's not supposed to do what you're doing. You may actually have to untangle Mari's fingers from Paul's curly locks.

Because toddlers can't absorb a lot of input, there's no point in long lectures to them about antisocial behavior. A short statement—"You can't pull Paul's hair"—as you're putting a stop to it, will help to clarify the action.

You may have to run interference as Tom and Jerry head for a collision. And you may have to protect the puppy from Josh, as much as Josh from the puppy. This kind of anticipation may sometimes be the only practical way to handle a toddler's antisocial behavior. Some parents feel that it's taking the easy way out: "If I remove the puppy, he'll never learn." The rule of thumb at this age should probably be that if someone is liable to get hurt—puppy or baby—and you can anticipate it and do something to prevent it, you should.

Youthful turbulence is a normal part of social development. The worst thing you can do is isolate your toddler from other children. He needs those contacts. He needs to discover, through firsthand experience, what actions he finds socially acceptable from his peers, and what behavior they find socially acceptable from him.

Friendship in the Daycare Setting

In daycare settings, like our Bank Street Infant and Family Center, we're seeing other kinds of friendship-play patterns. They're not so much new as they are newly documented among children in the United States. Some researchers had previously noted that children in kibbutzim in Israel and daycare settings in Japan and the Soviet Union were relating to their peers at an earlier age than those raised in individual families. Now we're observing it, too. It may be a tribute to the endless adaptability of humans. Or it may be simply that kids mature at different rates. But the most logical explanation of this earlier social behavior is that it is due to new social patterns. Kids who have been with groups of other children from an early age seem to be able to handle "friendship play" earlier.

Friendship with Grownups

Toddlers are equally unpredictable about making friends with grownups. Every parent knows the embarrassment of hearing Tony scream, "No! No!" as Aunt Sophie leans over to embrace him. Yet Tony may have, that very morning, taken an instant liking to the telephone man and made a pest of himself.

Common sense will tell you that you can't anticipate how your very individual child will react to each person. But you may be able to make meeting adult friends and relatives smoother. Here are a few strategies:

> You're having company for dinner. You know there's no time to tuck Tammy into bed before the company comes. You're concerned (rightfully) that Tammy, who loves company, will be an all-evening addition to the party.
>
> You can tell Tammy about the upcoming festivities shortly before they happen. Make it clear that she can greet people, but that it's not her party. After the greetings and a few minutes of talk, you can escort Tammy to her room quietly, preferably with a small toy that you've saved for this occasion.
>
> "Now it's time for bed, Tammy. Say good night. You can play with your new toy for a while, I'll leave the light on."

The important part of this social encounter is not to let Tammy get overstimulated. Once she's running around with the guests, being admired and eating hors d'oeuvres, you're going to have a tough time separating her from the party. Two parents working together is ideal in this situation. One parent can stay with the guests, the other can tuck Tammy in. And once she's down, the rules have to be firm. No popping up.

> Grandma and Grandpa are coming for a visit (or you're going there). Two-and-a-half-year-old Brian knows Grandma and Grandpa, but he doesn't give them the respect they expect. Talking about this behavior beforehand won't make much of an impression. But talking about other positive things may.
>
> For one thing, you can talk about how you feel about Grandma and Grandpa. "I'm so happy to be going to Grandma's. I haven't seen her in such a long time . . ."
>
> Just before arrival, you can prepare Brian for anything that might be startling or unexpected. "I'll bet Grandpa's going to want to give you a big bear hug." "You know, Grandma hurt

her foot, and she has a big bandage on it. We need to be careful not to hit that foot by mistake."

You can also encourage healthy social encounters between grown-ups and toddlers by some frank talk with grownups. If Aunt Rose always insists on paying more attention to the baby than to toddler Evan, you can mention it to her. If Uncle Irving's beard makes Jenny unwilling to kiss him, that's a legitimate complaint. Jenny may not tell him why she's crying, but you can.

Friendship with Siblings

What about friendships in the family, particularly between brothers and sisters? Toddlers can develop friendships with a caring older sibling. The unruly toddler can even sometimes be snapped out of a temper tantrum better by an older brother or sister than by a parent. Friendships with siblings are encouraged by a firm foundation of love and respect in the family. If a new baby is on the way, for instance, your toddler needs as much information as she can comfortably handle, along with the general assurance that this welcomed family event will in no way displace her.

After the baby arrives, expect that your toddler may not be any more attached to it than to her side-by-side pals in the playground (and maybe less).

Everyone who addresses the subject of siblings admits that how children learn to socialize with one another in the family depends on many factors. One of the most important is how the children are regarded by their parents.

In the case of the toddler, if he is looked on and talked about as difficult, pesky, wild, then older children will have the same views. The label may stick long after the toddler stage is over, coloring sister and brother relations.

Parents can do much to set the tone for sibling friendship, and it's never too early to tell toddlers that they live in a family that loves one another.

Summing Up

Friendship is a give-and-take affair that toddlers need to practice.

The necessity for your intervention in your child's peer relationships will probably crescendo when your child is around two and a half. But sometime after that, usually before he turns three, your admonitions—"Touch Paul's hair gently"; "See, we pat the puppy"; "Now it's Jerry's turn"—will begin to register. You'll see William and Wilma playing with the doll instead of stepping on it, bringing Mom a Band-Aid for her "boo-boo," tucking tired Daddy into bed and offering him a precious bit of blanket. You'll see them greet Grandpa with a warm hug and help pass the cocktail napkins to the dinner guests. You'll see sister and brother cuddle together on the couch, the older sibling helping the younger one. It's the beginning of the child's concept of caring, sociability, civilization, taking hold.

4

Alternative Childcare

Daycare: Pros and Cons

Daycare,* like television, is here to stay; and like television, it has its detractors and its advocates.

The societal needs for daycare for infants, toddlers, and pre-schoolers increase as more and more mothers join the work force. Yet the younger the child, the greater is the concern for good daycare that is responsive to the needs of these youngest members of the community. Let's take a look at some of the controversies over this kind of care.

AGAINST DAYCARE

The antidaycare group's position is stated by William and Wendy Dreskin, who conducted a daycare group, as well as a successful preschool program. The point of view presented in their book, *The Daycare Decision: What's Best for Your Child?* is endorsed by a noted educator, Dr. Burton White. He also agrees with the Dreskins that children are better off with their parents and that parental support should be available to this end.

The authors admit that while preschoolers (ages two to five) may benefit from a half-day preschool program, such as that offered in a

---

* By daycare we refer to various childcare arrangements, from large daycare centers to daycare in the caregiver's home.

good nursery school, they feel that a full-day program (daycare) has negative effects both developmentally and socially. Let's look at their concern for the social effects of daycare.

Generally speaking, the Dreskins feel, both from their own experience and from certain studies, that

- Long hours of separation from their parents create emotional trauma in young children.
- Children in daycare become more aggressive.
- Children in daycare relate less to adults.
- Many daycare children become unhappy and withdrawn.

FOR *GOOD* DAYCARE

The first reaction of the pro-daycare advocates probably would be, "Wow! that sure sounds like bad daycare!" It certainly does project a negative picture of an overcrowded, poorly programmed, uncaring daycare center, which every parent fears.

The proponents of daycare would go on to disagree with the Dreskins on other counts, too. Specifically, they would state that

- The studies quoted are not conclusive; other studies show that good daycare produces sound social benefits.
- Parental separation, because it's gradually introduced in good daycare, helps the child to deal positively with this inevitable event.
- Good daycare has beneficial effects, physically, mentally, and socially.
- Good daycare programs make children less aggressive, though usually more assertive, because they are beginning to learn satisfactory social interaction with adults, as well as with their peers.
- Children in good daycare programs are more responsive and outgoing toward adults because they have learned to depend on and trust those in charge.
- Good daycare doesn't interfere with the bonding process, but enhances it through developing the child's trust and love for adults.

Why? Because, basically, a good daycare center replicates the extended family. It resembles the old family situation, where Grandma or Grandpa was on hand; when older siblings, as well as widowed Aunt Sophie, Cousin Tom, or bachelor Uncle Ned, helped care for babies and youngsters. None of these helpers replaced the parental bonding; nor does a good daycare center today. Ideally, it enhances it by broadening the child's experience with caring adults.

Babies, of course, need special treatment. Good daycare provides not only the necessary physical equipment—refrigerator for juice and bottles, formulas, rocking chairs, cribs, diapers—but plenty of tender loving care. The caregiver, in a good program, provides a strong physical and emotional one-to-one relationship: plenty of holding, patting, soothing, rocking, singing, and talking. The presence of slightly older toddlers and preschoolers enhances the baby's interest; from time immemorial, babies have been drawn to young children. The interest is reciprocal; young children learn to care about the babies' needs, as if they, the preschoolers, are reexamining and reliving their own babyhood through these infants.

In one good daycare center for three- to five-year-olds, each group of youngsters "adopts" a baby, usually from one of the group members' families. The children visit the baby's home, watch how she is cared for there, observe her visits to the group. Then the children reenact such care with their own dolls, their "surrogate babies." They celebrate the chosen baby's birthday and such special occasions as baby's first toddling step or comprehensible word. Both child and baby blossom in the process.

If so many benefits accrue from attending a good daycare center, the question remains: how do we know what makes a good one?

One Model Center

The Bank Street Infant and Family Center at Bank Street College exemplifies these requirements. Amy Dombro, the head teacher there for seven years, says:

> "Basically, we are an extension of the home, devoted to providing similar security, caring, and attention to individualized needs, and working closely with the parents. But we are able to provide something extra—an environment where children can

come together in a group designed to promote positive growth socially, mentally, emotionally, physically. The child's entrance into our center is of the utmost importance, for it is the beginning of that giant step from home to out-of-the-home. How do we provide for this transition from parental care to center care? By going very slowly, very carefully, very sensitively.

"As head teacher, I support the parents, as well as the children and staff, during these beginning weeks and throughout the year. I perceive parents as a child's bridge from the safe and familiar world of home into the unknown world of the family center. We ask the parents to stay with the child for the child's first week here. By playing here with the child or having a cup of tea, the parent transmits the important message that 'this place is for us' to their young child. They [parents and child] come only for short time periods during this first week; this is to allow time during the rest of the day for the teacher to make brief home visits to each child, thus strengthening the connection between the child's two worlds; and to give the small child time to begin adjusting without being overwhelmed. At the end of that week, each parent and I plan together for the child's second week. Thus we can respond to each child as an individual."

Dombro's statement allows a brief glimpse into the foundation of any good daycare program:

- The child's slow, unhurried introduction into the program.
- The complete involvement and cooperation of the parents.
- The establishment of individualized care for each child.

The Bank Street program is for children from six months to three years old; it never has more than nine children in it at a time; there are always three caregivers. When a child enters the program, he is not arbitrarily assigned to a specific caregiver. Rather, the caregivers take their cues from the child himself and allow him to choose his own special adult. Only when this relationship does not develop is the child assigned a special caregiver. Each caregiver has two or three children as his or her own "special" children, thus giving each child a strong relationship with one caring adult, as well as developing relationships with the other adults and children.

The "curriculum" of this family center is that of "living together": the room is set up to encourage children to explore their new world, not only in manipulating many materials but in developing human relationships. The children constantly order and reorder their growing insights, not only through their physical experiences, but by their social activities.

Five or six years ago, educators thought that children under three played only side by side; that is, they didn't actively engage in shared play but performed independently, though close to another child. The Bank Street center's experiences endorse the newer perception that young children under the age of three years can and often do begin to develop a social concern for their peers. Dombro gives many examples, such as this one:

> "I was rocking weeping nine-month-old Karen when I felt a small hand tapping me. Two-and-a-half-year-old Roberto wanted to give Karen her orange rattle, her favorite toy. When Roberto's mother came for him, he told her about Karen. 'She was sad. I gave her rattle. She was happy!' "

In a good daycare center, children learn even sooner to understand *yours* as well as *mine;* it doesn't deprive them of their own self-esteem, or fulfillment of their own needs. Children at home alone or with devoted parents must wait longer to begin understanding and caring for other children.

Thus can one observe from one center setup the strong social components that make up good daycare:

- The development of a strong, caring relationship with and dependency on one adult.
- The development of ongoing relationships with other adults in daily interchange.
- The development of interest in and gradual concern for peers.
- The ongoing development of self-esteem through the care and support from all the adults in the child's daily routines.

Dombro briefly rebuts the charges made by the Dreskin antidaycare group (separation trauma, development of aggressiveness, less relationship to adults):

"Separation is a lifelong process, not a problem that is solved once and for all. In the group, it can be compassionately handled so that the child learns gradually to accept temporary separation from parents with less stress and emotional upset because of the supportive adults. This experience with gradual separation will help both children and parents with the inevitable separations that are yet to come.

"In its nine years of activity, the center has seen children develop positive friendly relations with both other children and adults. Aggressiveness is handled on a daily basis, and the child is offered alternate methods of behavior."

Finally, as interested observers who initially doubted the wisdom of establishing a day program for the very young, we have come about 180 degrees from that position. Frequent observation of the group, including reading aloud to them, for more than nine years has made us enthusiastic supporters of the Bank Street Infant and Family Daycare Center. The obvious development of the children's cognitive, physical, and verbal activities, their increasing physical skills, their friendliness, their outgoing interest in other children and adults, their concern and care for each other convince us that a good daycare group can produce wonderful results; that babies and toddlers and preschoolers can gain greatly rather than regress in such an experience.

DAYCARE FOR THE OLDER PRESCHOOL CHILD

For the four- to five-year-old child, social skills are even more enhanced in a good daycare program.

Initially a four-year-old entering the program will encounter the same kind of "social shock" that the toddler and baby experience: the anxiety of separation from a parent and from familiar settings; the confusion of a new setting and unfamiliar material; the lack of a special caregiver who knows one's special needs.

The response in a good daycare center is the same as with younger children: a gradual introduction to the center, with Mama staying close by until the strangeness wears off; the formation of a new tie with one special caregiver; the dependability of the new routines; and plenty of loving attention to the newcomer's needs.

Once the child feels at ease, social relationships and socializing encounters usually occur more rapidly than with the younger children. The four- or five-year-old has a strong drive to play with others, to make friends, and to test his own abilities and ideas against those of his peers. Now he has a safe place and continuing opportunities for expanding his social growth. There are opportunities in this sheltered society of peers for the child to learn and practice the social skills of give-and-take and the sharing that is necessary for satisfactory group life. More isolated children will be slower and take longer to acquire these social skills.

Two four-year-old boys, Sean and Taylor, attend Marie's birthday party. Marie's mother invites them to give her their coats, then join the other children at a table filled with games and toys. Sean, who has attended a daycare center, shyly yields his coat and sidles over to the table. After a short while he is playing a game with another child.

Taylor, however, who stays at home, has not had much group experience. At first he seems a little overwhelmed, refusing to doff his coat or go near the table. Finally he lets his mother remove his outdoor clothing, but remains close to her for the rest of the afternoon, watching the other children.

In the presence of caring and understanding adults, the preschooler struggles to reconcile her own social needs with those of her peers and begins the lifelong experience of understanding and caring for others. We believe not only that a good daycare center enriches and supports this process, but that it may provide a richer environment for the child than some homes.

EVALUATING DAYCARE CENTERS

But the key word, again, is *good*. How do we know what constitutes good daycare?

First, by our immediate initial feeling when we observe the center.

Then by careful observation of the children's and adults' interaction, with each other and with the materials.

Amy Dombro agrees with the two researchers Ellen Galinsky and William Hooks, who state in their book *The New Extended Family: Day Care Programs That Work* that this initial impression is an amalgam of positive answers to such questions as:

- Do the children seem busy, happy, interested in each other, in their activity? Does the look and feel of the place please me?
- Are the adults involved with the children in a friendly, caring way? Do the adults seem at ease with the other adults?
- Is the ratio of children to adults a good one? (An ideal ratio is one adult for every three children.)
- Are the groups small enough, even if the total number of children is large? That is, are the children divided into smaller groups with their own space?
- Would I want to work here? for a day? a week? a year?
- Would I want my child here? for a day? a week? a year?
- Do I think my child would learn here? be happy here? (One clue: If the children stop activities when you enter, the chances are that their activities do not interest them.)

If your initial impression is favorable, a further investigation is in order. Even though our emphasis is on social development in daycare, you will, of course, want to check the physical plant—is it safe? healthy? spacious enough?—the materials and caregivers, and the program and goals of the preschool.

You will also need to know the place of parents in the program. Are they involved with the caregivers in their child's program and well-being? Do they exchange notes daily? weekly? confer often? Do they and the program agree in principal aims and methods?

Your last check will be with outside sources. Talk to other parents, ask the licensing agency about the stability and reliability of the center, and check with respected professionals who know the program.

Galinsky and Hooks remind us that there is no one program that is a suitable model for *all* daycare programs. They found that "good daycare programs were organic outgrowths of a specific community and stayed responsive to and completely in tune with the people they sought to serve."

Furthermore, not all children are ready at the same time for a daycare experience. If your child still doesn't want to stay in the center after you have both visited it together for a week or more, talk to the head teacher. You both may conclude that your child isn't ready yet for this giant step. The teacher probably will suggest that you both return later—two weeks, two months, or even more. Give your child a chance to mature a bit longer. Don't think that she (or you) have "failed" because other children entered more readily. Each child is a success when she progresses at her own rate.

If you have difficulty finding a good daycare center, or if they are all too expensive for you, don't lose heart. Try to find a parents' group that is doing something about it—perhaps setting up centers, pressuring civic and religious groups to do so, or demanding centers from their elected officials. Where do you find such groups? Ask around. Ask in the playground, in the supermarket, call schools, colleges, churches, hospitals. And when you find such a group, support it. Interested, involved parents are the ones to establish not only daycare centers, but standards to which they must conform.

You are the final decision-maker. You alone know your child best, and alone can decide:

- when your child seems ready to leave the home nest;
- what program seems to best suit her and your needs;
- whether you and she can be comfortable with this choice.

Whatever you decide, become involved with your choice. Work closely with the caregivers; support them and your child. Trust your instincts—enjoy and learn along with your child.

The Babysitter: An Important Caregiver

At one time or another, most parents need the services of a babysitter. Some families employ this parent substitute only occasionally, but many parents count on such a service regularly, from once or twice a week to full-time daycare. Then the babysitter has a real impact on the social life of the child.

Whatever your needs, there are two basic preliminary steps to take:

- Choose your babysitter well ahead of the time you call on her for her services, just as you choose a doctor or dentist.
- Choose a babysitter that is right for you and your child.

The type of babysitter you need largely depends on your child's age. The baby under a year old needs an alert, caring person, attentive to his needs and ready to give lots of cuddling and rocking. An older person, including Grandma, is just right for giving this kind of personalized attention. Young teenagers might be too absorbed in the telephone or television to hear the baby. Of course many young people are very responsible, but it's best not to entrust the baby to anyone under fifteen or sixteen.

Babies also need consistency, as they can't accommodate rapid switching of caregivers; try to have the same person care for the baby when you're not there.

The toddler, on the other hand, may need a more active caregiver. But like the baby, the toddler and preschooler need consistency and react best when the same person's in charge.

Older children may respond well to teenage caregivers. Eight- to ten-year-olds often look up to this age as role models for themselves.

The most important quality to look for in all caregivers is their ability to keep your child happy and safe.

Finding a Babysitter

The usual method, and perhaps the most successful one, is to ask for names from parents, friends, and relatives. Not only will they have experienced the babysitter's services, they'll be frank about his or her qualifications. If you are new to a community, however, or away from home, you will have to find other sources of information. Perhaps your new neighbors will be able to help you, or you can get in touch with the local high school or college, church or synagogue, women's club or community center. These are good sources of finding out the prevailing wage scale, as well.

Look also at the notices pinned on bulletin boards or in newspaper ads, or insert an ad yourself. These rather haphazard methods will require a lot of reference checking and personal interviewing, but may prove as rewarding as any other way of getting in touch with a good sitter.

The traditional babysitter was a grandparent or other close relative. For some this is still a preferred choice, especially if Grandmother or Grandfather lives nearby and agrees with your methods. However, they may not be able to manage an active toddler. One solution is to hire a younger babysitter to work under the charge of your older relative. This arrangement works very well for overnight care, too, whether the babysitter (and the baby) stay in your house with the grandparents or they all stay in the grandparents' home. You can also work out other variations on this theme.

Choosing the Right Babysitter

The first step is to call the babysitter to set up an interview. Even such a preliminary contact may give you some clues about your prospective employee. Is she reluctant to have such an interview? Does she find it hard to make the time for one? After you have explained the situation, does she have any questions to ask you? If your reaction is negative, however, don't let this first impression weigh too much with you—she may seem quite different in person. (Since the majority of babysitters are women, from teenagers to those of more mature years, I am using the feminine pronoun. Many boys and young men are proving to be excellent caregivers, though, and may be just right for your needs.)

When you have the interview, plan to have enough time—not only for you to be alone with her but also for her to socialize with your child. The point of the interview is to look for a "match" between you and the applicant. Try to elicit some of her feelings about childcare. How does she feel about pets, TV, naps, diapers, toilet training, eating habits, crying babies? What is her idea of discipline, of getting children to bed, or reading to or playing with them?

You, of course, will be telling the babysitter what you expect from her—not only the chores that need to be done, but also how you want her to handle any negative behavior on your child's part. Tell her how to meet the child's emotional as well as physical needs, and what you expect her to do.

Explain your rules about her bringing a friend, using the television, or having prolonged telephone conversations. Assure her that you'll provide snacks, prompt payment, and an escort home. Let her know ahead of time first how you feel, and then what you expect from her, so you both will have a clear understanding of the job.

If you feel that she and you generally agree on the basics, that your first impressions of her are favorable, and that she and your child seem compatible, engage her at the agreed-on rate to spend an hour or two at your house with you and your child. This "paid visit" is an important step to take. The main purpose is to let your child become accustomed to this new adult who perhaps may be taking your place at some future time. The secondary benefits are getting to know your new babysitter better; letting her know your child better; and letting her become more familiar with the household. This is a good opportunity to show her how the stove works, where the telephones and the light switches are, the arrangement of your child's room (where you keep fresh clothes, linen, toys, books). End the visit on a freindly note by having a "tea party" with her and your child; it will also give your child an opportunity to be alone for a short time with the sitter while you are in the kitchen arranging the "tea."

This rather prolonged paid visit depends on whether you find the visitor congenial; if you don't, you may cut the visit short with your thanks and payment of her fee.

If the visit ends with warm feelings on both sides, plan to engage her services fairly soon, while the visit is still fresh in your child's memory. The first engagement should be fairly short—perhaps for your going out to dinner—and should allow for an extra hour ahead of time, to reacquaint your child with the sitter, and for her to socialize with the child while you are still there. This first visit should be fairly simple also, without asking the sitter to feed your child or take her out —just a quiet time together, which might include a nap or even going to bed if your child could do so without becoming upset. You know your child best and can plan the least upsetting experience for this first visit.

Consider hiring a babysitter if you are giving a dinner or party; this way the children are welcome to meet the adults but have their own needs met without disturbing the parents. It also might be a good way to introduce the babysitter's services to your child; you would be in the house and available if needed.

If you plan to leave the house, leave written notes: give the telephone number where you can be reached, a close friend's number in case you are unavailable, the doctor's number, the fire and police numbers. (Actually, the last three numbers should be posted by the phone at all times.) Write down what chores you want done, what time your child is to eat, go to bed, go to the toilet, or whatever the routine is; indicate where the refreshments are for both sitter and child. Be sure to return promptly, pay promptly, and see that the sitter gets home safely.

ALTERNATIVES TO HOME BABYSITTING

Sometimes you must make alternative plans to having a babysitter come to your home. Perhaps your babysitter is based in a nearby house, where you can bring your child, or you can leave your child in the house of a friend. Usually these options are used to solve the problem of providing all-day care for your child on a regular basis. Such an arrangement often occurs when both parents are working, and is one type of home daycare. In these cases the babysitter often has another child or two there also.

Whatever the arrangement, the same standards hold: a slow, easy introduction to the new person and situation, with your standing by until your child feels more at home; a sense of harmony and shared ideas of childcare between you and the babysitter; and a clear understanding of what your wishes are and what the babysitter's role is. Remember that she will play an important role in your child's life; on a daily basis, she will be transmitting ideas and social mores to your child.

ASSESSING THE BABYSITTER

Part of your assessment is done beforehand, when you and the babysitter discuss your goals and methods of attaining them. Your approval of the sitter's intentions must have been positive or she would not have been engaged. The next judgment of the babysitter's performance will be the matching of her previous statements to her actions. This assessment may take longer to evaluate, since you will know the worth of her performance only after some time has passed.

The last measure for assessing your babysitter's suitability is not only the most important, but probably the easiest to do: How does your child react to her? Does the child look forward to her coming, or does he react negatively? Does the child seem relaxed and at ease after the babysitter has left, or is your child cranky and tired?

You know your child best. You will know through your child's attitude whether you have been lucky enough to find someone who will "keep your child happy and safe."

5

The Preschool Years

THREE TO FOUR YEARS OLD

A Time of Ups and Downs

Human development in preschoolers goes through fairly predictable cycles, though not always according to predictable timetables. Preschoolers go from stormy intervals to periods of calm; from periods of discord to more harmonious stages; from warm sociability to antisocial behavior.

These changes are often unsettling or downright discouraging to the unprepared parent. The enthusiastic mother of a three-year-old says, "Max is such a doll now! Doesn't fuss and carry on about eating or sleeping the way he used to." But the father of three-and-a-half-year-old Denise shakes his head, saying, "Yeah, Denise used to be like that, too. But a lot of times now she acts like a regular brat!"

Take heart. Remember the popular saying, "He's just going through a phase." Most children do go through phases, and knowing this, we can accept the cyclic changes as we accept the seasons. Maybe we can relax a little during our youngster's stormy growing times, knowing that sunnier times will follow.

(Of course, some children go through these phases at an earlier or later age than others—and a few parents report that their children don't seem to go through noticeable mood or behavior changes at all!)

The Terrific Threes

The year of most noticeable change in your child's life is from birth to one, but the following two years are a time of flowering that culminates in the Terrific Threes. Finally, masters of their own bodies, three-year-olds are able to walk, talk, run, communicate, and otherwise express their own wishes.

For most children, this is a period of sunshine. No longer so frustrated by their physical inabilities, nor by their lack of speech, they are able to turn outward from their intense personal needs and become more sociable beings. Now they can enjoy their own abilities, and they can also share them with others—with their parents and with their peers.

PLAYING WITH PARENTS (OR OTHER CAREGIVERS)

This is a time of enjoyable relationships between adult and child. Your child is often willing to let you take the lead, but also enjoys taking the lead himself:

Three-year-old Leslie (to his mother): "Let's make a dinner. You be the baby, I'll be the daddy." (He stirs his pail of clay balls and lifts up some on his sand shovel. Mother puts down her paper and enters the game.)

Leslie: "Now, baby, you eat up all the peas. Gonna be a big girl, gotta eat up peas."

Mother (smacking lips and pretending to eat clay balls): "Thank you, Daddy. These are delicious peas—delicious! I'm eating them all up!"

Leslie: "Good baby!"

Mother: "Did you eat up your peas, too?"

Leslie: "All eated up! Daddy burp baby now." (Leslie smacks Mother hard on her back, saying, "Burp, burp.")

Mother: "Hey, go easy! Daddies don't burp babies so hard."

Leslie (laughing): "Yes, Daddies do. Daddy burp baby hard!"

Mother (swinging Leslie up in her arms): "Well, this baby *kiss* Daddy hard." Leslie squeals with delight as he is lifted up, hugged, and kissed.

This incident reveals Leslie's desire to relate to and play with a favorite adult, and shows his budding skills in social relationships. He is now able to verbalize a lot more of his feelings. He can speak in his own voice and through the voices of his make-believe characters. He is willing to be kissed, instead of brushing off such loving expressions as he did six months earlier. He is also able to use play to explore a broader range of feelings in a socially acceptable way. The hardness of his hitting may show that he has some hostile feelings toward his real baby sister, who has usurped his place as the baby in the family. Spanking Mother, even in the guise of play, also turns the tables for Leslie. It lets him pit his powers against Mother, the all-powerful adult in his life, and win. Since he doesn't actually hit his younger sister or hurt Mother, he is working off some of his hostility without being antisocial.

Leslie's mother seems to understand and accept his need for playful relations with her; she ends the scene not in recriminations, but with a hug, leaving Leslie in his cooperative mood. She is willing to be interrupted in a moment of her own leisure to play with her son; she seems to sense his need to be the commander rather than the commanded; she turns off his increasing hostility with a loving rather than a scolding reaction. Even in the "reasonable three" stage, the adult is in charge of the event, and it's the adult display of cooperation and manners that is the most convincing example to the child.

Andrea Pearson, a working mother, related an example of combining some leisure time with the needs of her three-year-old daughter, Chris:

"I was stretched out on the lawn hammock reading the *Times*. Chris and her friend Peter, bored with sandbox play, asked me to tell them a story. At first I resented their interruption, then realized their need and my responsibility. The story I told wasn't terrific, but as it centered on their imaginary adventures in the Land of Toads, they were delighted.

" 'Where toads live?' demanded Chris.

" 'In cool shady places. Maybe under those bushes,' I answered.

"Soon Chris and Peter were being toads, hopping under the bushes, acting out the story. I enjoyed watching their play, listening to their inventive ideas so much I forgot the paper. Later when they went back to build a toad castle in the sandbox, I returned to my reading. It was a great afternoon."

Glenn Wylotsky is delighted with his three-year-old son Adam's developing sociability. Glenn says:

"He's a real person now. We can communicate, even play together. Last week at the beach, he asked me to help him build, not a sand castle—what does he know about castles?—but a firehouse. We worked together, taking turns lugging wet loads of sand and making the walls. Adam found the right sticks to be the fire trucks and ladders, and shells for the fire bell. He kept a running monologue going:

" 'You be the tiller man. He drives the back wheel on the hook and ladder. Don't turn the wheel fast! Look out! There's a car. Don't bang it, Daddy! Hitch up hoses. Turn on water. Sssshhhhh. Daddy's all wet!'

"He's really a neat little kid now."

James Canolli says about his three-year-old daughter, Carola:

"When we went to the skating rink last year, Carola stayed with her grandmother. Now she wants to skate, too. She's scared at times, but I tell her. 'It's okay, Carola, you can do it.'

"She tried again. She's so little, hanging onto our hands, but she's a big sport. 'Carola do it,' she says. 'Carola skate with Daddy and Mommy.' She talks so much now, we can't get a word in most of the time."

PLAYING WITH PEERS

Though three-year-olds tend to like their special adults and want to please them, their biggest social interest is in their peers. Your child may have associated with other children frequently before this stage, but most of her relationships with other children her age up to this time involved watching them, or playing beside rather than with them, much of the time. As a baby she knew only her own needs. It took her a long time to understand that other people were separate entities, and even longer to know that they had their needs, too. Like all toddlers, she was ego-centered, not from selfishness but from an immature inability to comprehend fully the needs of others. Strongly self-centered, toddlers have little understanding of cooperative play and few skills for coping with it.

Educators say that in supportive settings toddlers do begin to develop some concern for and social interaction with others, but on the whole they tend to play independently—near, but not with another child. This stage is called lateral rather than cooperative play.

> Jeffrey, aged twenty-two months, squats on the floor, pushing a toy engine back and forth. Twenty-month-old Joanne plops down beside him, a toy car in her hand. Jeffrey looks at her, then continues pushing his engine and making engine noises. Joanne watches him. She spins her car's wheels, then runs it back and forth. Now both are absorbed in moving their little vehicles. To the observer, they seem oblivious to each other.

At three, your child will begin to talk *with* other children rather than just talking *to* them. Though she may change friends rather quickly, she is beginning to form more lasting relationships than formerly, and she is able to play in a small group more cooperatively. Sometimes children explore their bonds with peers by excluding others from the play. Cries of "Go 'way!" or "You can't play here!" are often heard. Unless the excluded child is really unhappy and can't be slipped into another activity, there's not much sense in scolding the young excluder. Her sensitivity to others is not yet developed, and neither is the sensitivity of her peers. But their eagerness to play together causes them to regroup quickly and try playing again.

TALKING TO PEERS

Three is a great age for talking; and talking, rather than action, is often the focus in play groups.

In this group of three-year-olds, Donna and two friends are sitting at the table, playing with clay. Another three-year-old boy watches:

> *Donna:* "I'm making a big wiggle snake! It's gonna wiggle over Mike and eat him up!"

Mike (lifting his clay high in the air): "No, it's not! This big bomb will drop on it and ka-boom! that snake will be all smashed up." (Laughing, he drops his clay—but not on Donna's snake.)

Kareen (rolling clay into a big ball): "Here comes roly-ball. Rmmmm, it rolls all over."

Donna (her long snake breaking up as she rolls it even thinner): "Now I got free [three] little snakes. All gotta go to bed now."

Kareen: "Roly-ball got to go to bed, too."

Each child is engaged in an individual pursuit, yet is socially involved with the others. Donna says she is going to interact with Mike's material but doesn't actually do it. Mike reacts verbally but doesn't touch Donna's clay. Kareen's last remark shows that she has heard what Donna said about bed, playing along with it. All three children are physically close, and attentive to each other's play, but they interact only verbally. The fourth child, standing close by, shows his interest in the play at the table but is not yet ready to join in.

VERBAL FANTASY

Sometimes a three-year-old's talk takes the form of stories, told aloud while he paints or crayons. The drawing he works on is usually related to his story in theme and action. If he's telling a story about a house burning, his drawing will get wilder and larger as his tale gets more dramatic, and he may end up with a huge scribble over everything he's painted or drawn. You may be taken aback by the violence of the story in contrast with the usual amiability of your child's social play. Other children listening to the story don't seem disturbed at all, but are often inspired to relate their own imaginary dramas. Here are a few typical three-year-old stories:

Malcolm: "This boy in this house. The house gets on fire—engines coming." (Makes siren sound.) "The house all burned up, the boy all burned up. Fireman goes in, he gets burnt up too. Clang! Clang! The ambulance comes, takes boy away. Ambulance bangs into car, all smashed up. But doctors make boy better."

Gary: "This fire engine racing down the street—"(Siren sound.)"—so fast it can't turn corner. Crash! Smashes up the corner. The fireman throws it away in the river. Then he runs and runs and gets the people out of the house."

Margret: "This girl has a black—no, a brown—horsey. The horsey breaks his leg off, the girl puts on a bandage. The spaceman wants to eat horsey, the girl chops him [the spaceman] into pieces. Then the horsey eats the space monster. And hay and Jell-O soup."

Hearing such stories, parents often become concerned about their child's inner world. Does Margret really need to see herself as someone who chops up a spaceman? Do Gary and Malcolm find pleasure in gruesome destruction?

Children have confusions about the world, vague fears of imagined disasters and of their own helplessness. The stories they tell help them diminish those fears because they can create a monster and then have the child hero subdue it. Stating a horror, then resolving it, is very satisfying, and allowing the child to release his fears in stories may help him develop socially without resorting to antisocial actions.

Children don't carry the ruthless actions of their make-believe world into their everyday social relations.

Play Fantasy

The preschool years are full of imaginary friends. Some children develop elaborate relationships with imaginary friends who may live in the body of a beloved toy—a teddy bear or doll—or may be totally invisible to the rest of the family.

Child psychologists give different reasons for the existence of such richly detailed friendships. For some children, an imaginary beast, such as the Laughing Tiger in Selma Fraiberg's classic book *The Magic Years,* is a child's way of resolving her fear of real animals. Laughing Tiger, as his name indicates, never bites or roars. He is completely under the child's power. She can order his behavior, or punish him. When she becomes more comfortable with and less afraid of the neighborhood's real squirrels, cats, and dogs, the imaginary tiger will fade away. A Laughing Tiger could also reflect the ongoing efforts of adults to "civilize" the child. On an unconscious level, the child enforces these civilizing taboos on her imaginary companion. She makes him eat neatly, wash up, keep his clothes spotless, and never never yell, lie, or fight!

On another level, the imaginary animal or playmate represents the budding of the child's conscience. As she begins to comprehend society's requirements for social behavior, which often conflict with her own desires, she is caught in a dilemma. One way of resolving it is to have an outside entity responsible for her antisocial actions.

Such imaginary playmates may present problems in the family circle: not only are they the "fall guys"—the "perpetrators" of the child's antisocial actions—but they frequently require constant recognition from other family members. Children often use the imaginary friend to deny their own actions, blaming him for all mishaps. "Isn't this just lying?" parents ask. "Should we let our child avoid the consequences of his own actions? Isn't that establishing a bad principle?"

Actually parents can comfort themselves by recognizing that this kind of projection is a sign that their child is becoming aware of wrongdoing. By turning over his misdeeds to this imaginary playmate (who can represent the dark side of his own character), the child shows that he has knowledge of right and wrong—at least according to his parents' moral views. No longer does he have to be told, "Don't pull the tablecloth." He knows better, and when he does pull the cloth, either inadvertently or purposely to get the butter, he recognizes his error and turns the guilty action over to his double. He isn't lying deliberately; he is perhaps recognizing that his character has two sides—a good, obedient one that follows the rules, and a stubborn, egocentric one that "wants what he wants when he wants it!" He is still learning the difference between how he is expected to act, and how he wants to act. Making his imaginary friend (or double) responsible for what he is beginning not to accept in himself is a giant step toward developing a moral order in his own independent conscience.

Though you can relax and enjoy the vivid imagination of your offspring, rather than scolding him or accusing him of lying, you will still need to confront the fact of your child's outrageous behavior (or that of his imaginary friend) and you will have to offer commonsense rejoinders:

- "So, Gerta Potty [the friend] spilled all the water on the bath-room floor? You better show your friend how to mop it up, okay?"
- "Hey, tell Petey Dink [the friend] to keep off those new seeds in the lawn, or he won't be able to use your trike any more!"

Your child will learn what behavior is unacceptable without suffer-ing the intense shame of a personal scolding. Eventually, as a sense of logic and conscience develops, both Gerta and Petey will depart.

The second problem—the child's demand that everyone recognize the imaginary friend at all times—is often a huge nuisance. The beloved friend must go on every family outing, have its own chair, be taken into account in family councils. While such insistence can be irritating, it's usually easier and more fun to go along with the intensity of your child's imaginings. And you can often take advantage of the friend. Using it as a go-between, some parents can issue requests or ask for information with better results:

- "Gerta Potty, do you think Sheila is getting cold? Can you bring this sweater to her, please?"
- "Petey Dink, your friend Paul seems a little unhappy. Maybe you can tell me what's bothering him this morning."

If the imaginary friend gets too out of hand or too demanding, parents can always order it, and its friend, to go to their room and play for a while until they are ready to behave more sociably. This usually works better than sending your child off by himself. Perhaps the two of them can complain about their parents together! This gambit also gracefully gives a child time alone to play out fantasies, to think, to day-dream, to enjoy his own company. A child must learn to play alone as well as with others—an important goal of maturing.

SOCIAL SKILLS THROUGH PLAY

Around three, children begin to recognize that they are complete in themselves, not extensions of their caregivers. They reach a first plateau of competency in mastering the needs of their own bodies, in knowing what they want, in using their physical abilities, and in expressing many of their feelings verbally. They are able to take longer steps away from their mother or their primary caregiver, and social relations with their peers become a major interest. Although they are still basically self-centered, they are beginning to understand that they must recognize the needs of their peers if they want to play with them. You can learn about your child's level of maturity by watching the social skills she is developing in friendly play. Mary-Jo's mother says:

"Mary-Jo is such fun now. She really plays with the other children instead of wanting her own way all the time. Today when playing with her friends, Adrienne and Stevie, Adrienne became fussy. Mary-Jo said to her, 'You feeling sad? Don't cry, dear.' Then she patted Adrienne on the head and said, 'I'll be the mommy. You wanna be the daddy? Bootsy [our fox terrier] can be the baby. No, Bootsy better be Grandpa. We make Stevie the baby.'

"Stevie, however, objected, and chose to be a dog. Mary-Jo didn't seem upset by this change in her plans, but accepted it equably. Soon Stevie was barking on all fours, as a smiling 'Daddy' Adrienne took him for a walk, while Mary-Jo made a family car from blocks. Then Stevie changed the car into a fire engine driven by him, with the girls as firemen; then the engine became a jet, with three pilots and one passenger [Bootsy]. Mary-Jo stayed friendly, accepting changing roles, absorbed in the play. Yet just a year ago, she would have been quarreling and crying to have the play going the way she wanted. Oh, yes, Stevie socked Adrienne at one point. She started to cry. Mary-Jo looked on for a moment, then said, 'Dogs don't hit people.' In a few more minutes, all was peaceful again. I don't know how they worked it out—but it was great!"

Let's look at another example taken from a nursery-school teacher's notes. She writes:

"In the play yard, Stuart still tries to draw others to him by acting silly. He makes funny faces and noises. Today Timmy and Jetta watched him for a few moments, then returned to making sand cakes. Stuart followed them and mashed in one cake. They drove him away angrily.

"*Timmy:* 'Get outa here. Get away from our bakery.'

"*Jetta:* 'You're a bad boy.'

"Stuart then wandered over to a group making a garbage dump. They were filling pails with spoons, shovels, blocks, then upending them into a square of blocks as they yelled, 'Dump the garbage!'

"Stuart followed suit, yelling and dumping. Then he hit Tony and dumped a pailful on Tony's head. 'You're a garbage dump,' yelled Stuart. Tony hit back. I started forward to prevent further fisticuffs, but Stuart ran away. After a few minutes he came back to watch the garbage play. Then he went over to Roselinda, who was watching, too.

"*Stuart:* 'Wanna make garbage for the dump?'

"Roselinda nodded. For twenty minutes they worked together, tearing up old newspapers. Together they made a tall receptacle out of blocks for the torn paper, which was blowing away. Stuart didn't yell, make faces, or hit Roselinda, but quietly played with her the rest of the morning. For the time being, Stuart had figured out one way to have a friend."

THE CAREGIVER'S ROLE

In both these examples, the children deal successfully and independently with their social situations. Mary-Jo had reached a level of social maturity—at least in this instance—where she could stop Stevie's aggression in an amiable way.

Stuart, however, is still trying to achieve satisfactory social relations and to control his own aggressive tendencies. When his antisocial act was met with similar hostility, his physical aggression collapsed at once. Yet his need for social play drove him back to the group. This time he chose another, more successful approach to re-entering the group. Stuart is obviously less socially mature than Mary-Jo, but he is learning.

Adults, observing the children in both incidents, refrained from interfering, even when some fighting began. Why? Because in both cases, the children themselves contained the aggression to one or two harmless blows. The teacher was ready to intervene if the fighting had continued. Both she and Mary-Jo's mother would have prevented further fighting by saying something like "You cannot hit each other," or

"We don't let children hurt each other," or "No hitting or hurting each other allowed." If one or both children had persisted, the adult should have removed them without scolding, but insisting on quiet isolation until they were ready to re-enter the group on more socially acceptable terms.

Usually the child's own need to play with others will effect the desired attitude. Sometimes, however, the child's mood doesn't change, and the wise caregiver or parent will substitute independent play for social play for as long as necessary, again without scolding the child, but stating the reasons if the child asks.

Providing Playmates

The strong drive of three-year-olds for establishing social relationships with their peers should be encouraged by thoughtful parents.

The first step is to provide a playmate or playmates. A good nursery school or daycare program offers the necessary children. As long as parents practice "easy does it"—introduce their child slowly into a daily group for an hour or two at first and stay with their child as long as needed—the group experience is usually a positive one. Daily visits to a playground may provide other opportunities. The one drawback may be a changing cast of characters. Children improve their social strategies best when they can meet the same group daily.

Finally, parents can form their own group, in which their own and their friends' children meet regularly, usually with different parents in charge and in different homes. The challenge is due to the changing cast of caregivers, as well as different locales. Studies of these kinds of groups show that changes are acceptable as the children become accustomed to the routine. For the children, the most important factor is the nucleus of familiar children as daily playmates. For the parents, this play offers a wonderful day of freedom at least once a week.

Preschool children will need little encouragement to play with each other as long as you

- Provide some appropriate materials: small and large blocks, toy people, crayons, paints, paper, a box of scraps, modeling clay, blunt scissors, simple toys.
- Refrain from interfering with their play and/or quarrels unless they start to get out of control.

- Make sure that the play area is safe.
- Always be sure that the children are under a watchful adult eye.

Expanding Social Experiences for Three-Year-Olds

The friendly and sunny three-year-old often accepts reminders about saying "please" and "thank you" that he hasn't been ready to deal with in the past. Children this age are more willing to wait their turn—if the waiting isn't too long—and to accept a little more philosophically that life doesn't always let people have what they want "right now!" Threes are eager for new experiences: a ride in a train, a visit to a downtown store, to Mother's or Daddy's office, to a restaurant—all are opportunities for trying out new social skills.

EATING AT HOME

A child who has only recently learned to cope with table utensils can't be expected to have excellent table manners, such as keeping food on a spoon, or refraining from spilling, dribbling, or upsetting glasses or dishes. Some general guidelines can be given:

- "We don't eat applesauce with our fingers."
- "If you put the edge of your cup a little farther into your mouth, you won't spill your milk."
- "It's easier to talk if you swallow your food first."

Many three-year-olds can eat at the family table with a little help, and will learn by observing others at the table. However, don't expect the three-year-old to remain at the table while adults linger over coffee or extended conversations. When the child has finished his own meal, he should be excused and allowed to leave. And if your child's lack of skill is likely to be ridiculed by his siblings, it may be easier on everyone if you feed him first.

Mrs. Dolan, a parent who had taught in a nursery school, became concerned over her three-year-old daughter's inability to join the family at mealtime. She expressed her dismay, and her solution to the problem, as follows:

"Helena kept acting up whenever she ate with the whole family. She was fine at breakfast, alone at her play table while the others rushed off to work or school; she was okay at lunchtime, with her brother and me. But the minute we included her at dinner time she became very silly. She made faces, interrupted our conversation, and dumped food on the floor—food that she handled perfectly well alone.

"She really annoyed me, but I was tired of feeding her, then the family. I had to think about the reasons for her antisocial behavior.

"Why did eating with the family excite her so? Why did she feel the need to show off and disrupt us? How could I help her adjust her behavior to conform more with ours?"

Mrs. Dolan though over some reasons for such behavior, then answered them as well as she could:

Question: Is Helena too young to socialize with the whole family?

Answer: No. Helena is fine socially when the family goes on trips, picnics, visits to grandparents.

Question: Does the closeness of mother, father, brothers, and sister at the dinner table upset her?

Answer: I don't think so. We are so close together on trips or going shopping, and Helena behaves then.

Question: Does she feel left out because the group is interested in other things, and is she using this chance to impress them —even if unfavorably?

Answer: Maybe. She doesn't play games very often with the other kids in the family, or enter easily into their activities. She is very much younger than the rest of the children.

Question: Is she too immature to accept such a close social setting easily?

Answer: Maybe. I don't really know.

Having looked at these questions and answers, Helena's mother decided to concentrate on her daughter's immaturity and her lack of social position in the family setup. In response to the first issue, Mrs.

Dolan decided to reduce the time that Helena would spend at the dinner table. The Dolans always ate salad first, so Helena would join them only during this course. Mrs. Dolan would plan to feed Helena most of her meal before the others ate.

To help her daughter feel more at ease in the social setting, Mrs. Dolan encouraged Helena's participation in the family conversation by telling the others of Helena's daily doings and encouraging Helena to contribute also. Slowly Mrs. Dolan's plan began to work. Helena's mischievous behavior at the table subsided as she was excused when the rest had finished their salad. Mrs. Dolan's insistence that the other family members listen to Helena's daily interests and activities gradually induced Helena to contribute to the general discussions and to remain longer at the table.

Mrs. Dolan also found that she had to speak privately to Helena's brothers and sister to enlist their cooperation. "I should have thought of that earlier," she said. "But it's okay. Now Helena's eating the whole meal with us."

Parents who want to help their children eat meals with the family may want to use Mrs. Dolan's list of questions as a guideline. These— and more mundane suggestions, such as helping your child cope with utensils—can serve as introductions to solutions that will facilitate successful family eating.

Remember always that your aim is to prevent creating a stressful situation at mealtime. Your urging a child to eat can quickly slip into nagging. Parents' concern over the amount and kind of food their child consumes is picked up by their offspring's parent-attuned invisible antennae. Children often use this parental anxiety as a weapon to confront, dismay, placate, or displease the adult in charge. Constant parent-child emotional confrontations over food consumption are a basis for long-term eating problems.

Eating Out

We want to enjoy our children and share experiences with them during this brief period of childhood. Yet we also want the trip to the restaurant, to the shop, to Great-grandma's house to be as felicitous as possible. It is usually helpful to tell your child ahead of time about tricky moments that may occur, and explain how he can cope with them.

If Great-grandma's way of life is quite different from yours and your child's, you can prepare him for the change:

Mother (to her three-year-old son Adam, on the way to visit "Omah" his great-grandmother): "Omah is pretty old, Adam. She does some things another way."
Adam: "What way?"
Mother: "She thinks boys are happier eating lunch before the grownups eat. You can eat first in the kitchen with Cordelia [the maid]. Then you won't have to wait at the dinner table while the grownups talk and talk."
Adam: "Bozo [Omah's dog] eat in kitchen, too?"
Mother: "I'm sure he does. That's a good idea."
Adam (with satisfaction): "Good."
Mother: "Omah thinks you still take naps! She takes a rest herself."
Adam: "Silly Omah! Big boys like me don't take naps. Don't rest at all."
Mother: "Maybe you and I can think of something quiet to do while Omah is resting."
Adam: "We take Bozo for a walk. He wants to see rabbits."
Mother: "Great! Maybe we can look for some flowers for Omah, too. You certainly have some good ideas, Adam."
Adam (with satisfaction): "Yes I do. Bozo wants to see flowers, too. Flowers and rabbits."

Adam's mother doesn't tell Adam about the change in eating arrangements until they are actually on the way, because there's little point in telling three-year-olds about proposed changes until the change is imminent. But she does give him some time to accept the new idea. She also encourages his method of acceptance, commending his ideas and helping him become interested in what he can do at Omah's.

The first trip to a restaurant is another experience that will be easier with preparation. For instance, we can explain that since many people are sharing the restaurant with us, we try to keep our voices low; we don't crawl under the table or run up and down the aisle. John Unger, a single parent, tells what he did:

"I only see Jon on weekends, and like to do different things with him. Last week he had his first restaurant experience. I'd been through a lot of embarrassment with Margot (Jon's older sister), so I laid it on the line with Jon ahead of time.

What we did was play-act restaurant visiting first at home. I was the waiter, Jon the patron. I made a menu of pictures for Jon to study and told him, 'Young sir, in here kids don't run around and yell. Peeking over the back of the booth is okay—but only once or twice, all right? No running up and down, but getting up to stretch is okay. And going to the bathroom is okay, too, but keep it cool—no back-and-forth.'

"Jon chose his food with dignity, then made me be the patron while he waited on me. Mostly I got served a lot of giggles and silliness—but it paid off when we went to a real restaurant. He was a little awed but acted with such propriety I felt like a Victorian papa. He became more normal on subsequent visits but never acted up like some kids I see. So both he and I can have fun when we go out."

Jon benefited from the chance to play-act a new experience before actually going through it. Not all new experiences can be dramatized ahead of time, but usually they can be explained and appropriate behavior suggested. Some rules can be laid out, but not too many to remember. On a first visit to a library, it's enough to remember to "talk softly" and it's hard to do! On first visiting a place full of grabable and tempting displays—whether books, toys, or delicious foods—the three-year-old needs to be reminded that she can't grab everything. Chances are she'll also need some physical help in not doing so. Sometimes the best solution is to postpone such temptations until your child can handle them. But it is always helpful to decide ahead of time what the most important rule is and not to worry about the other ones.

Jon's father's attitude brings up the point that the feelings and expectations—whether valid or not—of the adult in charge also affect which new experiences might be attempted. If Jon's father is disturbed by childish behavior in restaurants, he is right to help his son behave properly, perhaps more properly than most three-year-olds would. His preparing Jon makes the father-son relationship friendlier, especially since Dad presented the practice in such a playful way. If, however, a parent can offer only strictures or scoldings, it might be wiser to forego a new experience until later. Three-year-olds will act like three-year-olds—full of lively activity, friendly curiosity, uncertain table skills, and impetuous statements.

POLITENESS TO ADULTS

Nancy, riding on a crowded bus with her mother, suddenly exclaimed, "Dat man fat! Why dat man so fat?"

Embarrassed, Nancy's mother said in a low voice, "We'll talk about that later."

The man, however, smiled at Nancy and answered, "I'm like Santa Claus, that's why I'm fat. . . . In fact, I'm his brother."

That silenced Nancy, though she looked puzzled. Later her mother tried to explain that though some people looked very different from others, it wasn't kind to point it out. "You know," she added, "the way you don't like it when Uncle Ned calls you 'baby girl' when you're not a baby."

But Nancy was interested in one thing only: "How dat man is Santa Claus's brother?" she demanded. "He got to be in North Pole, not in bus."

Children will understand the feelings of others as they grow out of the totally self-centered stage. In a situation like that one Nancy got into, parents have two options. They can do what Nancy's mother did: hush the child, change the subject, and explain later; or they can just apologize to whomever the child might have offended, without trying to make a lesson of it for the child. But never should a child be punished or ridiculed for such an innocent and truthful observation. Three-year-olds can't be expected to understand that truthful remarks often hurt other people's feelings.

HELPING CHILDREN COPE
WITH FORMAL OCCASIONS

Children are having so many new experiences at this age that they have a difficult time figuring out how to respond, and parents can't always anticipate what kinds of comments or questions their children will ask publicly and loudly. What often helps is recognizing a child's limitations, and preparing for them and for the unexpected.

Sometimes parents will feel it necessary to stress manners prior to certain occasions or new experiences, especially when the parents know that more formality will be expected. A child who can't observe at least half an hour of these social demands would be better off left at home. And even for the child who can cooperate, limitations should be set. After a short time you should probably plan to have an older sibling take the younger child out to play, or have a friend involve the child in more appropriate activities.

How does a parent decide whether his child is ready to attend formal occasions—family gatherings, funerals, weddings, plays, parties, visits to friends—even for a short while? Basically, by evaluating the degree of his child's ability to tolerate strangers, unfamiliar places, and new experiences and situations.

Furthermore, the social requirements of the specific situation must be considered in relation to the child's personality. For instance, attendance at a wedding requires a child to sit still for approximately half an hour, to whisper, not talk; and to tolerate large crowds, new situations, and meeting strangers. Jeremy Brenner, facing this situation, made the following decision about his three-year-old daughter, Claudia:

> "Claudia is a restless kind of kid. She doesn't settle down to any activity very long. She also is a social butterfly, loves visiting my friends, as well as her friends. But she can become really absorbed if the event is full of rich sounds and sights.
>
> "My older boy, Jay, didn't want to go to our cousin's wedding at all. So I worked out a compromise with him. Both children would go to the church service—I found it would last only twenty minutes—then our babysitter would take charge of him and Claudia; Jay could invite a friend to our house for supper. In church, Jay would help me keep Claudia quiet.
>
> "This program worked out fine. I told Claudia that morning what would happen at the wedding and how she was expected to behave. As I guessed, she remained quiet at the church, fascinated by the pageantry. Jay kept a tight eye on her all through the service."

Finally, adults should be prepared to have their most careful tutoring go awry:

> When Amy Downes took her three-year-old granddaughter to meet her great-great-aunts for the first time, Amy knew that the aunts were representative of a more mannered time, so she thought she should coach Linda a little before the visit. At that time, Linda was a silent child and might not have responded at all to the aunts' overtures. They probably would have interpreted silence as rudeness.
>
> Amy tried to teach her some polite responses ahead of time. She told Linda that the aunts would say something like, "So this is little Linda! How are you, Linda dear?" To which she would respond, "Fine, thank you. How are you?" They played this as a game, taking alternate parts, until Amy was sure that Linda caught on.
>
> The great visit came, and the aunts started off as expected. "So this is little Linda!" But then they threw a curve ball and came out with an unexpected question: "How *old* are you now, Linda dear?"
>
> To which Linda politely responded, "Fine, thank you. How old are *you*?" Luckily, the aunts didn't hear very well and just beamed at Linda, assuming that she had answered correctly— and politely.

DIFFERENT SOCIAL RESPONSES
FOR DIFFERENT OCCASIONS

Of course, Linda didn't understand her grandmother's desire to please the aunts by using the social customs they understood. Normally, we don't endorse teaching just surface politeness to children but hope, by our example and natural discussions, to nurture their regard for the needs of others. Some social responses, however, are part of children's early learning experiences, whether or not they understand them. Almost all parents want their children to say please, thank you, hello, good-bye—meaningless phrases to children and perhaps to some adults.

Why, then, do parents persist in requiring children to say them?

First, these words are an accepted way of greeting people or of showing gratitude to others. S. I. Hayakawa, the noted semanticist, calls them "the establishment of friendly communication," a basic requirement for satisfactory social relationships. Adults murmur, "How are you?" or "Have a good day," without expecting answers. This habit of making agreeable noises to another person is a reassurance that we come in peace, that we are friendly. In the same way we can encourage children to make a few "amiable noises" without fear of overstressing surface politeness.

It doesn't have to be under the stress of a special occasion that you introduce your three- or four-year-olds to the idea that there are different social codes for different occasions and situations—such as, running is not for church, yelling isn't done at libraries, grocery boxes aren't for throwing on the floor.

These reminders come naturally to most parents and caregivers. Denise Moreau says that for a time she felt she spent all her days correcting her three-year-old son, Tommy. She remembers incidents like these:

Tommy pinches the cat.
Denise: "Bootsy is not for pinching—you hurt him, Tommy! You can pinch stuffed toys, not real animals."

Tommy hits his playmate Frances.
Denise: "You can't punch Frances, Tommy; you hurt her. I can't allow children to hurt each other."

Tommy, at his birthday party, plunges his hand into the cake to play with the merry-go-round decoration.
Denise: "Cakes are for eating, Tom, not for playing in. You can have the merry-go-round when I've cut the cake."

Tommy starts to put unwanted grocery articles into the shopping cart.
Denise: "We don't need those, Tommy. You can take down the things we do need and put them in the cart, okay? Let's find the bananas. Help me look."

After some personal experiences of codes of behavior such as these, you can usually remind your child by a casual remark, such as:

- Where do mud pies belong? Yes, outside!
- What do we do to our hands before we eat? Yes, wash them.
- Which clothes will you wear to Timmy's party? Yes, your clean ones.
- If you don't want more cake, what do you say to Timmy's mother? Yes, you say "No, thank you."
- What's important to remember before you cross the street? Yes, take my hand [or look at the light, look out for cars, wait for me].

Helpful Points to Remember
about Three-Year-Olds

Not all three-year-olds are alike.

Your youngster's "up time" may be another three's "down time." All assumptions (while based on reliable research) are just that—assumptions, not facts, and are offered to *help* you understand your youngster's behavior, not to confuse you.

Jonathan and Bette race from one activity to another, talk constantly to each other and to themselves. They are noisy, whether delighted or otherwise. They are often verbally stubborn in rejecting parental suggestions, but are not above screaming and kicking to make their points clear. On the go all day, they can exhaust the adults in charge.

These children respond more easily to changes in environment or routine activities, and seem to welcome a bustling, energetic day. They also can successfully engage in more than one activity at a time, such as listening to a story while drawing or throwing a ball. New children or adult strangers don't upset them. They either ignore newcomers or draw them into play. They often do better outdoors than indoors. They also need warning ahead of time to conform to the day's schedule: "In ten minutes, you will have to come in for dinner."

Parents can save themselves a lot of unnecessary emotional fatigue by going with the seemingly ceaseless flow of these small activists, insisting only on a few firm rules—bedtime, mealtime, bathtime, departure time (for school, shopping, visits).

Harvey and Jeannine, on the other hand, are much slower-moving, more placid children. They usually stick to one activity at a time, resisting attempts to involve them in other children's games. They, too, verbalize a lot, but much of their speech is directed toward their activity: "Here's the boat coming. Now it's getting loaded up. The captain has to watch so nobody bangs the boxes."

They, too, need time to break off their activity and should be given notice of impending change. Trying to modify their concentration on one play area is a hard task. Parents find it easier to let them play out their interest, and even broaden it, by supplying equipment for it or reading stories about it.

Children like Harvey and Jeannine are often upset by changes in their daily activities. They are apt to be shy with strangers and will cling to familiar adults in new settings. They need plenty of time for everyday routines, may be poky eaters or dressers. These are the youngsters who are the "dawdlers." Parents often find it easier to dress these three-year-olds than wait for their slow performance. Being patient with the slowpoke is sometimes hard.

But, as with the more active child, parents must adapt to the child's timing and activity pattern. Trying always to force a faster pace can lead to further frustration, crying, or even stuttering.

Parents can discern their three-year-olds' behavior, either in Jonathan and Bette's very active patterns, Harvey and Jeannine's slower pace, or somewhere in between. Whatever your child's style, your best line of action is to go along with his or her own pattern and save your energies for enforcing the rules for social behavior that are important to you—and the fewer the rules, the better for you all.

The best method still for inculcating the kind of social relationships we want our children to attain is by our own modeling. Our caring concern for our children, our respect for their needs and ideas, and our attitude toward others, including animals and the environment, will demonstrate our idea of "good manners." We needn't expect social graces from three-year-olds, but we can expect them to mirror our concerns—at least some of the time.

Three-and-a-Half-Year-Olds—A Stormy Scene

After a time of some stability, many three-year-olds seem to enter a period of insecurity as they move toward their fourth birthday. Physically they may begin to stutter, to become more uncoordinated than they were; socially, they become more negative, more insistent on their own way.

"No!" resounds again as it did at the age of two, but now it often accompanies indecision, or anxiety and fear. A three-and-a-half-year-old may demand carrots for supper, then at their arrival, tearfully announce that she really wanted green beans. Another time she may tell her family, "Don't anyone look at me!" but a short while later whine for attention. It seems to be a time of irrational feelings, of "bears under the bed"; a time when a child can develop an incomprehensible fear of such diverse objects as flies and airplanes.

"A bud [bug]! Get that bud away!" yells Jenny, pointing to a microscopic speck on her floor. Or Jeremy may cry at night, "There's 'nooks' in the room. Get the 'nooks' out of here!"

Parents and caregivers can be upset, annoyed, or bewildered by such unpredictable behavior, even if they understand it's "just another phase." The most effective handling seems to consist not of arguing about the situation or trying to convince the child that her fears aren't justified, but to deal with them as quickly and calmly as possible. At this stage, children don't think logically, so trying to persuade them that the bug is harmless or that nooks don't exist is a useless task. Jenny's father bends down, picks up the unseen "bud," and throws it out the window. "There, all gone now," he says. "No more bugs here any more." Jeremy, the "nook" fearer, is given a flashlight to shine in all the corners where nooks may be lurking.

The three-and-a-half-year-old can verbalize his anxieties and fears better than he could in his last stormy stage, making the situation somewhat easier for parents to understand, if not always to handle successfully. But it is still necessary for parents to listen extremely carefully. They must use their "third ear" to account for the child's particular use and understanding of his newly acquired language. This bewildering stage of "yes, I will—no, I won't" is often a trying one for the child's caregivers.

STRUGGLE OVER ROUTINES

Routine jobs, such as dressing, undressing, eating, bathing, or going to bed, can become real combat zones at this time of antisocial behavior. Children also tend to revert to a negative state in times of stress, such as a move to a new house, an upset in the family, or starting nursery school.

The growing need for the older three to take more control of his destiny often underlies such rebellions, and the persons he turned to for assistance in the past—his parents—may be the very ones he most rebels against now. His burning desire to show his competency, and his overestimation of his ability combined with his lack of emotional control, make things difficult for his parents at this time.

The best way to handle this daily struggle may be to let someone else take over the routine for a while—an older sibling, a housekeeper, or grandmother. This will dissipate a lot of the heat, and relations between the parent—or whoever the principal caregiver happens to be —and child will benefit.

If a parent has to handle the routine alone, however, the best bet is to get through as quickly and as quietly as possible, eliminating unnecessary demands. Examine the routine to see which parts of it are most distasteful to the child. If it doesn't really do any harm, let the child do it his way. All too often both parent and child can let a battle of wills become the dominant factor, while both lose sight of the original issue. If Howard sleeps in his clothes tonight, okay; he'll go back to pajamas in the future. If he sleeps with his light on or sleeps on the floor, it won't last forever. The important thing is to get him to bed, to keep the routine going smoothly, even if there are a few small changes.

Some parents might ask, "Isn't it setting a bad example to Howard to let him get away with doing only half his job?"

Such worriers may be reassured to know that children do get through this period and resume the old routines. Letting children assume some degree of power, at a time when they desperately need to, may be a plus. Such minor victories may enhance their uncertain self-esteem, though, of course, parents will want to encourage other, more positive ways of accomplishing this goal.

BEDTIME. For most children—and many adults—breaking off daily activities in order to go to bed is not easy. Children seem to need a familiar social routine for going to bed: an established ritual that eases the changeover could be undressing, bathroom chores, prayers, a glass of water by the bedside, a good-night story, and the recitation of some magic incantation, such as "Good night, sleep tight. Don't let the bed-bugs bite!"

But there are times, like the late three-year-old stage, when the child strongly rejects the usual pattern. What to do then? The following anecdote may be helpful.

Chris Thornbury tells of his struggle to get his three-and-a-half-year-old son, Michael, to bed:

> "It helped to remember that our older daughter, Mavis, went through a similar fight against the routine of bedtime, and showed the same bad social behavior. We remembered that Mavis's struggles were directed mostly at her mother—especially this 'I won't go to bed' business. So I took over the job with Mike—and it's a pain in the neck! Even though I tell him I'll read to him when he's in bed, he still can't resist stalling and whining. So I kind of hustle him through: 'Okay, Mikey, let's go! Off with your shirt and vest. Zip. Off come your pants and socks, and into your pj's.'
>
> "I wash his face and hands fast; the nightly bath has been changed to a morning job—he's more amiable and social then. The only thing I do insist on is his brushing his teeth—he knows I'll do it for him if he slacks off. Then into bed, and storytime. I usually try to read to him; it calms him down and changes the direction of his thinking. I think it's important in its own right, too. I don't punish him by cutting out storytime, except if he's too tired or resistant to listen, anyway.
>
> "One night it was fight, argue, and yell all the way. I was fed up and getting boiling mad, when I thought, 'Is brushing his teeth worth all this fuss? Is this fight really important?' I felt calmer right away, picked Michael up, still kicking and yelling, and deposited him under the sheets, without the usual prayers or storytelling.
>
> "'You really need your sleep, Mike,' I said, still calm. 'Good

night, now, sweetie, and pleasant dreams.' I kissed him and left.
Lo and behold! in about four minutes, the tumult and the shout-
ing died. And in about seven minutes, Michael was asleep—and
I didn't feel like a dragged-out survivor!

"I guess once in a while just moving out of the scene without
anger really works."

Some points to remember from Chris Thornbury's experience:

• Recognize a rebellious situation for what it is.
• If possible, let a less-involved person handle it.
• If not, get through it as quickly and as easily as you can.
• Don't let the situation develop into an emotional confronta-
  tion; skip whatever threatens to become an impossible de-
  mand.
• Remember—some things are not worth fighting about.

TOILET TIME. By three, most children are dry during the day, and many
stay dry all night. But in times of stress, some older threes revert to
babyish ways, even to the extent of soiling their pants.

It's hard to accept this step backwards, but scolding or shaming the
child only increases the tension and anxiety which may have caused the
reversion in the first place. During the day the adult in charge can
usually judge when a child needs to use the toilet and can get him there.
If the child refuses, present him with a potty and walk off. At night you
may have to start doing away with that last drink. And if all else fails,
you can put paper on the bathroom floor under his potty, and leave
him to it. It may help to repeat to yourself, "This won't last! This won't
last!" It usually doesn't.

DRESSING. Often the negative attitude of this age rears up in the dressing process. The three-and-a-half-year-old wants to do everything herself, and this includes choosing her clothes. She may want to wear a
flimsy dress and sneakers in the snow or no raincoat in the rain. Again
it's easier if a sibling rather than a parent works with the younger child
when these problems come up. But there are also some precautions you
can take to avoid as many confrontations as possible:

- Put away all but the right kinds of clothes for the time of year (or day).
- Provide the easiest-to-put-on kind of clothing—elastic instead of buttons on underwear, zippers in pants or shirts.
- Give a choice: "You can take the umbrella or wear your raincoat with a hood today."
- Accept the child's choices if possible—even though they aren't yours.

EATING

Another area of social conflict can be the family table: the child may reject the family meal, demand other food, and then reject that, too.

Some parents ask the child to leave the table. Others let him stay but insist he not disturb the rest of the group; while still others decide to feed the complainer early. The best thing to do is ignore the varying demands as much as possible, and decide on a minimum standard of behavior and which choices you will insist upon.

One inventive parent placed small packages of nourishing food in the refrigerator, *e.g.,* a bundle of cheese strips and cherry tomatoes; a little jar of mixed salad with a vial of salad dressing and a hard-boiled egg; a brown-bread, ham, and lettuce sandwich; a half cup of milk pudding; half-pint cartons of milk with straws. She let the child help himself during the day and thus eliminated the problem at the family table, except for those times her child chose to join them with his food choices. And his feeling of independence—arriving with his own food —made him much happier when he did come to the family gatherings.

The point is not to let mealtime—one of the lifelong social occasions—become a testing ground for antisocial behavior. The most nutritious diet will be adversely affected by stress at the dinner table and may encourage the child to use mealtime as an effective weapon against her adult caregiver.

Remember:

- This phase won't last.
- It's not worth a lot of anger and strife.
- Keep calm, even if it means leaving the scene.
- Don't worry about your child's food intake; children usually

take what they need. A baby's fierce demands for food usually taper off in the first few years, and children often seem uninterested in eating. If your child picks at one meal, she will usually eat more at the next. It's the rare child who starves herself.

Signs of Stress

Most three-year-olds are physically and socially quite competent, yet six months later they may seem to regress. At three and a half they often stumble, stutter, or temporarily lose the fine-muscle coordination they use in block building or coloring. But what looks like backsliding is usually caused by the child's desire to push faster than he can manage. The three-and-a-half-year-old who suddenly begins stuttering usually does so because the words are tumbling out faster than she can pronounce them. This is not a true stutter and should not cause concern, though may parents do become anxious about the cause of this ineptitude and of the general nervousness exhibited by their youngsters. The following typical report shows the kind of puzzled disturbance that many parents feel!

"I don't know what's gotten into Shana. She seems stronger in some ways—she can climb to the top of the Junglegym now. But she seems so nervous—about what, I don't know! She blinks a lot, and every once in a while she complains she can't see. At other times she says she can't hear. But she really can see and hear perfectly well. And we're back to that old NO stage! I thought we were all through with that negative attitude. But when I ask her to do something, like come to the store with me, it's 'No, I don't want to! I won't!' Yet if I start to go without her, she gets upset! Does she need to go to the doctor? Is something wrong with her?"

Probably not. It's more likely that she's trying to do more than she can. This means you're in for a stormy time of change, of disharmony, of antisocial behavior, which will lead, in turn, to a more harmonious stage. If you need reassurance, however, you may want to have your physician check her out between her regular examinations.

VISITS TO DOCTOR, DENTIST, AND BARBER

Even though your child has visited the doctor—and possibly the dentist —as an infant and toddler, you can still expect this kind of trip to be fraught with stress. The same may be true for visits to the barber for haircuts. Be prepared for possible antisocial actions and emotional upsets.

The best way to handle these possibilities is to prepare your child ahead of time:

• Explain just what the doctor (dentist, barber) will do.
• Try not to let your own anxiety about shots or doctor visits color your child's attitude.
• Role-play the visit ahead of time—with puppets, dolls, or you and your child as the actors.
• Read stories of visits to such offices.

Most important, if your child hasn't been to one of these places, or if the doctor, dentist, or haircutter is new, take her there ahead of time. Then she can accustom herself to the office, the personnel, the equipment. The easiest way to do this is to take your child along when you need one of these services, so she can have a firsthand view of what goes on.

Even after all this preparation, remember that your child may still "act up." If so, try not to preach or punish, stay as calm as you can, and complete the visit as quickly as possible. After all, these visits are often genuinely upsetting, and most doctors or dentists are accustomed to the ways of three-year-olds.

VISITS TO STORES AND OTHER DAILY OUTINGS

We know the importance of providing preschoolers with the best kinds of materials, places, and experiences to help them develop physically, mentally, emotionally, and socially.

Taking small trips into the outside world is a valuable and necessary activity in raising a social child. Most children love these experiences. They learn how people work and live; they observe differences in appearances, ages, and life styles; they learn how to interact with all kinds of people; and they learn how the community expects them to behave.

Yet in stressful periods, children revert to behaving the way they want to, not the way others want them to. If your three-and-a-half-year-old carries on about going shopping with you, don't take him unless it's absolutely necessary. Coping with a kicking, screaming, stubborn child in the supermarket is an experience nobody needs. Plan ahead for a babysitter your child knows and likes, or plan to leave him regularly at a favorite friend's or relative's house, perhaps on an exchange basis.

When you can't avoid taking a reluctant child on these errands, try to make them as short as possible. Save the long shopping expeditions for a day when Johnny or Janey can be left elsewhere.

Since exploring the outside world with your child is so valuable an experience, however, you will want to keep trying to include her in as many expeditions as possible. Perhaps you can anticipate ahead of time some things to avoid, such as lengthy waiting in line, large crowds, overlong expeditions. There are also some useful strategies to use to divert antisocial behavior, such as:

- observing the imminent signs of collapsing self-control (restlessness, whining, dragging of feet, snappiness);
- suggesting diversionary action (stopping for food, resting, going to an alternative activity, carrying your child, letting another handle your child);
- leaving the scene altogether;

But always remember that this stressful stage will pass, and soon your child will be that curious but pleasant trip taker once more!

A Special Stress: Sibling Relationships

Probably children with siblings have always wanted to be only children, and only children have always wanted to have siblings. With siblings come problems as well as satisfactions, especially that familiar problem called sibling rivalry.

Experts say that sibling rivalry is greatly lessened when there is at least a five-year age gap between the children. Those siblings with only a one- to three-year difference are more apt to experience rivalry.

The two- or three-year-old has been King of the Castle, the focus of parental and grandparental attention, all his short life. Suddenly along comes the Dirty Rascal, the new baby, who demands attention too.

The preschooler, still in the ego-centered stage, can't understand that parental love expands to include both children. In her illogical thinking, the attention shown the newcomer must be subtracted from the attention previously shown to her. No wonder she's resentful. Many preschoolers also think the new baby will be an immediate play-mate, and they are disappointed by the helpless infant. There are many steps parents can take to help smooth the way for a soon-to-be sibling: they can explain the expected arrival when the changes in the mother's body become evident, and again as the delivery date nears. They can answer all the child's questions and invite her help in preparing for the baby; they can consult the child about using her discarded possessions (crib, highchair); they can have a favorite relative or sitter move in before Mom moves out; and they can tell their child not to be surprised if Mom leaves at night. All these preparations will help the older child receive the newcomer more easily. When the new baby comes home, the older child should be included as often as possible in the baby's routine, helping to wash, dress, and hold him, under supervision. It's when the baby becomes the Creeper that rivalry between siblings most often begins in earnest.

"My four-year-old Debra was just wonderful when we brought Henry home! We let her tell the relatives and friends, and help put Henry to bed; we saw that she had a small gift when Henry was given gifts. We even encouraged Debby to imitate our baby care with her doll care. And it all seemed to work! Sure, at times Debby objected to the baby. Take the time we were going out to eat, leaving Henry with a sitter; but Henry developed a fever and we had to stay home. 'Take that dumb baby back,' Debra yelled then. But most of the time it was okay, until Henry began to crawl, then to creep.

"Not only did he attract a lot of attention and praise from the grownups; he disrupted Debra's things, knocking down her blocks, chewing on her stuffed dog. He adores Debby and creeps after her. Sometimes she seems proud of his regard for her and plays with him, but often now she complains of his interference, of the time I have to give him. She loves books like Martha Alexander's *Nobody Asked Me If I Wanted a Baby Sister* and wants me to read them again and again.

"She also has begun to act more babyish herself—climbing on my lap, sucking her thumb, wanting her milk or juice in a bottle. I guess we'll have to make sure that she gets enough time alone with us, to feel that she's still special. But it will take a while."

Yes, it will take time. And a certain amount of sibling rivalry will undoubtedly continue. Debra will often see Henry as a tagger-on, or as an interferer. At times, Henry will see Debby as someone he can't catch up to, someone "better" than he is.

Maria and Joseph Caprio have four children, ages one, three, five, and eight. How do they find time to give each child individual loving attention? Maria says:

"Morning is usually my time with my three-year-old, Rita, and JoJo, the baby. Rita helps me clean and make beds, while JoJo naps. Rita loves this time together and feels she's doing something really grown up as she holds one end of a sheet. She loves to punch up the pillows for me.

"After JoJo's nap we all go shopping (I'm a daily shopper) and stop by the park. Rita has other three-year-olds to play with in the park, and she looks forward to seeing them. So it's JoJo's special time. I bounce him and play finger and toe games with him, and point out lots of things in the park to him. He doesn't know most of what I'm saying, but he loves it, anyway.

"At noon, Tommy comes home from kindergarten. I listen to him a lot as I get lunch ready; he's nearly always stirred up by the morning's events. He's ready for a short nap; so is Rita. JoJo is, too. And I'm sure ready to rest! As I say this, I'm amazed that I've given each kid some special time already. And I'm usually there with snacks and open ears when Anita, my eight-year-old, comes home after school.

"Joe, my husband, makes the rounds at night. He puts each kid to bed after reading a story to them all, JoJo included. It's a three-ring circus at times, but the kids know we have time for each."

Avril Leslie has a different problem. She is a single, working mother with two children: four-year-old Jamie and three-year-old Andrew. She says:

"Mornings are rough. I have to dress Jamie and help Andrew, who both want to dress themselves. I used to make breakfast, but it didn't work well. Now I take them down the street to Petra's house, where they spend the day. There she gives them and some other kids a leisurely breakfast. She only takes care of five kids altogether, which allows each to have enough attention, as well as someone to play with.

"I eat my dinner at noon, so I can spend more time with my two at night. We have an unhurried light meal, then they get ready for bed. I try to get both sides of any squabble that arises, then make as fair a decision as I can. We have a short 'talking time' when they are in bed. I bring up whatever bothers me and encourage them to do the same. I read a story out loud, then hugs and good-night kisses end the day.

"Like they say, since I don't have too much time with the kids, I try to make the best of it and give each one a little special attention. I get cross, tired, yell sometimes, but I do try."

Another single, working parent, Richard Epps, says:

"Sure, I have my hands full with three boys, a ten-year-old, an eight-year-old, and a three-year-old. I couldn't do it if my mother didn't live with us. She's great with the kids, though she spoils them a little—especially Teddy, the youngest. The others complain that Grandma's not fair sometimes. So I have to be strict and fair. Teddy has to try to stick to our rules. If everybody has to make his bed, nobody complains. The boys accept Teddy's messy job—and Teddy feels like a big guy. Sometimes they all gang up against one of my rules (like no more than one hour of television daily), but I don't mind. It gives them a feeling of comradeship, one for all, and all against one—namely, me."

From these brief glimpses of several different kinds of family groups, we can see some of the effective ways that understanding parents can help children develop a caring regard for each other:

- By showing their love and concern for all their children.
- By trying to be fair with all their children.
- By making parental rules apply to every child.
- By insisting on fairness and sibling consideration from all the children.
- By trying to give some personal attention to each child every day.
- By allowing and encouraging siblings to develop relationships that exclude the parents.

A tall order? In theory, perhaps, but not in practice; for such treatment comes naturally to most parents who really care for each child's well-being. Fair treatment and loving concern seem to be the qualities most children desire from their parents. And if a little rivalry still persists, that might be a plus in preparing kids for real life.

Four-Year-Olds—Time for Preschool?

Most children enter their fourth year in a period of emotional and social equilibrium. They are in control of their physical activities, and they seem to be in emotional harmony with their families and peers. They are adept at language and fairly capable of good body control. They also are more accepting of others' needs and viewpoints, although they have developed their own preferences. Quite a well-rounded person is this four-year-old.

At this time, many parents are thinking of the advantages or disadvantages of sending their youngster to a preschool program. Of course, many children younger than four may have been attending some kind of preschool already, at least for part of the day. But because kindergarten is now only a year away, parents, including those whose children have attended a preschool program, may wonder if their child will be ready socially, emotionally, and intellectually for entering kindergarten. They wonder if their child would be best prepared by entering a preschool, and if so, what kind? A formal one? A play school? A

Montessori school? The answer depends not only on the parents' preferences, but also on their understanding of the important factors in
their child's development.

PRESCHOOL EVALUATION GUIDES

There are many guides to assessing a preschool program, in terms of
considering not only its setting and the materials used, but also the
program's philosophy, as it enhances the cognitive (or intellectual) development, the physical development, and the emotional and social
development of the child. Since our interests lie in the child's social and
emotional development, we will concentrate on this area.

A good social climate in a preschool will provide

- opportunities for social interaction. For instance, if the teacher
  appears always to direct the play, to organize the day by
  assigning children to groups, obviously children won't have
  much chance to initiate and explore social relationships on
  their own.
- materials that encourage social play, such as blocks and family corners (stove, cribs, dolls, a refrigerator).
- opportunities for group discussion, during which the child is
  encouraged to volunteer his ideas.
- clearly understood directives for social behavior, which are
  protective rather than restrictive.

STAFF-CHILD RELATIONS. A good preschool has a staff that

- is sensitive to individual needs.
- encourages but doesn't force participation in group activities.
- provides opportunities and materials for social interaction.
- uses group trips and group projects to include the shyer and
  the bolder child.
- encourages group discussions.
- has a general attitude of "informed permissiveness" that encourages individual exploration of materials and social relationships.
- protects children from their own and others' overagressive
  behavior.

The best way to judge the staff is to see it in action. As you watch, ask yourself these questions:

- Is there a caring relationship between each teacher and child?
- Does the staff show respect for each child? Encourage and listen to his questions and comments?
- Are boys and girls treated equally?
- How are behavior problems handled?
- Are children allowed to work alone, as well as with others?
- Do the caregivers encourage children to understand their social problems and to seek solutions?
- Do the caregivers understand the child's need to blow off steam or show negative emotions?
- Do they console unhappy children?
- Do they help children develop their own self-control?
- Is the physical space adequate?
- Do children work on their own sometimes?
- Do children do different things? Have a variety of activities to choose from?

CHILD-CHILD RELATIONS. A visit to the preschool will also let you observe the social interaction among the children. Ask yourself the following:

- Do children enter the preschool happily or eagerly?
- Do they get along with the other children? Have fun and play together? Seem at ease?
- Do the children help each other?
- When they fight, are they treated fairly and with understanding by the staff and the other children?

You will also want to find out how parents interact with and are treated by the staff. If all or most of the previous questions have positive answers, then you can be fairly sure your child will develop emotionally and socially in such a preschool setting.

WHY PRESCHOOL, ANYHOW?

Some parents wonder if it's in the best interests of their children to start preschool.

One mother, Eleanor Sanchez, notes:

> "My four-year-old Lucia seems so happy now. Each day is so full of activities for her, she seems busy all the time. She's very outgoing, enjoys meeting and greeting people in the stores and at my friends' houses. And she does have plenty of opportunity to interact with other children. We go to the park almost every morning, where she plays with a familiar group. In fact, she plays so vigorously that she takes a long nap after lunch.
>
> "I'm afraid if she starts preschool now, she may not be able to have this needed rest. And maybe being thrust into a strange setting with strange kids will upset her wonderful equilibrium. Is it worth this kind of possible trauma? Wouldn't it be better to wait till she's a year older and ready for kindergarten?"

Perhaps Lucia is one of the lucky children who has enough peer contacts to meet her needs for a larger social world. No doubt she will do well at home and in kindergarten; at the same time, she will miss out on some of the important adjustments that the preschool offers— adjustments that sooner or later she will have to make.

THE SEPARATION PROCESS

One of the great steps preschoolers must take is the first prolonged separation from their prime caregiver, often their mother. Individual children respond in a variety of ways to separation. Some do it easily, with a minimum of stress and anxiety. But others need a lot of attention, much reassurance that they are not abandoned by their principal caregiver, and a gradual easing into longer periods of separation. Sometimes this step is taken earlier, with entry into daycare or nursery school, but for many children it occurs in the year before kindergarten.

Children who, like Lucia, stay at home miss this early experience of separation and reunion with the parent in a familiar structured setting. Lucia also will miss the prekindergarten experience of relating to peers and adults without Mother's help in a similar structured but caring setting. (Of course we take it for granted that these children are in the kind of preschool that has the desired setting, the necessary number of helpers, and the sensitivity to respond to each child's needs.)

Recently in a preschool program I watched Bella, whose mother, after a week of staying with her, had finally decided to leave Bella on her own. Bella kept on working with others on a puzzle. When her two playmates left, Bella worked alone for a while. Then, finger in mouth, she wandered over to watch a building in progress. When the teacher asked her if she wanted to join the construction workers, Bella shook her head. The teacher kept close to her as Bella stayed apart from the group. Then the teacher asked, "Would you like me to read *Mouse Tales* [a favorite book by Arnold Lobel]?" Bella nodded. The teacher's reading attracted others to the reading corner. At the story's end, the teacher asked the listeners, "Vanessa, Philip, and Bella, would you help me get the tables ready for lunch? Vanessa, you get the napkins, Philip can lay out the spoons and forks, and Bella will set out the dishes."

Bella worked happily with her peers, joking and giggling all the time. She had, for the time being at least, forgotten Mother's departure.

LANGUAGE FOR REASSURANCE. One of the reasons for deferring a child's entrance into preschool is to allow for his growing use of language to support his acceptance of separation. The three- or four-year-old is aware of himself as a complete person and he has been through many short separation periods, which have taught him that mothers don't vanish but do return. Though he knows these facts intellectually, repeating them out loud seems to help him grasp them emotionally.

Here are some typical statements made by older three- and four-year-old children. They were said while the children were crayoning together.

Lana: "My mother is at work. She's coming back after lunch."

Alan: "My mother's coming back, too. She's coming back for me the minute I get up from nap."

Lana: "My mother brings me here after breakfast. My mother brings me to Nana's [Grandma's] after lunch."

Alan: "Yeah. After nap and snacks. That's when Mommy comes."

By stating this timetable in words and relating it to events, children reassure themselves, and each other, about the predictability of Mother's return. Staff members also repeat these assurances to anxious children until they have enough experience to accept them as true.

Lynn, who was engaged in dramatic play with some other four-year-olds, suddenly rushed to Russell, the teacher's aide. "My mommy is coming back soon," Lynn said, tears brimming in her eyes. "She's coming right back."

Russell squatted down by Lynn and put an arm around her. "Sure she is, Lynn," he said. "She brings you here in the morning. You play and play while Mommy goes to work. You eat lunch and go to nap time. What happens when you wake up?"

"Mommy is here?" Lynn asked, wiping her nose.

"Something else first," Russell said. "Something you pop in your mouth."

"Snacks!" Lynn cried.

"Right!" said Russell. "And then what happens?"

"Mommy comes," Lynn said, with deep satisfaction, and went back to her play group.

A PLAN FOR SEPARATION. Good preschools plan carefully with parents so that separation causes the least amount of trauma possible. Here are some guidelines for a smooth transition:

- Parents stay with their child each day as long as is deemed necessary.
- Parents gradually lessen the amount of time they spend in preschool.
- Parents confer with the caregivers daily about their child's adjustment.
- Both parents and staff observe and interpret to themselves and each other the child's reactions and needs at home and at school.
- Both parents and staff are prepared for and accept a certain amount of the child's regression to more babyish ways, and

other behavioral changes, in response to the emotional stress of the separation.

A working parent recalls:

"When my daughter was young, I worked in the nursery school she attended. I wasn't too pleased with the school's philosophy, but she seemed happy. Then I had to leave for a better job. Her reactions at home began to disturb me. She was cranky, cried easily, looked sullen, acted babyish. Yet the staff assured me that all was well. A week of this behavior, along with my intital misgivings, led me to search for another preschool more in accord with my beliefs.

"I transferred her there as soon as possible. With the school's help, we took all the steps outlined for coping with separation. In a week, my child was her old sunny, happy self again, and I was enormously relieved. I knew then, as I know now, that a child's attitude and behavior are a parent's best measure of her inner turmoil or satisfaction with life."

SETTING BEHAVIOR LIMITS

Though verbally adept, four-year-olds are still learning language by imitating the speech of others, playing with words, and trying out the effect of words on others. Just as toddlers tested the limits of their physical capabilities, preschoolers feel out the boundaries of their newly acquired language. At this early stage it is only from adults that children can learn what is appropriate and what is inappropriate. And it is a complicated business for the young language user; he must also learn that what is appropriate for one social situation might be inappropriate for another. Getting all this sorted out is no mean accomplishment.

"BAD" LANGUAGE. As their social world expands into the playground, the street, and the preschool setting, many youngsters are exposed to "four-letter words" and swear words. Unlike the innocent toddler, the four-year-old soon becomes aware that such languge has an emotional overtone: adults use it to express feelings of dismay, dislike, or anger. No wonder a child is tempted to try out these words himself. If when he does use them they evoke strong emotional responses, the child may well feel that he has discovered a powerful tool for causing adult reactions, even if such reactions are negative.

Sometimes parents are shocked to hear their own heated words— or even their more careless ones—being repeated by their children. One parent ruefully admitted she hadn't realized how often she swore until she heard her daughter repeating her language.

Other parents, though accustomed to hearing language that once was called vulgar, and though often using it themselves, are uncomfortable when they hear it from a young child. Such parents have to recognize that they are models for their child's language as well as for their child's behavior, and they must decide to clean up their own speech or be prepared to hear it from their kids. It really doesn't work to demand that children not use language that parents use. If children are punished for doing so, what conclusions will they draw?

If, however, children are picking up language outside the home that disturbs their parents, the parents have not only a right but a duty to let the children know how they feel about it. The following scene is typical of family reactions:

> *Father:* "Come on, Josh, time to go home, now."
>
> *Josh:* "Aw, let me stay. Don't want to go home now."
>
> *Father:* "Sorry, son, we have to get going. I warned you we would, five minutes ago."
>
> *Josh* (stamping foot): "I won't go. You're a mean old fart!"
>
> *Father:* "*What* did you call me?"
>
> *Josh:* "A mean old fart."
>
> *Mother:* "Where did you hear that, Josh? Who says that?"
>
> *Josh* (sheepishly): "Billy says it. He says it when I won't play with him."
>
> *Father:* "Well, *we* don't say that! Not in this family!"
>
> *Mother:* "Right. Josh, did you ever hear Daddy or me call anyone a fart?"
>
> *Josh:* "No. But Billy says it."
>
> *Mother:* "Billy's not in our family. And we don't call people that."
>
> *Josh:* "Why not?"

Mother: "Well, what a fart means is passing gas—you know what that is."

Josh: "Yeah, you gotta say 'Excuse me.' "

Father: "Right. But do we want to say anyone is like passing gas?"

Josh: "No—too smelly, too pewy!"

Mother: "Okay, let's get going, gang, or we'll miss the bus."

In this episode Josh certainly learns both by words and by his parents' reactions that they don't like his new expression. His father seems almost angry, almost threatening. Mother backs up Father, but lets Josh tell where the word came from and explains what it means. She also stops the discussion when she feels it has gone far enough.

Josh's own attitude indicates a certain sly expectation of his parents' negative reaction to his expletive. And the message he receives is a mixed one:

- This phrase is not socially acceptable to his parents—and probably not to most adults.
- He now has a social weapon to use when he wants some powerful, though negative, adult reaction.

On the negative side, a less shocked and heated response from Father might have defused some of the phrase's power. On the positive side, Josh has a trusting enough relationship with his parents to try out such words with them. He seems to know they won't punish him, but he learns something about the limits of their tolerance. The immediate result of this experience probably will be that Josh will not call his father that name again, but may try it out on Billy.

Rather than yelling at your child, try telling him how you feel:

- "Adam, when you use those words over and over, I really feel annoyed. I can feel my neck getting hot. I've told you so many times how boring it is to hear them. So I want you to go off by yourself if that's all you can say."
- "Marny, I can't accept that language. I don't say it, your father doesn't say it. We don't use it here. It makes me feel depressed and annoyed to hear you. Do you think you can stop talking like that?"

Or you might help your young child develop other epithets, less offensive to older family members and appealing to the child's love of wordplay:

> *Four-year-old Christa:* "Aunt Mindy's a big poo-poo. You're a
>   big poo-poo!"
> *Mother:* "And you're a little mushy mushroom."
> *Christa* (laughing): "You're a big fat potato!"
> *Mother* (picking Christa up and dumping her in bed): "You're
>   my kiddly, koddly, kuddly kitten Christa!
> *Christa* (sleepily): "You're a big pinker potter potato head!"
> *Mother:* "And you're my sweet succulent slippery sloppery slap-
>   pery sleepyhead. Good night, Little Fish!"

Most children, even at six or seven, respond to and copy silly jingles like this, much less hurtful than real name calling:

> Ala-ka-zee
> Ala-ka-Zony! [or Zebby or Zeter or Zarilyn, etc.]
> Tee-legged
> Tie-legged
> Two-legged Tony! [or Debby or Peter or Marilyn]

EXPLORING SEXUAL SIMILARITIES AND DIFFERENCES

The four-year-old is still in an experimental stage, learning best from firsthand exploration. Most young children explore their own bodies, noting how they are alike and different from their parents' bodies and from those of other children. In previous generations, such exploration probably took place in secret, since the culture frowned on it. Now children are more likely to see and ask questions about puzzling anatomical features; and many parents can more easily and comfortably answer them, though there are still many adults who find it difficult to discuss human sexuality with their children. For these parents there are some fine books on the market, with helpful illustrations (See Bibliography). Looking at such books with your child is often a good starting place for discussions. The important thing to remember is to answer only what the child asks. Deal with his questions about bodily functions directly, simply, and matter-of-factly. There is no need to develop the conversation further, or to add information beyond the child's comprehension. Often in-depth information serves only to confuse the child and discourage further questions.

> (Billy's mother was giving him a bath. Billy was playing with his penis.)
>
> *Mother:* "Here's the washcloth, Billy, if you want to wash your penis."
>
> *Billy:* "Marilyn doesn't have a penis. How come?"
>
> *Mother:* "Because she's a girl. Girls don't have penises, only boys."
>
> *Billy:* "Oh. Does Hamish have a penis? Does Joanne have a penis?"
>
> *Mother:* "Joanne doesn't, she's a girl. Hamish does because he's a boy. Your penis must be all clean now; how about washing your toes?
>
> *Billy:* "How does Marilyn peepee?"
>
> *Mother:* "She sits down, like Joanne, like all girls and women. Only boys and men stand up."
>
> *Billy:* "Look! I cleaned out all my toe holes!"

Billy's mother answered his questions in a matter-of-fact way; she didn't add more information than he asked for and, curiosity temporarily satisfied, Billy's attention shifted. His mother may have had some uncomfortable feelings about his penis play, or she may have felt "enough was enough" and diverted his actions. But she didn't make him feel that he was "bad" for playing with his sexual equipment.

Since most children find that stimulating their sexual parts results in pleasant sensations, they are apt to masturbate at some time or other. Most experts feel that a moderate amount of sexual activity is not harmful, that it may even relieve some stress, and that parents should accept it as a natural event. They also say, however, that obsessive interest in masturbation may indicate some emotional need, which deserves closer investigation.

If parents are made very uncomfortable by masturbation or other sexual explorations, they'd do better to ask the child to stop, to tell him that they don't care for it, rather than attempt to hide their feelings.

Children pick up how parents really feel, on their marvelous invisible parent-attuned antennae. Receiving a mixed message often makes them feel confused or guilty and anxious.

Most parents do feel embarrassed or angry if their child masturbates in public. As privately as possible, they should let their child know this behavior is not an acceptable public activity, without condemning it altogether. Most children catch on quickly.

The important factor in all these instances is not to punish the child or make her feel wicked or disgusting for her curiosity. Harsh treatment may diminish the child's sense of self-worth now, and lead to sexual problems later. If you tell your child directly how you feel, she will respect your confidence. Children do want to please their parents and to be commended by them.

ANTISOCIAL ACTIONS

When you are away from the home and your four-year-old is cross, tired, oversocialized, overstimulated, or feeling ill, he lets you know about it. He may begin to rebel, cry, fuss, whine, become logy, or even strike out. Whatever he does, you must learn the best way of coping.

Unfortunately many parents still use a quick slap as their first reaction. This may stop the behavior momentarily, but usually the child just shifts from one negative behavior to another, from whining to dragging behind, from fussing to crying. And slapping certainly is negative modeling.

The important thing to remember is that your child can't help exhibiting his feelings. He is still strongly egocentric, not by choice but by nature. Unable to conceal how he feels, to rationalize it away, to predict a more comfortable future, he acts. We, the rational adults, must try to figure out what his trouble is and how to help him. The more we can anticipate his behavior, the easier it will be to avoid. Ask yourself:

- Has he been socializing too long?
- Have I taken him on too long a shopping trip?
- Have I been ignoring him too long for my own concerns?
- Is he hungry? Is his nose getting stuffy again?

Once you have a clue or have made a reasonable guess as to his difficulty, what do you do next? The best solution, of course, would have been to prevent the situation. But here it is, and you must deal with it as quickly as possible by

- picking up, carrying, or soothing the child.
- taking him to the nearest restroom, restaurant, or bus stop.
- grabbing a cab and getting him home as soon as possible.
- not scolding, but giving him firm directions: "Okay, Tony, I know you're tired. But you cannot lie down on the sidewalk or kick me—I won't let you do that. Here's the bus, I'll help you on. When we get home, you can have your supper [or look at TV for fifteen minutes, help me feed Rover, play with your train set]."

BEING A SOCIAL MEDIATOR. Though most fours are able to play reasonably well with friends, they are still self-centered, and at times they will fight to have their own way. Observing how preschool caregivers handle antisocial situations can be very helpful. Sometimes they just stand by, ready to intercede if the argument gets too heated. Often they will state the problem and ask the combatants to think of better ways to solve it.

In the following scenario, two preschool teachers, Tony and Lisa, are with their group outdoors. They act as social mediators, comforters, and rule affirmers, responding to a variety of situations:

- *Lisa:* "Emmy, that swing is for sharing. Now it's Timmy's turn. Here, I'll help you down. You can use the swing later."
- *Tony:* "Zeb, you have all the blocks and Tina wants some. Do you want her to help you? Or will you give her some of your blocks?"
- *Lisa:* "Debby, I can't let you hit Gregg. No [restraining her], you come sit by me. We don't hit people here." (Pause) "Let me see your hands, they're folded up so tight. You have strong fingers, don't you? I bet you can do lots of things with them."
- *Tony:* "That hurt, didn't it, Matt? I'm sure your thumb feels as big as the moon! [He takes Matt on his lap] Let's wave that

ol' thumb in the cool air for a minute. Think that will blow some of the hurt away?"

- *Lisa:* "Gregg, all that noise you're making really bothers the children. Go way down to the corner of the playground if you want to stamp and yell. You can't do it here."
- *Tony:* "Jon, we don't use words like that here. So please don't say them anymore. I bet you can think of some funny words instead. I can—how about this: 'tee-legged, tie-legged, two-legged Jon!' "

These few glimpses give you some clues about how you can help your own children in the ongoing job of becoming socially mature. The teachers are firm about what is not allowed, but they don't denigrate or shame the wrongdoer. They either present two choices to him, suggest substitute actions, or change the subjcet.

TEMPER TANTRUMS. At home, temper tantrums may still occur occasionally. Though the four-year-old can use language to express her problems, sometimes she reverts to more babyish reactions. She may want to attract your attention, defy or annoy you, or she may be feeling left out or just at odds with the world.

In most cases, you can guess the cause and try to answer it by:

- including her in some immediate activity: "Want to bake some cookies? You can make faces on them." "Want to help me in the garden? You can find worms for it." "Let's return our books to the library, okay?"
- cuddling and hugging her, or spending a little time rocking quietly.
- having her play alone in her room for a while; giving her some time and a place to quiet down, with a firm statement that she needs to cool off before you and she can talk.
- helping her accept a delayed gratification of her needs: "You look at 'Sesame Street' while I finish my work—then we'll go get your shoes." "We can't do that now. But we can do it when the clock's little hand is on three and the big hand is here—on four."

Don't threaten to abandon her or to stop loving her. This is the fate a child fears most, and the suggestion of it may well be psychologically damaging.

INCULCATING "GOOD MANNERS"

A decade or so ago many adolescents abandoned good manners, declaring them to be "hypocritical and sanctimonious," and saying that "actions, not words, define good manners." Indeed, words spoken without sincerity are not good manners, and verbal expressions of politeness mean nothing unless backed up by caring actions.

Our definition of good manners means respect: respect for yourself and for others, both in speech and in action. And the most important place for a child to learn and to imitate caring respect is at home, especially from his role-model parents.

Respect means not only the familiar "respect for your elders," but also the consideration that elders show for their children and that children show for each other. While adults traditionally have demanded respect from their children, they may not always have returned it to their children. You can evaluate your own efforts to show your children respect by the following questions:

- Do I usually give my child's questions serious consideration?
- If he is present, do I include him in conversations I have with adults?
- Do I introduce him to people I meet in the supermarket?
- Do I ask his preference on matters relevant to him, such as food for dinner, the kinds of clothes he wears, his ideas for the weekend?
- Do I allow him his choices as much as possible?
- Do I show him, especially by example, the manners I expect from him in greeting people, in eating at the table, in public conveyances and restaurants, or just while walking down the sidewalk?
- Do I show consideration for others (animals as well as people) as I expect him to?
- Do I show him by my standards how I expect him to treat our environment—to pick up, not throw down, trash? to treat the park, the flowers, the trees, as well as he treats his home?

- Do I allow him the same chances to "let off steam" that I allow myself?
- Do I really listen to him? hear his side in disputes? hear his comments or his expressions of anxiety?
- Do I praise his efforts and accomplishments? encourage his growing independence?
- Do I let him know I appreciate his attempts at good manners (sharing, helping, waiting, showing concern)?
- Do I show him my love? Do I hug him or hold him enough?

You may have been doing some of these things since your child was a toddler, but this is a good time to look at your side of the relationship. If you find that you answered yes to most of the questions, you shouldn't have to worry much about your child's manners. You are saying "please" and "thank you" to him as a genuine expression of your respect; you are sharing with him as you expect him (eventually) to share with others; you are treating him with the consideration you want him to have for others. And the respect you have shown for him will slowly, slowly become the respect he has for others.

SPECIAL OCCASIONS

The young child's mastery of acceptable social behavior often slips when big occasions occur, like holidays, birthdays, or going to some special entertainment (the circus, shows, movies).

There are several steps we can take to help young children experience momentous occasions more easily:

- Be sure the occasion is suitable for the child's age or stage of development.
- Help the child prepare ahead of time.
- Be alert to signs of stress.
- Adjust the occasion to fit the child's individual personality.

Most of the time, we have a simple choice: we don't have to take our child to a planned event if we feel that she or he is not mature enough to handle it. There are other times, though—her best friend's birthday party; a family gathering at Christmas or Hanukkah; or the special circus for children to which family and friends are going—when not taking her would be awkward or difficult or would mean a real loss. On these occasions we must make a value judgment: which will be worse, to allow the young child to miss the event, or to permit her attendance, even if she becomes a little raucous?

Most of us would make the choice to include the child, and if we do, some beforehand preparation is essential to help her understand— even if only dimly—the expected social behavior.

> "Jayne had the wildest idea of a wedding," her father said. "I don't know where she got it—maybe on the TV cartoons she loves. But when she told me everybody gets up and dances around the bride and groom, I decided she needed a more realistic idea, especially as we were going to her aunt's wedding. I enlisted the help of my older daughters: they staged a mock wedding, constantly changing parts. Jayne and I were the guests —until Jayne decided to be the bride! Later on I saw her enacting the scene with her dolls. I didn't tell her about the need for quiet and sitting still till just before the wedding—and she was a doll!
>
> "Oh, yes! We went to the reception, too—but I took her home after she had some food. So she missed the cake-cutting and the dancing—but she came home happy, if tired."

Jayne's father gave her information in a way she could understand, and he didn't wait for her to begin acting up but correctly judged how much partying she could take.

We all know our own child's signs of stress. Some kids begin to whine and cling; others get overexcited physically or vocally; others get cross and cranky. Whatever your child's signals, you usually know when it's a good time to remove him—even if the ball game or show is only half over. These stress signs also help us realize that the particular event was probably beyond the child's level of interest. We can use them to choose a more successful outing the next time.

THE SHY CHILD. Mrs. Busch talks about her four-year-old son and how she handles birthday parties:

"Scott, my four-year-old, is a shy little boy. He hangs back from playing with other kids, even runs off sometimes when he's welcomed by them. So I keep Scott's own birthday parties short and sweet! I let him invite only the few children he seems most comfortable with. I encourage him to help with the preparations. This year he made placemats covered with boats. He chose the menu—peanut butter-stuffed celery, ice cream, and ketchup sandwiches! He helped hang up the pin-the-tail-on-the-donkey picture, even helped me turn around each blindfolded child attempting to pin on the donkey's tail. But he wouldn't try it himself, he just enjoyed watching quietly.

"Going to other kids' birthday parties—that's a tougher problem. So far I have to go with him. He tends to hang around me a lot but makes little sorties into the social activities. At the last party he played jackstraws with another child and colored some pictures with the other kids. But when they had circle games or marching, he stood by me just watching. When it was time to eat, he said he wanted to go home, so we left. But I made him thank the hostess.

"I wish he would be more outgoing—sometimes I feel like pushing him into more social activities. But that would only make him shyer. You have to take a kid as he is. When he's a little older, with more confidence, I think he'll make his own social relationships. Probably he won't ever like big crowds or events. So what? Everyone's got to be his—or her—own person. As long as he's comfortable with himself and understands others, I don't care if he's not outgoing."

Mrs. Busch has adjusted to her child's personality and accepts his hesitation to enter more actively into social occasions. Scott may become more outgoing, or he may not. Raising a social child doesn't mean raising a social butterfly; it means raising a child who is aware of and respects the needs and rights of others.

INDIVIDUAL DIFFERENCES. Some four-year-olds are ready to enjoy entertainments directed at their older siblings, such as some children's movies, puppet shows, circuses, and some kinds of legitimate theater. Four-year-old Joanne may be laughing at the clowns, while four-year-old Jerry is screaming with fear. Harrison can sit quietly through a showing of *Peter Pan*, but Helena wiggles and squirms long before the end. Such reactions don't mean that Joanne and Harrison are smarter or better behaved than Jerry and Helena; it means just that they are in different developmental stages. Or they may simply have very different personalities. Their interests also vary: Jerry and Helena may well play with concrete materials more happily and for longer periods than do Harrison and Joanne. Jerry and Helena are still in the stage of firsthand learning, while the other two children have begun to appreciate and learn from a more abstract, yet lively and vivid, experience.

Again it helps to know which state of growth or development your own child is in to best determine most accurately the suitability of a "big occasion" for him. Often in an attempt to attend the needs of older siblings, some parents take their children to films that are much too mature for them. Not only do they require the child to be quiet far beyond his physical development, they often frighten the child so deeply that the negative impact lasts a long time. Such parents may have no one to leave the younger child with and may want to give the older children (and themselves) a treat, and they don't realize the damage that may be done to the preschooler. Luckily the child often falls asleep, but since you can't count on it, you should leave the child at home with a sitter. If that is impossible, perhaps it's better to postpone the treat. No one can blame small children who cry, run up and down the aisles, or distract others by constant questioning; they are being asked to behave in a more mature manner than they can manage.

Young preschoolers don't need to be excluded from all big social occasions, nor should they be. They need to learn how to act in these situations, to be part of the company. If they don't experience them, how can they learn about them? Just remember how to help prepare your child, and choose the big occasions carefully, so that you and your child can enjoy them, even if only for a limited time.

Ready, Set—Go?:
Evaluating Readiness for Kindergarten

As children near the end of their fourth year, parents are thinking about the imminence of kindergarten. Most schools have established five as the minimum age for starting kindergarten. By now you will have found out the requirements of the school; more important, you will be acquainted with the school's first year's program and will feel comfortable with it.

Now comes one of the most important decisions of all: is your child ready to enter "real" school? Probably you'll consult with others—the new teacher, your pediatrician, your family, other knowledgeable people—but the final decision rests with you. (Don't depend on an opinion poll.) You will evaluate your child's physical, mental, emotional, and social development.

How to Decide

We believe the stage of your child's social development is a crucial consideration. If your child doesn't get along with other children; if she has difficulty relating to adults in authority; if she doesn't join in, in her peers' interests or play; if she is unable to sit still or follow instructions, what does it matter if she has a good fund of information, knows her numbers and letters, or can even read? Her first encounter with school will make her unhappy, and she will not benefit fully from it. In fact, her initial negative experience may damage her future success there.

The first step is to compare your child's physical age with the stage of her mental and social development. Let's take for granted that her mental age is comparable to her physical age. At five years old, she has the general fund of information known to most five-year-olds: her reasoning and her mental skills are developed; she knows some numbers and letters; she can read her name and simple signs. She is also well developed physically. But how can you assess her social skills?

Let's look at two cases. The first report is given by a public-school teacher:

> "David was one of my second-grade pupils. According to all the tests and according to my opinions and those of his parents, he should have been doing well in schoolwork. Instead he was barely scraping by, a withdrawn, silent child, largely ignored by his classmates. A review of his school record helped me understand his problem.
>
> "David turned five a month after he entered kindergarten,

and he was the youngest child in his class. Mentally he was well prepared; he knew his numbers, could do simple computations, and could read at a beginning level. He had some computer experience and seemed to function mentally on a first-grade level.

"Physically he was slight, delicate, and underdeveloped. He had spent most of his time engaged in academic pursuits rather than in play. He was awkward with, or unable to use, the physical equipment in kindergarten, because his large- and small-muscle development lagged behind his age level.

"Socially he was at a less advanced developmental stage than his classmates. Having spent most of his time with adults rather than with children, he was unaccustomed to their more outgoing, lively activities. He tended to watch the other children play, to let them order him around. He was happiest listening to stories or working by himself. He was a loner the minute he entered school, ignored or teased by his peers.

"David probably should not have entered school when he did. He needed the opportunity to play with other children before he confronted the pressures of kindergarten. He needed to develop his social and physical skills, which he might have done in four or five months at a preschool. Delaying his entrance to kindergarten until the following term would have greatly benefited him.

"Unfortunately David's parents were not aware that social and physical development are as important as mental development for success in school. They had a kind of tunnel vision all too common today: 'prepare your child for college at age four or five by drilling him in the three R's.' These parents ignored the fundamental importance of the child's other needs. 'Play is the work of childhood' is not an idle statement. Play is the method by which the whole child is developed.

"Fortunately David's parents cared enough about their child's well-being to accept our advice about giving David more opportunity to play with other children and to develop his physical strength. He joined an after-school play group, which had been set up for working parents. He also joined a small gym group of boys slightly younger than himself.

"His parents still worried about his academic achievement but went along with my suggestions. Since I was able to reassure them that his schoolwork was first-rate, they read to him at night and let him play with blocks, paints, and clay. He has improved his social position in the classroom but may always be shy and somewhat of a loner. We can't always fully make up for earlier deprivation."

The second report is from a mother who considered her daughter Betsy's readiness to enter kindergarten in the fall:

"Betsy had played and worked with children and adults for two years in a nursery group. She seemed to have concern for others; she would pat their heads or give them a toy when she saw them crying. She seemed ready to substitute words for antisocial actions, was ready to arbitrate rather than to snatch. Generally, she seemed as compassionate as most four-year-olds, with a beginning awareness of others' rights.

"She related fairly well to most children, though she had always had favorite playmates. She enjoyed their interests and seemed welcome in their play group. When Betsy fought with children, it was because she thought they were unfair (usually when they grabbed her possessions). She was willing to help figure out solutions, however, and generally agreeable, neither demanding to be first, nor dropping out of the group.

"Betsy seemed independent and liked working alone as well as playing with others. She didn't cling to me and seemed to have enough confidence to enter a new group.

"She liked and accepted most adults in her placid, friendly way, and usually listened to and followed directions. The few times she balked at adult authority, it was because she thought their behavior unfair, or when she was deeply engaged in a creative activity or absorbed in dramatic play. At these times, her concentration was intense, and she didn't respond quickly. She seemed to need time to change gears or interests. She was often the last to leave her work after repeated reminders, but would do so without complaint if allowed enough time."

After carefully reviewing Betsy's social attainments, her mother decided that even though Betsy would be in the younger group of children in kindergarten, she was as socially competent as the older children, and, what with her physical and mental maturity, would be ready to enter kindergarten when she was five.

Making Your Own Decision

These two examples provide guidelines for evaluating your child's social readiness for school. Perhaps the best way to make your decision is to ask yourself the questions that Betsy's mother asked about her social development. Only you know how to compare your child with his peers in terms of social, emotional, intellectual, and physical development. Once you have determined that your child is intellectually and physically prepared for kindergarten, here are some questions you can ask to assess his social-emotional development:

Age Level

- Will your child be among the youngest in his class?
- Is your child bossy, trying to dominate others much of the time?
- Is your child a follower rather than a leader?
- Does your child fight a lot with other children? Does he initiate the fight?
- Does your child react to rough peer treatment by crying? by running away?
- Do your child's interests differ from most of his peers'?
- Does your child speak less often, less clearly, and seem to have a smaller vocabulary than his peers?

If four or more of your answers are yes, the chances are that your child is too young for kindergarten. He would benefit from six months to a year more in a play group, nursery school, or daycare situation.

Social Level

- Does your child share with his peers without being reminded at least half the time?
- Does your child try to make friends? Is he successful?
- Does your child willingly enter the dramatic play of other children?

- Is he able to accept others' ideas in play at least part of the time?
- Can he wait his turn? Not interrupt others constantly?
- Does he listen to stories? to discussions? Does he contribute at least part of the time to the discussion?

If you answered yes to four or more of the questions, probably your child is ready, other matters being favorable, to enter kindergarten.

INDEPENDENCE

- Can he go to the toilet by himself?
- Can your child put on and take off his outdoor clothes? Can he hang them up with little or no adult help?
- Does he enjoy working by himself (painting, looking at books, block building) as well as with others?
- Does he stay at one job or follow one interest for at least fifteen minutes?
- Does he show independent thinking some of the time?
- Can he be relied upon to carry out a simple, assigned job (helping set the table, watering flowers, fetching cookies or pencils)?

If you answered yes to five of these quesions, your child is ready for kindergarten. If not, consider carefully why he isn't competent in certain areas before deciding to enter him in kindergarten.

RELATING TO ADULTS

- Is your child at ease with most adults?
- Is he fairly amenable to trying new experiences?
- Is he able to leave you without excessive clinging?
- Does he seem to trust adults in authority? Is he fairly free in asking them questions or for help?
- Does he listen to adults and follow directions?

If you think your child would feel comfortable in four of these situations, he probably is ready for kindergarten.

These questions are not all inclusive. You will, no doubt, look at other facets of your child's social development as well. But after considering the answers to these questions, you will be better prepared to judge for yourself if your child is competent enough socially to enter kindergarten.

Remember—school is *not* a race: the child who gets there first is not necessarily ahead of the game. What counts most is a broad, deep preschool preparation; the child who is fortunate enough to have this background will do well in school in both early and later grades. Hold back from the national rush to push kids into and through school. When your child is in college, who will care if he entered kindergarten at five or five and three-quarters? You can take this step slowly. When your child is ready socially, emotionally, intellectually, and physically, that's the right time for him to enter kindergarten. Being prepared beforehand is the best guarantee of success in school.

The preschool years pass quickly—though harried parents may not think so at the time. But the school years really bring a change: your child will increasingly be influenced more strongly not only by his peers but also by a new authority—the teacher. If his social relationships have been satisfactory at home, you can be fairly sure that your child will enter new relationships easily and eagerly. The basic habits and value systems you have gradually instilled will now be your child's tools and strategies for coping with his new and expanded social world.

6

Early School Years
FIVE TO SEVEN YEARS OLD

School—The Start of Something Big

"Brian's been going to the same school for three years. It's just a few blocks from home, but you don't send a seven-year-old out alone in the city; at least I won't. Of course, Brian keeps telling me, 'I can do it alone.' He walks ahead of or behind me —definitely not with me. I used to get a good-bye kiss at the door. Now I'm lucky if I get a 'See ya, Ma!' "

—Mother of a seven-year-old

Brian and his mom have come to a developmental crossroads. Like it or not, Brian is taking long strides on the road to social independence. Public displays of affection just don't go with his growing sense of himself as a big and separate person. Without relinquishing her responsibility, Brian's mom understands the ongoing process of holding on, while letting go. In spite of his cockiness, Brian is not ready to walk himself across two congested city avenues. Yet he is ready to walk there without having his hand held, his lunchbox carried, or a big farewell production.

At the same hour, Brian's country cousin Karen is climbing on board a school bus. From 7:30 A.M. until about 4:00 in the afternoon, six-year-old Karen will spend her day away from home and family. Much as she looked forward to going to "real" school, some of her earlier enthusiasm seems to be evaporating. Karen comes home tired and often tearful over "this big kid on the bus who calls me Shrimp." Her mom suggests that she sit somewhere else on the bus. But Karen says she has to sit in the same place because "It's the rule."

Rules to Be Learned

For both Karen and Brian, entrance to the primary grades signals the start of a big and sometimes awesome adventure. Even if they've been to nursery school and kindergarten, real school begins now and brings with it a new set of expectations and demands. A whole new set of social codes must fall into place. There are rules to be learned for walking on line, talking in the lunchroom, riding on the bus, fitting into the group. Tattling is one of the typical ways children have for classifying all the new rules. By "telling" on others, they prove they know the rules and watch to see if the teacher is going to enforce them.

Knowing the rules, however, is a lot easier than living by them. Brian is not above cheating to win a game of checkers, and Karen can't see why the rules can't be changed to solve her problem on the school bus. Together, they can spend more time arguing over rules than actually playing. And often the important rules of conduct that the child's peer group imposes are not clearly spelled out. Karen and Brian must learn most of these from experience, some of it bitter, some of it sweet, but all of it a necessary part of becoming a member of their school society.

Skills to Be Mastered

Then, too, there are skills to be mastered in the classroom, in the gym, and on the playground. Karen thought learning to read happened automatically when you entered first grade. Although she is making steady progress, her friend Jennifer is fifty pages ahead of her in their reading books. Karen has begun to compare herself to others and to measure her own strengths and weaknesses. Her assessments of herself are no more accurate than Brian's belief that he is able to get to school independently. Nor does Brian see why the teacher makes such a big thing out of writing numbers neatly. Sitting still in his seat actually gives him a cramp in his leg. And he didn't mean to take somebody else's turn in math—he just couldn't help blurting out the answer to $7 + 5$.

Extending Skills in a Social Setting

Don't overlook the possibility of both building skills and having good times together with books and games. Often parents stop reading to their young schoolchild, expecting instead that the child will read to himself. The fact is, beginning readers are pretty limited in what they can read independently. Sharing picture and storybooks that are beyond their decoding skills helps to stretch their listening antennae and speaking vocabulary. It's also an opportunity for one-on-one time— enjoyment of a good story, new ideas, and each other.

Games, too, may provide a chance to extend their knowledge of or practice in simple math, reading, and gamesmanship skills. Five- and six-year-olds don't take defeat easily and are not ready for complex rules or strategy. Games of chance that end quickly give everyone extra odds at winning some as well as losing some. They also provide a time set apart from other distractions and obligations, a time for laughter and suspense that puts adult and child on equal footing for a little while.

Bridging School and Home

While school is not your child's whole world, what happens there will certainly be reflected in his relationships at home. Brian's parents may feel a bit displaced by new authorities—"My teacher says . . ." and "Everybody in my class does." After so many years of being the seat of all wisdom, parents can now expect outside figures (both positive and negative) to touch their lives. In the early grades, what the teacher says and does is often quoted as gospel, although the quotes may not be entirely accurate or entirely honest.

> "Meg kept coming home from school with wet pants. She insisted that the teacher wouldn't let her go to the bathroom. So I called the teacher and discovered there was no such rule. Children were free to go to the bathroom when they needed to go. Meg just wasn't taking the time, and she was blaming the teacher." —Mother of a six-year-old

Rather than jumping to the conclusion that Meg's teacher was an ogre, Meg's mom got the facts from both sides. Cued in, the teacher realized that perhaps she wasn't allotting enough time for dismissal and getting to the buses. By restructuring the last ten minutes of the school day, she was able to relieve some of the pressure-cooker atmosphere that previously led to kids' running for coats and buses when the bell rang. By sharing mutual concerns, parents and teachers can often remedy problem situations with simple solutions.

What happens in school will certainly be evident in new attitudes and behavior at home. You can't expect Karen and Brian to leave their newfound independence in their school locker every night. Their new and necessary self-reliance finds expression in demands for small freedoms at home. It's not that they want total independence and power— but they do want some say in small matters that affect them directly. Oddly enough, along with this newfound independence, there may be a greater need to cling to some childlike things again. A well-loved teddy bear or doll may become a comfort and a piece of the past to cling to while facing the rigors and demands of first grade.

New Classmates, New Friends

New, too, are the classmates. One can stay up until ten; one took my crayons; and one gets everyone else in trouble. Karen's best friend this week may be Ann and next week, Jennifer. Brian's worst enemy in October may be his best buddy in December. Since they are still to a great extent self-centered and see things from their own point of view, first and second graders can be painfully honest (and dishonest). They have not yet developed much in the way of tact or diplomacy, so they are hard on each other. Although some friendships formed in these years will continue throughout childhood, most primary-grade friendships are temporary and experimental.

Like most children of this age, Brian and Karen are moving into a new and expanding social world. While home and family remain the secure base they return to for support and guidance, increasingly their attention and goals will center on the world of school and friends. It is in the company of their peers that school-age kids measure themselves. How they think their friends see them is how they see themselves. In the classroom and on the playground they develop a sense of themselves as reader and runner, leader and follower, friend and foe. Inevitably they will meet children who are stronger, weaker, faster, slower, friendlier, or less friendly. Given their limited experiences, Brian and Karen often lack perspective about themselves and others. So some of their goals are inappropriate and some of their expectations unrealistic. They lack strategies for coping with their feelings about themselves and others. They learn a great deal through experience—you might call it the school of hard knocks—but parents can play a supportive role in softening the blows, helping the child reach the central goal of becoming competent and confident, physically, socially, and intellectually.

Shy Kids

Some kids hang back, watching and waiting for a way into the games on the playground. They hold back in classroom discussions or even casual conversations. Timid kids may really need some assistance from caring adults who can gently steer them through this awkward stage. They may need an adult who sees an opening and suggests that "Karen could turn the jump rope," or "Kevin could help you paint the puppet stage." Opportunities to play with age mates on a one-to-one basis are often less threatening in the familiar setting of home, and help build the shy child's sense of being able to hold his own. He may also benefit from playing with slightly younger children with whom he can take the role of teacher or leader.

There's no way to cure the shy child once and for all. Parents sometimes look for a quick solution, hoping to pull the child "out of his shell." The fact that always-shy Andrew plays the piano beautifully does not mean he's ready to perform for the whole family at Thanksgiving. Indeed, putting shy children on the spot, pushing them into the limelight, may do more harm than good. Under the pressure of performing by parental command, Andrew's nervousness is likely to lead to goofs that sound twice as bad to Andrew and rob him of confidence for future performance as well.

The Flip Side of Shy

In contrast to Andrew, Emily is the kind of kid who carries her own spotlight and expects to be the center of attention at all times. Emily is the super friendly, slightly pesky, drop-in-on-everyone, all-over-everybody kid. In family situations she may outtalk and outshine her little brother or sister. In the classroom she may be so eager for her usual, oversized serving of attention that the teacher complains, "Emily has no self-control." Helping children like Emily strike a balance, to listen as well as talk, to follow as well as lead, takes time and repeated reminders. Performances can be cut short gently but clearly. A simple "let Susie finish what she is saying," tells Emily to stop, without calling her rude and without switching the attention away from Susie. After you've heard Susie out, be sure to find out what Emily wanted to tell you. Showing both children respect teaches more about social responsibility than lecturing on "not interrupting" and "being polite."

Of course, teaching children to be wary of strangers is a necessity with all children, shy or not. But with outgoing Emily, learning to steer clear of candy, cars, and strangers may be a hard lesson that needs repeating.

What They May and May Not Do

- Brian may not be given a choice to go to school on Monday or not. He may decide if he wants to wear a plaid shirt or a blue one.
- Karen may not decide when it's time for bed. She may decide whether she wants to hear a story or play a game before bed.
- Brian may not decide if he needs his hair washed. He may decide if he wants it washed in the tub or in the sink.
- Karen may not make the final decision that she should have an expensive video game that is beyond the family budget. She can be included in an honest discussion about what her family can afford and what alternatives there are to items they can't afford.
- Brian may not be given the choice of using profanity in verbal exchanges with his family. He can be given appropriate language to express his feelings of anger and frustration.

By including children in large issues and giving them some choices about small ones, we help them to feel less powerless. We also give them opportunities to make less-than-earth-shattering decisions—even mistaken ones. Rather than turning little battles into a war between parent and child, you can shift the power to encourage a natural boost in social development. These confrontations are part of the ongoing business of redefining roles in the parent-child relationship. During the early school years children need parents who lend support to their emerging (but still vulnerable) sense of themselves. It's not a question of parental surrender; it's a salute to a new level of competence.

The Physical-Social Connection

Think back to your early school years. Remember recess on the playground, gym class, bikes and skates after school? For the young child, physical activities have a meaningful social dimension. Physical competence is one of the tickets kids need to enter the group. After all, climbing the monkey bars, throwing balls, playing tag or marbles or jacks, riding bikes, and jumping rope are physical things that children do together. Being "able" is one of the yardsticks they use to measure themselves and others. They don't need to set any world records. They don't even need to be terribly good—just willing and able to get into the action.

For some children these activities present no problem. They'll get back on their bikes with skinned knees; trip on a rope and start again; run the treads off their sneakers to build up speed. For others the hurdles seem higher. Within this age group there is a tremendous spread of abilities. There are fives who take the training wheels off their bikes and ride off to glory. And there are many perfectly normal sevens who still need those wheels to balance. Individual differences in developmental timetables are not at all unusual, and for many children a bit of parental help may be needed to smooth the way.

"Annie was invited to a roller-skating party. When I got to the rink to pick her up, I found her going round and round the edge, holding on. I figured, poor Annie, this party must have been a disaster. But she didn't seem at all troubled; she was working at it, and so were some of the others. A week later, though, my sister took her skating with her seven-year-old, who's a terrific skater. That was the problem, I guess. Annie refused to skate all afternoon. She just couldn't stand her cousin's skating circles around her."

—Mother of a seven-year-old

For many kids like Annie, being "no good" means giving up altogether. They hang back or claim they don't "like" to do things that they don't do well. They don't yet understand the cause and effect relationship between working at something and succeeding. They expect instant results, or it's no go.

Recognizing this, Annie's mom found a way to provide more practice without pressure. She borrowed a pair of used skates and encouraged Annie to practice in the garage at home. So Annie is growing in her "I can" skills and learning that progress comes in slow but sure ways. She's not training for a gold medal, just getting ready for the next party at the rink or the next outing with her cousin.

There are times when simply providing space, equipment, and encouragement will do the whole job. But sometimes children need direct instruction. Often a parent or older child can offer a steady hand, helpful tips, and slow-motion demonstration. If a child is left-handed, however, another left-handed child can teach her how to bowl a lot better than a right-handed parent or teacher, and in some cases there's less emotional static if the teacher is a stranger.

> "Tommy couldn't wait to go skiing. But when we got to the ski hill he did an about-face on us. My wife and I both ski, yet we couldn't get Tommy to let go and try. We arranged for a lesson and left him with the pro. By late that afternoon, Tommy was really getting the drift of it."
>
> —Father of a seven-year-old

Neither Annie's mom nor Tommy's dad has turned their children's physical development into a quest for excellence. At this stage kids don't need any added incentive to compete. They need time to test and nourish their inner sense of themselves. An emphasis on competition can push some kids right off the track they need to run on.

> "All I remember about the physical fitness tests in school was the fact that I was certifiably unfit at an early age. I used to miss one day of school every year—that was the day after I had to do a hundred sit-ups. It wasn't just the ache of the sit-ups; it was the pain of being taunted with what I couldn't do."
>
> —Father of a six-year-old

Of course, there is no way to protect kids from all competition, nor would it be wise to. Five-, six-, and seven-year-olds are readier to handle competition than they were as preschoolers. Simple group games like giant steps and statues give them a joyful sense of belonging and playing together. Since almost everyone gets caught, there's no singular shame in it; it's part of the game. In our culture, children are competitive, and some of the striving that grows out of competing has real value. But parents don't need to add to the pressure by comparing kids or demanding triumphs. The main objective at this age is not to beat the group, but to join it; not to play against others, but to learn how to play with them. Parents also need to guard against pushing children toward goals that may actually endanger their health and safety. In their eagerness to live up to parental expectations, some children actually push themselves too far and end up with both physical and emotional injuries.

What children need most is help in making small (but often hard-won) gains. We need to avoid casting them prematurely as physically inept. Too often "klutzes" are made (not born) from overblown expectations and not enough instruction. By supporting the development of physical competence, parents can help children build their muscles and their confidence as both physical and social beings.

Kevin may never make the first string in any league. Indeed, he may be the kind of child who trips on a curb and slips on a pebble. Some children are going to take pictures of the basketball team instead of joining it. Others are going to play drum rolls instead of tumbling on gym mats. But parents can help their children evolve a positive, balanced picture of themselves by encouraging them to develop other interests along with their physical skills.

Peer Groups

Life in the peer group begins in the early school years. While peer pressure is less powerful than it will be in coming years, the primary grades mark an important shift toward a larger social sphere. These are years of significant social transitions.

Until now, home and family were the center of the child's universe. As Amy's mother put it, "Until kindergarten, I knew all the people in Amy's life. Now, it's a whole new ball game. She has this other world out there that I have no contact with." While the preschooler's concept of himself was largely a reflection of how his family saw him, the school-age child begins to look to his peers for a new self-image. It is in the company of age mates that the child begins to test, measure, and compare himself.

Finding their way into a variety of groups is one of the major developmental tasks for children of this age. On the playground, in the classroom, and in the neighborhood, they encounter acceptance and rejection. By the end of second grade Tommy sees himself as one of the smart kids, a social leader. An achiever himself, Tommy has begun to select those he considers "smart" (and therefore desirable) and to exclude those he doesn't. There are kids who can be in his club and kids who can't. Of course, his club may not last a week, and by tomorrow he may be excluded from someone else's club. These groups are rarely long-lived. They reflect, however, the child's desire to belong—to shift from "me" to "we"—even if the shelter is only temporary.

Seven-year-old Jonathan talks a lot about his "band," a musical group. According to Jon's mom, this ensemble has never played one note together. Music is not the important thing; it's who's going to play and who's not. This feeling of exclusivity and mutual admiration is a way of overcoming a child's vulnerablility and lack of power.

Almost all children at one time or another suffer the pangs of being excluded. "Nobody likes me—everybody hates me," is a typical complaint among five- to seven-year-olds. For most kids the pain is real but temporary, and a sympathetic parental ear can often help them clarify their problems. Six-year-old Keith may always be the boss in his own backyard, but on the playground he will have to follow as well as lead. Jeff may think the way into a game of catch is to snatch the ball. Lacking strategies and experience, Keith and Jeff are learning lessons that are taught in the reality of group life.

Children belong to many groups: the family, the classroom, the neighborhood. In large part, membership in these groups is a given; there are no choices about your position in the family, the block you live on, or the class you go to. While parents can't shield and protect their children from all of the painful moments, they can provide encouragement and understanding. During these years, home and family are the steady anchor that the kids return to at the end of each day's adventure in the sometimes bumpy social world.

SKILL GROUPS

School-age children also enjoy the ready-made feeling of belonging that comes with joining classes in gymnastics, swimming, dance, art, or crafts. Beginners' classes give children a chance to taste and test their interests and skills. It gives them another small group in which they can relate one-to-one and as a member of a unit. The big stumbling block is in finding classes that invite exploration.

Programs that stress competition, with medals, ribbons, and prizes, tend to value end products more than beginners' efforts. Pressure to perform publicly may take the pleasure out of performing altogether. It may also set kids up in competition that does little to encourage either social skills or any other skills. Six- and seven-year-olds are often put into social situations in which competition is a factor, but most are not ready to handle the externally imposed rules and regulations surrounding competitions. Kids may set up their own contests, but these are more in the nature of pretend play—of trying it on for size. In making up their own competitions, races, or shows, kids also make (and break) their own rules. That's quite different from living up to rules and expectations set up by others. Although a few years down the road many preteens begin honing preprofessional skills, these early school years are a time for discovery, not professional dedication.

Social Groups—Joining Up, Signing On

Cub Scouts and Brownies, 4-H Clubs, religious groups, and community-centered Y's bring small groups of children together with an adult leader to smooth the way. Through group projects and individual work toward badges, members share a common purpose that builds competence, confidence, and cooperation. In contrast with their classroom groups, these are generally smaller, with more opportunities to get to know others one-to-one. It is also through such groups that children often engage in activities for the benefit of the general community. Paper drives, park clean-ups, and planting projects give youngsters a sense of social service, of becoming helpful members of the community.

Social Overload

For many children of this age the formality of additional groups may be an overload. Being in school all day, as one of many children, may be enough to teach them about group activities. Such kids may benefit from the comfort of playing one-to-one with a playmate or with the neighborhood children. Certainly membership in one or more groups should not override the value of informal play with others. Indeed, kids of this age often get overscheduled, with dance on Tuesday, scouts on

Wednesday, crafts on Thursday, swimming on Friday. They need social calendars just to keep track of their busy lives, and they lack time to use their own ingenuity.

No matter how good the programs may be, all youngsters need time for doing "nothing." They need unscheduled time for daydreaming, and for absorbing and sorting out their experiences. Lacking that freedom, they may be unable later to use their undeveloped inner resources, to be alone or with other people.

Linking Two Worlds—Supporting Social Skills

"By the end of first grade, Jeff had terrible feelings about himself. He kept calling himself 'dumb' and telling us, 'I can't read.' By September he didn't want to go to school. Well, I had a conference with his second-grade teacher, and we worked together. She gave us things we could help with.

"Jeff is doing well now, but his confidence is still shaky. I wonder if he's ever going to feel 'smart' or at least 'not dumb.' "

—Mother of a seven-year-old

It may be a while before Jeff's attitude toward himself catches up with his new academic know-how. Few children breeze through the primary grades without some bumps along the way. By forging a strong link between school and home, Jeff's mother and teacher are providing the kind of support system most children need. Some need extra help with specific academic skills. Others have different problems. They may have a hard time completing tasks, getting along with others, contributing to group activities, or tying their own shoelaces.

"Billy just doesn't know how to get into the action. Peter and Kevin were playing dominoes after lunch, and Billy wanted in. He pestered them till Peter finally told him to go away and leave them alone. Billy's solution was to kick the dominoes across the room."   —Second-grade teacher

Instead of looking for another game or for other players, Billy let his angry feelings explode. His seemingly antisocial behavior really grew out of a genuine desire to be social. Like many others his age,

Billy may need some adult help in finding more positive ways to approach his peers. In this case the teacher stepped in and stopped the fight before the boys came to blows. She cleared the air by getting the boys to talk instead of slugging it out. "Billy ruined your game and that makes you angry," she said. Peter and Kevin agreed. "And Billy really wants to play. He wants someone to play with him." Billy nodded.

"He can play with me," Mike called from across the room.

Lacking experience, Billy needs to learn positive strategies for making friends. By acting as a model, his teacher lets him know how to say what's on his mind instead of striking out against the people he wants to join. The demands of being in a group and the expectations for greater independence and achievement are no small challenge for young schoolchildren. Billy's social problems are as significant as Jeff's reading problems or lack of confidence.

Talking face to face with your child's teacher can give you much more information than a monthly or quarterly report card. Although regular communication between school and home is generally limited to report cards or a "problem" that calls for a meeting, some schools schedule regular parent-teacher conferences. These meetings give parents and teachers an opportunity to share their concerns and chart a mutually satisfactory course of action.

It is interesting to note that in Japan, preschool children carry a notebook back and forth between school and home. Every day the teacher writes something in it, and every evening the child's parents write in it, too. These books are not "report cards" with A's and F's. They include little anecdotes about the child and focus on what's happening. Through these notebooks, parents and teachers are giving each other a glimpse of the child's world that the other does not see. Perhaps most significantly, the child knows that his two worlds are communicating (not tattling) about him.

While daily notes are rarely needed (or even desired) with school-age children, the underlying value of parent-teacher communication is real. Children don't leave their family problems at home or their school problems in their desks. Interests at home and at school are not compartments to be kept in separate places. By sharing information, parents and teachers can cue each other in. Teachers can't solve the breakup of a marriage, family illness, the death of a pet, or other family problems. But knowing about the crises in a family's life can help in handling the child who is living through them. Parents can't (and shouldn't) turn home into school. But they can enlarge upon and enrich the lessons their child is striving to master.

We Don't Say Things Like That!

"Sarah came home from kindergarten bursting to tell me the 'bad words' she heard. 'Can I just tell you what Randy said?' she asked.

" 'Never mind,' I told her.

" 'But don't you want to hear what she said?'

"Poor Sarah was just asking to try those words out—to say them out loud."   —Mother of a five-year-old

In her journeys into the world, five-year-old Sarah is going to be exposed to many influences, both positive and negative. While Sarah knows "bad" words when she hears them, the temptation to try them out for size is tremendous. Sarah's tattling on Randy isn't designed to get Randy in trouble so much as to get permission to use the tantalizing words. Her tattling has a double edge. On the one hand, she's looking for a way to prove she knows the rules. On the other, she's looking for a legitimate way to break them. She's testing which rules can be broken without making her world fall apart.

In contrast, her classmate Sam brought his newly learned vocabulary to the dinner table. When his three-year-old sister accidentally spilled her milk, Sam spilled a few choice expletives that led to an explosion that Sam was not expecting.

If Sam's parents had asked him what he thought the words meant, they would have discovered that he honestly didn't know. Nor does he need to be given a definition. Rather, he could have been told that smart people don't use words they don't understand. Sam could also be told that the words he used were not the kinds of words "we use in our house" (a fact Sarah already knew). Of course, if you do use such words in your house, you're probably fighting a lost cause. You can't teach children that it's all right for you, but not for them, and unfortunately, the child who imitates such language may be in for a rough time in school and in other social circles. On the other hand, it may also be true that a child who does not use such language within the group may be seen as a social outcast. While you know when and where such words are acceptable, the inexperienced child does not.

Neither Sam nor Sarah needs their mouths washed out with soap. They don't need long lectures, or a "spanking they'll never forget." They do need a firm, consistent, and clear statement: "That may be the way your friends talk—but we don't use those words in our house" says it all. As new unacceptable language surfaces, the lesson will need repeating. Parental values are not transmitted on only one try. Lessons that are worth teaching are worth repeating.

Early Racism

Not long after the "bad" word incident, Sarah's stories about Randy took on a new dimension.

> "One night Sarah announced bluntly that she hated Randy. I asked her why, and she said, because Randy used bad words and she was black. 'I hate black kids,' my five-year-old bigot said confidently."

Sarah's mother and dad were appalled. "And," Sarah continued, "if I get a black teacher next year, I'm not going to school!" Sarah had made a sweeping generalization that needed to be clarified. Typical of her age, Sarah was defining people by simplistically sorting them into categories: good or bad, right or wrong, black or white. Yes, her parents agreed, Randy used "bad" language but that did not make her bad; nor did it make all black people bad.

Having addressed the issue, Sarah's parents let it rest for a bit. But during the weeks ahead they made a conscious effort to introduce Sarah to their black friends and colleagues. They took a fresh look at their world and realized that from their child's point of view they lived an insular life. They had assumed their own lack of prejudice was apparent, but obviously this was not the case. Recognizing the breach between what they believe and what they convey, they made a conscious attempt to demonstrate the ideas they value.

Sometimes the same kind of early racism can surface from other sources. Sarah may be eager to play with Randy, but her best friend

Annie refuses and won't be Sarah's friend. Or Annie's mom and dad
may not make Randy welcome. Without blowing the situation out of
proportion, parents can make their views clear and help kids shape
their own emerging value system. For the most part, kids of this age
are essentially color-blind, unless others have imposed their prejudiced
opinions frequently. Racism at this stage is neither rampant nor deep-
seated, but more a matter of imitation. Rather than ignoring it, this is
the easiest time to make corrections, when it surfaces.

Where Do Babies Come From?

Curiosity about where babies come from continues to be of interest to
five-, six-, and seven-year-olds, especially if a new baby is expected in
the family. Even if you've explained it all a million times, the questions
usually persist. Why do children have such problems understanding?
Basically, kids find it difficult to hold on to verbal explanations of how
things work. To the young child, "seeing is believing," but in this case,
seeing how babies are made or born is neither possible nor appropriate.

Answers to their questions need not be overly elaborate, just honest
and to the point. Parents who feel uncomfortable about answering
questions directly may feel better with a book that offers simple explanations without burdening children with more information than they
can handle. It may be that children who don't broach the subject sense
their parents' reluctance, so their questions go unasked and unanswered. Here, too, a book may help open the subject and relieve the
child from having to look elsewhere for information. Watching the
birth of kittens or puppies can also help children understand some of
the mystery.

Quite apart from the information conveyed in books or friendly
talks, parents convey deeper and more long-lasting messages in dozens
of everyday situations. Kids notice and learn from the way parents talk
to each other, work together, and touch each other. For many children,
their parents' living situations—a live-in boyfriend, girlfriend, or new
wife or husband—stimulate questions that might have been answered
once, but arise again in a new context. Indeed, parents' attitudes about
the human body—their own and their child's—are conveyed from infancy onward.

Most children discover the pleasures of their sexual organs during infancy. Although masturbation is neither harmful nor immoral at this stage or at any other, it is generally unacceptable in public. Rather than forbidding children to explore their own bodies, parents can make it clear that some things are done only in the privacy of one's own room. It's only when children seem to spend a lot of time pursuing their own bodily pleasures that parents need to be concerned. Kids who are excessively turned in on themselves may need extra help in finding ways to relate to others.

You Want to Play Doctor?

The age-old game of doctor and other forms of sex play between children is common at this stage. Boys' and girls' curiosity about their bodies is as normal as their interest in all sorts of information. Naturally, these games of exploration don't warrant the Parents' Stamp of Approval. On the other hand, they should not be treated as great criminal acts that foreshadow a life of sin.

- You don't let the game go on, but you don't need to lecture at length about immorality and shame.
- Don't assume that the whole thing was the other child's idea. Both kids were probably equally curious and mutually involved.

Simply stepping in and saying, "That's enough of that game," is usually enough to deliver the message without threats or displays of anger. It's only when such games persist over a long period of time or when they are the chief source of entertainment that parents really need to be concerned. In such instances, you may need to examine what your child is really looking for in the way of sexual information. Eric's curiosity about how girls are made may be answered best by a visit to a friend's house, in which a baby girl is bathed, diapered, and changed.

It helps to look at the big picture and to remember that if this age-appropriate and natural curiosity is not satisfied when your child is six or seven, it may continue into the preteen years and become a real social liability.

Going Places

There are a lot more places you can go comfortably with a school-age child than with a preschooler, providing your outings are planned for mutual pleasure. Jenny may not be ready for three hours of *Madame Butterfly*, but *The Mikado* or *The Pirates of Penzance* may be exactly the right ticket. Doing the entire Egyptian collection at the museum may lead to "When are we going home?" But an hour with the mummies can change the response to "When can we come back?" The biggest danger lies in giving children too much of a good thing. Enlarging the child's view of the world demands juggling events into child-sized and appealing portions. You're more likely to have a good time if you cue in on what interests the child. This may not be the age to try to get your child to share your own tastes.

Whether you're at the museum, circus, ballet, or amusement park, it's important to read children's signals to tell

- when they're hungry and need a snack break.
- when they've been trudging along and need a sit-down break.
- when they've been cooped up too long and need some time to run around.
- when to say, "We can't do it all in one day; we'll come back another time."

BENEFITS VS. BOTHER

Outings with children are rich with potential for growing both intellectually and socially. Along with the fun of sharing your enthusiasms, such excursions can strengthen the bonds of mutual satisfaction between parent and child. Given school, jobs, and other obligations, you now have less time together, so the quality of that time carries greater importance.

These small journeys into the larger world also demand new levels of social competence. Being a passenger, part of an audience, or dining in a restaurant call for a variety of social skills different from those your child needs at home. There are acceptable and unacceptable ways to behave. You can and should talk about such things at home, but talking is different from trying, testing, and teaching in the real world. No one is suggesting we revert back to the maxim "Children should be seen and not heard." But well-behaved kids are not an anachronism, nor are they an accident. Knowing how to behave is taught by parents who respect their children. While social graces may seem old-fashioned, there's nothing outdated about respecting other people's space and rights.

SOCIAL RECIPROCITY

Being sensitive to others and the ways we conduct ourselves is basic to becoming a social person. It's not just knowing what spoon to use or chewing with your mouth closed. Being sociable goes beyond manners. It must also embrace the larger concept of social reciprocity, of understanding how our actions and interactions affect others. This is a tall order for children, who are strongly self-centered, but it is not entirely beyond them. In fact, learning about social reciprocity really begins with parent-child reciprocity.

- It means adjusting your plans to suit your child's interests and style, rather than expecting your child always to fit into your plans.
- It meand adapting and readjusting plans as you go, rather than expecting everything to run precisely as planned.
- It may mean staying for only half a concert or not lingering over a second cup of coffee with dinner, when your children are sending signals that they've had enough.
- But it's also true that kids need to learn that, even in the best of all worlds, there is not always true reciprocity. There are times—at home and away—when adults call the shots and kids have to comply.

If all of this sounds like more trouble than it's worth, you may be happier staying close to home. The only problem is that some of these lessons can't be learned at home. The fact is, going on vacations or day trips with children is different from going out with another adult. It's not a question of better or worse— just different. There are adjustments to be made on family outings if they are to be successful and pleasurable, and usually those adjustments are worth making for everyone.

MUSEUMS

Many museums offer special exhibits designed to accommodate a child's natural desire to touch. Others also have weekend classes that invite kids to participate in scientific or artistic exploration. Even if there are no special programs, museum-going offers relatively low-cost, high-interest outings.

Parents who are tuned in to their children's new interests, from dinosaurs to baseball scores, can find exhibits to enrich their child's enthusiasm. Trips chosen specifically to match the child's interests don't mean you won't see other unrelated and interesting things. But it will be your job to keep the outing focused. It's also your job to explain in advance what the rules of the museum are and then to see that they are enforced. Touching, running, loud talking, and eating are not allowed in most museums. Given simple explanations in advance, children can begin to understand that many objects in museums are old, delicate, and very special. Teaching your child to respect the museum's collection need not dampen, but rather can enhance, his appreciation of seeing an ancient suit of armor or an oil painting. Children are not too young to understand that a visit to a museum with its vast spaces is not the same as a romp on a playground. As in all new social situations, children generally depend upon their caregivers for on-the-spot guidance. If you talk in a quiet voice, they will in most instances do so too. If you call across a gallery, they'll see no reason not to do the same. Sliding down corridors should not be shrugged off as youthful exuberance. Learning to respect other people's space is part of museum-going. For most kids, these are reasonable trade-offs for the opportunity to see new sights.

By all means point out the objects that are special to you at the museum's collection, but don't rush your child past something that captures his interest, even if it seems of minor importance to you. Take the time to listen to his assessment of what he's looking at. One eight-year-old wandering through a Norsemen collection asked, "Dad? Weren't there any female Vikings?" Obviously this youngster was looking and thinking beyond the labels and dates that are of less interest than the human connection children make with the past. Avoid reading every sign and telling your youngster everything you know on the spot. Better to cue in to what he notices and answer with simple explanations. They are not little sponges waiting to be filled up with unconnected facts. Listening and watching will tell you what information they are hungry for and ready to absorb. Don't drown them with more than they want to know, just because you know it. Do find a way of complimenting them on the way they're remembering the rules and now nice it is to be out with them. Don't expect them to walk a tight line for prolonged stretches. Better to break up your visit with a stop for a snack and change of pace. A cool drink and time to sit down give you time to reflect on what you've seen and plan for the next leg of the trip. Whatever else you do, don't overdo it. Better to leave before their endurance is used up. As they say in show biz, always leave them wanting more.

Remember, too, that if going to museums, concerts, or the theater are not your cup of tea, leave them out of your itinerary. It's better to let someone who does enjoy them take your children along than to go out of a sense of duty, hoping it will be "good for them." Kids are quick to pick up your true sentiments, and when they do, the trip is usually worthless.

THEATERS AND MOVIES

Obviously, selecting a show that will be appealing and appropriate is the first order of business. But your responsibility doesn't end there. Unfortunately, children see many more poor models in theaters today than good ones. Movie theaters have recently been running film clips reminding adult moviegoers that talking disturbs others. And not long ago, a *Playbill* distributed in Broadway theaters addressed itself to the same issue. It seems that courtesy has gone out of fashion. As usual, television is getting the blame for another social ailment. It's altogether possible to watch a television show, answer the phone, eat a snack, and spin a Rubik's Cube all at the same time. Unfortunately, doing these things at once in a theater disturbs the actors and the people sitting near you.

Teaching children how to be part of an audience starts when you enter the theater. This is the time for going to the bathroom "so we won't have to miss any of the show." Many theaters don't allow food or drinks inside, but it may be a good idea to have a quiet, wrapper-free treat you can offer if the need arises. If you're in a popcorn movie house, do your buying when you enter and make it clear that there will be no shopping during the show. Take the time to help your child settle in and settle down. A folded coat in his seat may give him a needed boost. Aisle seats or the front of the balcony may give him a clearer view without having to peer over and around the full-grown person in front of him. Before the movie or show begins, tell him there's no talking out loud once it starts, and whispering should be saved for emergencies. You may need to remind him again, but stick to whispered reminders that don't disturb others.

If wiggling or talking continues, it's your responsibility to take the child out of the theater temporarily or permanently. Establishing rules for behavior may mean leaving before the movie is over, but such lessons are less costly in the long run. Better to miss the end of one movie and establish your commitment to certain standards of behavior. Few school-age children will need a repeat performance if the lesson is confronted with action, rather than with prolonged recrimination or warnings with no follow-through. Remember, too, that positive behavior deserves reinforcement; praise your child for being an appreciative audience.

Of course, there are occasions when what you've paid for is not what you expected. When you've made a mistake, costly though it may be, it's better to admit it and leave than to brave it out. If the movie is "too talky" kids are apt to get restless, and if the scenes are too explicit or scary they may misbehave. Often in such situations the misbehavior of children is related to an inappropriate choice of entertainment. You can teach children to be selective by acting upon a bad choice, rather than just by talking about it later. In a few years, your child will be going to movies with friends. This is the time to establish standards and values that will influence independent behavior in a similar situation later on.

While stadium events, such as the circus, ball games, and rodeo allow a chance for more boisterous participation, the same precepts of courtesy need to be taught. Teaching kids to respect the performers as well as their neighbors in the audience won't diminish the pleasure.

Eating Out

Given the high cost of even fast food, eating out with the family is usually a special occasion. School-age kids are generally delighted with dining out, if it doesn't take too long. This is not the time for a five-course gourmet meal.

Even if they can't read the whole menu, kids like the status of having one to study. Fives and sixes are often finicky eaters, so choosing their own dish allows for individual preferences. That's a real treat compared to the usual no-choice, one-meal-for-all menu at home. Although many restaurants have kiddie menus, some children reject such offerings as "too babyish." Rather than turning it into a hassle, check the regular menu. Single dish items (burgers and such) are often no more costly in terms of dollars, and much less costly in terms of dignity.

In fancy restaurants where every dish is made to order, slow service is part of the ambience. Leisurely dining can be a problem. Ask your waiter to bring the bread and butter as soon as the order is taken. It helps, too, if you skip the soup or appetizer, or have the waiter bring the child's main (and only) course with your appetizers. Kids eat less but take longer, so with luck the time factor balances out by dessert.

If you're dining with several kids, use preventive measures in the seating. Don't sit kids side by side; opposite is better and safer. They should be close enough to talk without shouting or having to get out of their seats. Walking around the restaurant between courses is dangerous for both children and waiters. It also disturbs other diners. If it's a big family gathering, don't isolate the kids from each other or lump them all together. Scatter them so that they can enjoy each other's company without being silly.

This is not the time for major confrontations about eating and drinking everything . Save that for meals at home. Keeping your own voices low sets the tone for conversation, which should include the kids. You can't treat Jenny like an invisible person who's expected to sit still and be silent. You *can* talk about where you've been and what everyone saw and liked. Be sure to do some listening as well as talking. Carl may need an occasional reminder to lower his voice or to use the fork instead of his fingers, but correct him quietly, and don't turn the meal into a lesson in deportment. Setting a good example can be done in a friendly fashion that puts kids at ease, not on guard. What they want is your attention. If they can't get it positively, they'll find a way to get it negatively.

Of course, sometimes things get out of hand and kids test parents to the stretching point. Rather than blowing your fuse and disturbing everyone, take your youngster quietly and firmly to a private place, maybe the rest-room, the coat-room, outside the front door, or to your car. Talk (don't shout) about what's happening inside and about what it means to the other people eating at the restaurant. Either get a commitment that the misbehavior stop, or don't go back. Missing the rest of the meal may be the only way to deliver the message to the child who needs it. Most kids benefit from stretching their legs and knowing you mean what you say. True, you may miss part of this meal, but chances are things will go more smoothly next time.

Family Gatherings

Gatherings of the family clan represent major social events in the lives of young children. Even if your family lives nearby, the special holiday food and finery set the day apart. But spending the day with "their sisters and their cousins and their aunts" may be pleasanter to anticipate than the event itself, unless you plan ahead.

If the party is at your house, let your school-age child play a real role in making the day happen. Don't look for "make-work" pretend jobs. Kids are too wise for chores that are designed to get them out of the way. They're not too young to do real things like dusting, setting the table, or tearing the lettuce for a salad. If you're expecting young cousins, encourage your child to select games and toys to share, and put away private nontouchable treasures. It will save a lot of bickering later, when you'd prefer to be relaxing rather than refereeing.

Give your child a chance to play host. Before your guests start arriving, ask him to help take coats, pass the potato chips, and make guests feel at home. Kids don't need to be the center of attention, but they shouldn't feel like displaced people in their own homes.

Avoid making comparisons between the behavior, looks, and abilities of cousins. If the conversation moves in that direction, don't get drawn into it; try to divert it. Competition does not make for good feelings between cousins who may not know each other well.

Taking a child visiting requires some planning, too. Bringing a game or toy to share helps break the ice between kids who seldom see each other. But don't make a fuss if your child hangs back a bit and sizes up the situation. Being a bit shy is natural in new settings, and the less said about it, the better.

Of course, some kids get set off and start "performing" if there's a crowd. Rather than make a bad situation worse, take your child away from his captive audience. You don't need to scold and punish him publicly; help him save face and give him time to cool off. A crowd of cousins can get rambunctious, and that should not be the hosts' responsibility. Running through the house, standing on furniture, or playing under everyone's feet is not acceptable at home or away. However, hosts are often put in odd predicaments when young guests misbehave.

If you've been invited for dinner at an odd hour, plan ahead by providing a snack before you arrive. When it comes to eating, kids are very much creatures of habit. You can't expect them to hold out for lunch at three if they're used to eating at noon.

Whether you're hosting or guesting, remember to praise their positive behavior. Most of the guidelines for eating out apply to family feasts. Just because everyone knows everyone else, there's no reason to have confrontations at the dinner table. If you want family events to be days worth remembering fondly, you'll need to plan them for everyone's pleasure.

"Should We Take the Children?"

Where families gather, there may be adult tensions that rub off on the children. If there's an undeclared war going on between you and your in-laws, the artillery is apt to hit the wrong target—the kids. Adults have to be careful that their own sense of discomfort doesn't overshadow the tone of the day. If it's going to be unpleasant, but you must go anyway, better to leave the child with a sitter and pay the obligatory visit yourself.

This may also be a good idea when a family member is seriously ill. In such situations parents may need to consider several questions. Will the child's visit mean anything to the older person? What may it mean to the child? Will the visit be too puzzling or frightening? If you think the circuits are going to be overloaded, better to avoid the connection in the first place. When youngsters are faced with difficult situations they don't understand, they are likely to act up, and that will not help the person who's ailing or anyone else.

Friendship, Friendship—Not a Perfect Blendship

Friendship for five-, six- and seven-year-olds has more to do with proximity than deep-felt loyalty or affection. While some long-lasting friendships may blossom, most kids flit through a series of "best friends." Others have a circle of playmates rather than one best buddy. This ever-changing cast of characters mirrors the child's ongoing development. New interests bring new friends who share those interests. By six or seven, boys and girls begin to prefer playing with children of their own gender. Even when adults attempt to convey nonsexist attitudes, young Michael insists that "girls are yucky," and Michelle lumps all boys together as "dumb." These chauvinistic views go hand in hand with other typically rigid ways of thinking and labeling things; people are good or bad, smart or dumb, beautiful or ugly.

Although they look up to older kids and enjoy leading younger ones, for the most part they prefer friends their own age. An age mate is more likely to laugh at the same riddles and jokes; share the same excitement about secrets (that are still hard to keep); and enjoy a round of jacks or giant steps. Sharing goes beyond taking turns. There's usually an open sense of communication: "This is how you do it!" or "How did you do that?"

Much as school-age children want friends, they are not terribly adept at the business of being a friend. Michael still has trouble seeing things from someone else's point of view if it doesn't agree with his own. Because rules and routines give them a secure structure to hold on to, they tend to hold rigid views of right and wrong, fair and unfair. Games are apt to end with the response "You cheated!" or, "That's not in the rules!" The idea that there may be alternatives or more than one way of playing is still beyond them. Rules, they believe, come from some kind of divine source and are meant to be broken only if you don't get caught. It's not that they are unethical, just pre-ethical. Although they know right from wrong, their behavior has more to do with a subjective view of crime and punishment. If you can cheat and win without getting caught, that's good. A lie is bad if you get caught and punished, but it's all right if no one knows.

Through trial and error children discover that they can get away with lying sometimes but not always, and that sometimes they are the ones who are fooled. So the pre-ethical child often has confrontations that result in his being surprised or offended: "So, you're not my friend!" or "I won't play with you anymore!"

PARENTS' ROLE

Stormy and painful as these first friendships may seem, there is no substitute for learning how to lead and follow, win and lose, give and take or negotiate. Parents can't fight their battles or shelter them from inevitable hurt feelings. They can act as a sounding board, listening with a sympathetic ear and helping their child clarify what happened when he and his best friend had a fight, and why he thinks it did. As an interested third party, a parent can often suggest alternative ways of handling a "bossy" friend or an ongoing problem. For the most part, it's best to reserve judgment and not cast blame on the other kid. Remember, you're only hearing one side of a story. Chances are that an hour, a day, or a week from now, Mike and his "enemy" will forgive and forget and then go on to fight again. Remember, too, that both kids are still essentially inexperienced in the friendship department. The fact that they are temporarily incompatible doesn't mean that they'll never be compatible again. Indeed, learning to fight and make up is one of the skills that all children will need in future relationships.

While school and organized clubs provide group experience, children need one-to-one relationships, with time and space to flourish or flounder. Setting the stage for this kind of socialization means welcoming friends after school and on weekends. Busy as parents may be, juggling work, shopping, home, and their own social life, kids want and need to have firsthand and one-to-one experience both as hosts and as guests. Having a friend over may require some extra chauffeuring and an added demand on an already lively household. But these experiences add up to real benefits in social development, and the efforts you make are usually worthwhile. Indeed, research shows that children who have friends tend to have fewer social problems in adulthood.

BEING A GUEST

Going to a friend's house gives children a view of how other families live. It's a great opportunity for them to be on their own, to have a taste of independence. Of course, you'll want to be sure an adult is there to supervise. School kids often give on-the-spot invitations to empty houses, and that is potential trouble. While they don't need hovering caretakers, fives, sixes, and sevens do need adults to turn to when short fuses blow.

Eating lunch or dinner at a friend's house is special. Kids often taste foods they would reject instantly at home. Young visitors get an inside view of household rules and customs that are different from the ones in their own family. Sid's mom may be stricter, Sid's toy chest fuller and his TV diet heavier. Getting a view of how other people live isn't just a treat. It may lead to some testing and questions like, "How come I can't have . . .?"—but that's another side of learning that has real value. It takes time for kids to understand that we don't all have the same toys, skills, or priorities. The fact that Sally's family has a home video game doesn't mean you have to have one. The pressure of the insistence that "everybody has one" will become stronger as time goes on, so it's not too early to start dealing with these issues calmly but firmly.

BEING A HOST

Having a friend over gives kids new responsibilites and a new awareness of the importance of making someone else feel at home. Your child may need some help learning not to embarrass a friend who's visiting, and learning to respect the fact that not everyone does things the way his family does. Both the guest and the host have to figure this out. Being a host also means sharing possessions. For some children this is still difficult. You can do some preliminary peacemaking by encouraging the host to put nonsharable treasures away.

Having a guest over sometimes leads to show-off behavior and total disregard for house rules. You don't want to embarrass your child in front of his friend—but you can't let him run wild, either. Establish the areas where he and his friend can play before company comes. If the system breaks down, a gentle reminder to your child will generally restore order. Kids like having the responsibility for enforcing house rules if the rules are reasonable and they understand them.

If one activity leads to trouble, kids of this age may still need an adult to steer them toward another more cooperative or acceptable activity. You may need to step in and say, "Look, you can't play that game here, because it disturbs our neighbors" (or because someone will get hurt, or because it's too noisy). Follow through with a few suggestions for a change of pace, or help the kids set up a new game. Once the transition is over, move off-stage a bit. At this age, kids need adults they can turn to as resource people, rather than directors.

If Tony's buddy is staying for dinner, you don't need to turn the event into a flowers and candlelight affair. Keep it simple. If Mike usually sets the table or clears, give his friend a job to do, too. Try to avoid making comparisons about table manners or appetites that put your child or young guest in the spotlight.

SLEEPING OVER

Occasional overnight visits to Grandma's or a friend's house gives kids another taste of independence. It's a little early for pajama parties with several kids. That's a few years down the road. For now, two's company and three or more is a crowd.

If Michelle is going to someone's house to spend the night, and she usually sleeps with her doll, let her take the doll along with her. Kids this age often sound confident and they want to act grown-up, but when bedtime comes, they may need the comfort of a familiar token from home. If Amy calls from her friend's house, don't go on at length about what fun you're having without her. Chances are, no matter how much she wanted to go visiting, a small case of homesickness has set in. Assure her that all is well and that you'll want to hear all about her visit when you see her.

If your child is playing host, she and her friend will probably be most comfortable sharing a room. Relax about getting them in early. This is not an ordinary night for either child. Part of the fun is staying up later, giggling, talking, and nighttime snacks. If tensions start to build, you may need to step in and change the flow of events. A family board game, a storybook, or trip to the refrigerator may brighten everything up for the night.

Being together for prolonged periods of time can be tiring and demanding for both children. Arranging for some private time may require tactful manipulating, such as giving each child a separate job to do. Don't overlook the possibility of letting them help with some of the real chores around the house. Washing the car or raking leaves gives them a cooperative venture with a real objective. Helping you bake or prepare dinner also lightens the burden of too much independence.

That doesn't mean they won't enjoy some privacy together, too.

This is the age of keep-out signs and secrets that bring on the giggles. The trick is in keeping a balance so that the overnight visitor and host have a sense of success in being together. By being available, parents can offer guidance through the rough passages, but can let the kids feel they navigated on their own.

The Good Ol' Summertime

By the end of the school year, kids are as eager as ever to run free. "No more teachers, no more books" rings just as true today as it has for generations. Yet after a few days of sleeping late, o.d.-ing on TV, and looking for someone to play with, the sweet taste of freedom often goes sour.

Years ago rural children had real chores and the camaraderie of large families to take them through the idle months. Those in small towns and city neighborhoods were free to play hide-and-seek, roller-skate, and congregate within the bounds of what mothers called "close to home!" There were chores, friends, and a safe community to fill the child's energetic needs from sunup to sundown. Besides, Mom was usually available to soothe a bruised knee, go to the beach, and listen in between times.

Obviously the good ol' summertime is a thing of the past. More and more moms are working, neighborhoods have changed, and the freedom to "go out and play" is more restricted than ever. Urban crime and suburban sprawl have put roadblocks in the way of kids' free-flowing play. Even if Mom is at home, chances are her neighbor is not. And where are the kids next door? Probably at summer camp.

SLEEP-AWAY CAMPS

While there are some sleep-away camps that take young children, a prolonged separation from home and family may be difficult for fives, sixes, and sevens. If you are considering sleep-away camp, try to visit the camp the season before you send your child. Try, too, to talk with parents who have sent children there. Listen carefully to the things they valued and liked about the place. If your ideas on discipline, competition, and activities are different, the camp may have been perfect for their child—but not yours. It's not enough to know they liked it. Ask what they liked about it.

You'll want to be sure that the staff is mature and the program geared to building competence rather than competition. Kids of this age are not usually ready for specialty camps that emphasize a single skill such as tennis or gymnastics. These are the years for exploring a variety of activities and discovering new strengths, skills, interests, and potential. For some kids of this age, camp offers what they want most —a summer full of activities and age mates. For others, the need for less hustle and bustle is apparent. For such kids full-time life in a group may be too much of a good thing. If your child has a hard time spending the weekend at a friend's or prefers long sessions alone with only occasional company, then it's probably not the time for a summer away from home. Parents are the ones who must determine whether the child is really ready for such a long stretch of separation from home.

DAY CAMP

For most children of this age, day camp offers a more comfortable social setting. With group activities by day and the security of home by night, day camp may be the best of both worlds for your five- to seven-year-old. Again it's important to get some firsthand information about the camp's program. Visit, if possible, and talk with other parents and the camp director. You'll want to know what provisions are made for rainy-day activities; what kinds of indoor facilities are available for eating, resting, and play. Does the program emphasize group play or group competition? What will your child be doing during a typical day? What kind of staff run the camp, and what experience do they have with young children?

Unfortunately some day camps are essentially baby-sitting services for parents. They'll keep your child for the day but do little else beyond providing custodial care. Others offer programs that are overly structured. Team sports, for example, are more appropriate for kids eight years old or older. Fives, sixes, and sevens want and need to learn real skills, but they don't need the pressure of too much competition. They want to swim, but they don't need to race. Learning to kick, hit, or pitch a ball is challenge enough without setting some children up as winners and some as losers. In playing with others, kids this age still need some of that free-flowing play that helps them learn about leading and following, giving and taking, talking and listening. These skills of social competence are of no less importance than the physical skills that camps frequently stress.

OTHER ALTERNATIVES

If there are no appropriate camps or the fee will drain your family's budget, there are other alternatives to social isolation and boredom. Schools and community centers often offer swimming lessons, craft classes, and other group activities daily or a few times a week. For many kids, these provide just the right amount of structured activity. It gives them a ready-made group with a shared interest and plenty of free time in between. If none of these programs exists in your area, talk with your school principal, local librarian, or community service organization about organizing seasonal activities.

PARENTS, KIDS, AND SUMMER

Summer is a great time for some real connecting between parents and children. A weekend in the country, a day at the beach, a picnic in the park, an overnight camping trip, are rewarding ways to strengthen the bonds of that wonderful social institution, the family. Away from work, phone, television, and other distractions, a family outing can be a refreshing change. Pitching a tent, building a sand castle, or collecting stones on the beach gives you time when the real objective is enjoying each other's company.

Yes, there will be questions about "How long till we get there?" and "What can we do now?" A day with the children is different from a day alone with your spouse. It demands another kind of give and take and seeing things from the child's point of view. You may need a few games up your sleeve for making the miles pass. Counting cars, twenty questions, facts of five ("I'm thinking of five green things we eat"), are old favorites for young passengers.

An afternoon or evening at home can also be spent with a game board or in the backyard. Much as they enjoy being with friends, kids of this age still revel in spending time, one to one, with parents who are companionable. Painting the doghouse, planting a garden, washing the car, preparing a picnic, are just some of the activities that combine work skills and social interaction between parent and child.

Even if your child goes to day camp, weekends are prime time for family pleasure. As the values and pressures of group life begin, parents need to keep the family lines of communication flowing with positive feelings on both sides.

Birthdays

A birthday party is one of the big social occasions in a child's life. This is an event that brings together your child, her friends, and her family —all the important people in her social world. Making it a happy event means planning ahead.

A traditional party with friends and presents, cake and candles, ice cream and candy, hats and horns, favors and games, is a birthday child's dream. Of course, kids this age tend to dream big. Your space limitations and budget may force you to temper her fantasy with a touch of reality. But a big party need not be expensive. Homemade decorations and cakes can cut down the cost and add to the fun of preparation.

Right from the start, give the birthday girl a voice in planning. Anticipation extends the pleasure of the celebration, which comes so slowly and ends so soon. Children this age will enjoy planning the party list and menu, and deciding which games to play. They can help with the decorations and preparations, too.

Allow two to two and a half hours for your child's party, and be sure to include that information on your invitation. If you're planning a big bash, be sure to have extra adults on hand to help. Even if the party is small, don't try to do it alone. If a child gets hurt or ill, you may need to leave everyone and rush off to the emergency room, and someone needs to be there to take over.

Depending on the time of day, you can plan a meal or simply have a cake-and-ice-cream party. If you do want a meal, keep the menu simple and familiar. Pizza, burgers, peanut butter and jelly, or fried chicken are some of the favorite finger foods kids can handle independently.

While fives and some sixes may still want to invite both boys and girls, many sevens will choose a guest list of their own gender. You can design the party around a forthcoming holiday or pick a theme from your child's favorite play activity. Do some brainstorming with him about the possibilities of spaceships, trains, planes, boats, clowns, dolls, and storybook or cartoon characters. Paper plates and napkins may help set the theme and give you ideas to enlarge upon. A transportation or circus theme will help you choose the shape of your cake and the decorations and favors. If you have a circus theme, instead of pin-the-tail-on-the-donkey, you may want to pin the nose on the clown. Most of the traditional game favorites—musical chairs, hot potato, chief, statues, and giant steps—can be altered a bit to match the theme.

Party hats and favors for the guests sweeten their sometimes difficult obligation of giving a gift. The biblical proverb that it is "more blessed to give than to receive" is a lofty sentiment at this stage. To avoid friction among guests, keep the hats, noisemakers, and favors alike, and supply each child with a bag for storing his or her goodies. Brown lunch bags can be decorated before the party with thematic stickers or drawings. Printing each guest's name on each bag will save last-minute hassles over the protest that "He took mine!"

If it's a sunny day and there's a yard available, allow time for the party-goers to enjoy some freewheeling play. With a crowd you may feel more secure choosing games that involve everyone. Keep in mind, however, that if a few children are engrossed in a nondestructive game of their own, you may be better off letting it continue. Even if you've planned great activities, there are times when plans are better forgotten. There are some kids who won't enter in immediately; they need time to watch. Don't push too hard. They're more apt to join in as the fun becomes apparent. Outdoor games might include green-light-go and treasure hunt, blindman's bluff and follow-the-leader. These are all good, active games for running off energy and keeping the group together. (See directions for some of these games below.)

Indoor parties are more of a challenge. Too many kids running around the house can turn into chaos. Better to plan (even over-plan) a series of games that keeps the fun going. Sit-down games such as chief, hot potato, and telephone are simple to learn and can involve everyone in spirited but relatively quiet play. Simon says or musical chairs provide a little physical action in limited quarters.

Inevitably, there are some kids who either can't or won't join in on group games. Some need to watch from the sidelines awhile, to be sure they know how, and feel safe in trying. Don't insist. After a first round extend the invitation to join in again, but don't force the issue. Kids whose feelings are easily ruffled by win-lose situations can be "your helper" by counting or handing out the prizes. Find another way to involve them without embarrassing them into a corner.

You may also want to consider a sit-down show of some kind. Libraries often have films and projectors to lend. There are teen-age magicians and puppeteers who will entertain children at parties for a low fee. These are extras that may make your life simpler and add to the party.

There's no doubt that a birthday party for fives to sevens makes a vigorous, often exhausting day. After so much preparation, the birthday child is sometimes overexcited and may be less than his usual charming self. Try to avoid embarrassing confrontations in front of friends by anticipating when one activity is played out and a change of pace is needed. You can't expect the birthday child, or his guests, to sit still with company manners for two hours or more. Alternate sit-down games with some action. Juggling the activities demands having more games up your sleeve than you may need. It also requires some tact, a smile, and some flexibility.

Naturally, you'll want to have a camera handy to capture the highlights of your celebration. These are the mementos that can be enjoyed long after the thank-you notes are in the mail and the big day has become a happy memory.

In fact, why not use a photo of the birthday child and each guest as a thank-you note? A box of note paper, stickers, and preaddressed envelopes make the task simple and palatable. Indeed, think of thank-you notes as a finishing touch, another way to extend the happy occasion for guests and host.

Here are some activities and games to help you get started. You might even want to make some decorations with the children at the party.

Outdoor Games

GREEN-LIGHT-GO. One child is chosen to be *it*. Players line up at the opposite end of the yard, facing *it*. *It* turns his back and chants, "Red light, green light, one-two-three," while the other players move toward him. Then *it* turns quickly and everyone freezes. Anyone *it* sees moving must go back to the starting line. Then *it* turns again and chants. The object of the players is to be the first to tag *it* and run back to the starting line without being caught. If *it* catches a player, that player is "out." If the player gets back safely, he becomes *it*. Make a point of giving each child a turn to be *it* in this game or another. An adult may have to step in to help equalize the balance of power, so everyone goes home happier.

FOLLOW-THE-LEADER One child is the leader and runs, skips, hops, jumps, and leads the group around the yard, then picks a new leader.

STATUES. Again, someone is *it*. *It* closes her eyes, and everyone moves about. *It* counts to ten (or more) and then shouts, "Freeze!" When *it* opens eyes, anyone she sees moving is out. The game continues until everyone but one child is caught moving. The last child becomes the new *it*. This takes a long time, since everyone wants a turn at being *it*.

TREASURE HUNT. Set up a series of clues and hidden prizes (edible or otherwise) for each child. Give each child a clue that leads to a place where he finds another clue, that leads to yet another clue. Four or five clues should do. As an alternative, you can play this as a group activity. Clues lead to a group prize —a cut-up watermelon, or a bunch of balloons, or even the birthday cake.

INDOOR GAMES

MUSICAL CHAIRS. Set up a line of chairs. Alternate seats facing forward and back. Have one less chair than you have children. Play a record or the piano (you can even clap) as children circle the chairs. When the music or the clapping stops, they must sit down. The child left standing is out. Now remove one chair, and continue until all but one child is left sitting on the last chair.

HOT POTATO. Use a potato, a toy spaceship, or a beanbag. Have the children sit in a circle and pass the object while the music plays. (Again, you can clap or sing.) When the music stops, the person with the object is out. The game continues until only one child remains.

CHIEF. Have the children sit in a circle. One child goes out of the room. Another child is chosen to be "chief" (or clown or astronaut or president). The chief begins clapping, tapping, or winding his arms, and everyone must follow; he changes his type of movement from time to time. The child outside comes in and has three guesses to discover who the chief is. The old chief is the next child to go out.

Easy-to-Make Birthday Decorations

Party Favors

Save the tubes from paper towels and toilet tissues.

Cut strips of crepe paper longer than the tubes.

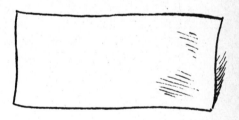

Put small toy favors or wrapped candies inside the tubes.

Roll tubes in the crepe paper, and tie bows at either end.

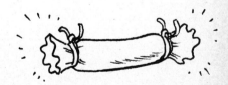

Paper Chain Streamers

Cut many strips of colored construction paper.

Put a dab of glue on the end of one strip, and form into a circle.

Thread next strip through, and glue in the form of a circle.

Continue adding links until you have a chain.

Clown Game Board

On a large sheet of cardboard draw a simple clown face— but leave the nose off.

Using red construction paper, cut out round noses, one for each child. Put a pin through these, and you're ready to play pin-the-nose-on-the-clown.

Easy Party Hats

From construction paper, cut strips about 2 inches wide and 2 feet long.

Decorate these with various designs, plus the name of each child. Then staple the ends together, for a snug-fitting, colorful hat. Variations can include crowns, tiaras, etc.

Goodies Bags

Decorate brown paper lunch bags with stars, flowers, and so on. Print the names of each guest in *large* letters on separate bags. The children can collect their goodies in these bags to take home.

Personal Place Mats

Hand out large oblongs of construction paper. Supply glue, stickers, marking pens, cutout pictures from magazines, etc. Let the children create their own place mats, complete with their names.

Name Balloons

Inflate balloons—one for each child. With a marking pen, print the name of each guest on a balloon. Tie these to the chairs, so the kids can all find their places at your party table. Have extra balloons and your marking pen ready in case a child's balloon pops.

Fortune Poppers

On small slips of paper, write out various fortune messages.

Roll these tightly and stuff inside deflated balloons. Then inflate the balloons.

After cake and ice cream, the kids will have great fun popping the balloons to find their fortunes (or small party favors).

7

Intermediate School Years

EIGHT TO TWELVE YEARS OLD

A Society of Peers

By the age of eight or nine, kids become old hands at the business of school and other routines. Much as they may look forward to vacations and weekends, boredom soon sets in if they are cut off from the social world of their peers for very long. Indeed, being with age mates tends to be the underlying motivation for going to school for kids this age.

While home and family continue to be the security base the eight- or nine-year-old turns to for support and approval, his energies are directed at finding acceptance and approval from his age mates. It is in the company of his peers that the child tests and measures his strengths and weaknesses.

Among their peers, kids continue to evaluate themselves and their friends against the yardstick of the group. Vis-à-vis an adult, the schoolchild is powerless and relatively incompetent. Within the circle of age mates, however, children gain a sense of their own abilities and a sense of themselves as others see them. Often the group motivates children to master skills in the classroom and on the playground.

A NEW ALLEGIANCE—"THEM" AND "US"

In contrast with the younger child, who frequently tattles to prove that he knows the rules and is being good, the older schoolchild considers tattling a breach of loyalty. Within the group there is a new allegiance to peers. The teacher, like other adults, is part of "them," while kids are united as "us." The group has its own standards, its own dress code, and its own language. Kids who don't fit the mold may be teased and ostracized. Secret codes and oaths are sealed with "cross your heart and hope to die."

Within the world of his peers the schoolchild continues to experiment with the roles of leading and following, being friend and foe, winner and loser. Since no one is an expert, there is a certain mutual acceptance of imperfection, and a camaraderie of striving. It's the extreme cases—the superbright kid (who's put down as the teacher's pet) or the superklutz (whom nobody wants on the team)—who have trouble "fitting in" as members of the group. For most children, however, the teasing and taunting, the rough-and-tumble, the put-downs and pats on the back are an acceptable price for admission to the community they care most about.

New friendships are built within the many groups, and the very nature of friendship changes dramatically. "Best friends" stay best friends longer, and the bonds between kids are based on mutual interest rather than on mere proximity. During these years the quality of these relationships takes on new depths of feeling. Kids are now better able to predict and understand what someone else is thinking or feeling. Younger children describe a friend in terms of their own needs: "Anne let me ride her bike" or "Jeff likes me." But the eight- to twelve-year-old describes his friend's particular abilities or characteristics: "Annie's a great swimmer" or "Jeff is a good sport!"

In addition to sharing everyday events, kids of this age begin to share their dream of the future. They are optimists and they sense that they can do anything and everything. This is the age when children find new adult models and heros. Athletes, musicians, performers of all kinds represent what they hope to become—famous! Yet few are ready to make the commitment to vigorous practice and the discipline of their new interests. Indeed, interests tend to change rather quickly. Today Joe is going to ski in the Olympics. Tomorrow he's going to be a rock star.

An Old Allegiance—The Family Anchor

Despite the powerful pull of the group, the middle-years child still embraces the family's value system as her own. Though she may struggle for a greater say in regulating her comings and goings, her bedtime, her chores, and her TV or movie choices, she is essentially testing limits rather than trying to take over. She wants her opinions to get a fair hearing. Although she may be argumentative, she doesn't expect to win all her cases.

The middle-years child uses new evidence found in the world to argue on his own behalf. He has a long list of "everybody elses," who are cited as the true authorities in all disputes. Everybody else gets more allowance, everybody else goes to the arcade, watches what he wants on TV, and goes to bed when he pleases. Everybody else has been to Florida, has customized ski boots, and is not nearly as deprived as you know who. This is the age when kids do a lot of "comparison shopping," finding out how other families work. Sometimes the grass looks a lot greener in someone else's backyard. These are the years when many kids have strong fantasies about their own history: "Maybe I was adopted by these poor and unglamorous dolts who claim to be my parents"; "Maybe I am really the child of someone rich and famous who could give me all the pleasures that are my natural birthright." For Snoopy's friend Lucy, and for many eights and nines, royal heritage is just a daydream away.

On the other hand, if you could hear your child describe her own family to others, your confidence would be restored. Critical and materialistic as they may seem, most kids paint a glowing picture of their own families to others. There is still little doubt in their minds as to your authority. It's just that they now want to know the "whys" behind your decisions, and "what would happen if . . ."

They complain bitterly about things being "no fair," and their antennae are always tuned in to injustice. Yet, in spite of all protests, the middle-years child finds comfort in knowing that he can turn to his parents for help and advice. In setting the stage for the coming turmoil of adolescence, these are important years for keeping the personal and social lines of communication flowing.

Physical Activities

One of the important arenas for group social life is team sports. While individual talent is admired, the team provides a safe haven for those who are not headed for the major leagues. No one wants to lose, but it's a lot less devastating when it's the team, rather than the individual,

losing the medal. While games with complex rules are beyond the
younger child, the middle-years child enjoys learning the system and
watches closely to see that rules are enforced. Although the rules for
informal backyard games are often made up on the spot, once agreed
upon, they are followed, and a sense of honor is expected of the players.
Cheaters and sore losers come face to face with a strong group ethic.
On the playing field the issues of fairness and justice are as important
as the score.

Organized Sports

Although many kids prefer the informality of backyard games, some
set their hearts on making organized teams. Little League baseball
and Pee-Wee hockey have the added pizazz of uniforms, a regular schedule, and adult involvement. When these organizations focus on the
kids (instead of on some need of adults to have "winning children"),
they can serve the developmental needs of this age group. A responsible coach can give kids the skillful tips they need for improving
their game. He can mediate disputes over form or rules, develop cooperation between teammates, encourage a sense of team loyalty, and
help youngsters swallow the bitter lesson—"You can't win 'em
all."

While youngsters of this age are ready for some competition, many
get put into no-win situations. Most often the root of the problem
lies not in competition between kids, but between adults. Ambitious
parents and coaches get caught up with teaching kids to play like
pros. It's as if the adults have to prove themselves through the kids.
If the kids score, the grownups take a bow. For the superjock as
well as the average player, such unrealistic expectations drive the joy
out of any game. They force kids to value winning rather than playing. Often the pressure to win (at any cost) undermines the concept
of fair play, and kids resort to cheating rather than developing sports
skills.

A young player usually can't recognize misguided leadership. As a
parent, you may need to run some interference if the values of the
league are getting skewed. In some cases parents have brought pressure
to hire coaches who value kids' feelings more than the score. Going out
to the games gives you a chance to see not just who wins and who
loses, but how the game is being played.

DEVELOPING SPORTING SKILLS

Of course, not everyone makes the team or wants to. In addition to team sports, middle-years kids are interested in swimming, skiing, skating, biking, riding, gymnastics, tennis, and a long list of other physical activities. Since "knowing how" is one of the most reliable tickets into group activity, kids often throw themselves into the sport of the season. They don't need to be champs, they just want to be able to play.

Group lessons give kids a chance to get some professional tips while trying out new experiences in the company of other beginners. For most youngsters the combination of camaraderie and a bit of healthy competition works. In some instances, though, there may be real benefits in a series of private lessons, particularly for kids who are late to learn sports that their peers can already play with ease. Often a few private sessions can build the child's confidence and competence quickly and can help him feel good about joining his peers.

Keep in mind that some sports involve a great deal of physical contact and others do not. If your child relishes the touch and tumble of soccer, football, and other contact sports, and thrives on rubbing shins and shoulders, encourage her participation in team sports. Other kids need more space. They prefer the distance that a bike or a pair of skates provides, the net that separates tennis players. There are plenty of ways for your child to develop physical competence on his own terms, in a sport he likes.

The pleasures of biking, hiking, and swimming can be enjoyed solo or with a friend. Whether your youngster is on the team or not, developing such personal skills has real value now and will serve her well into the future. This is especially true for kids who are essentially nonjocks or even downright klutzy. For such children, finding an individual sport may mean the difference between a totally sedentary life and an active use of their muscles. These are years when long-term attitudes as well as skills are being developed. Although it may mean some trial and error, nonjock kids this age need encouragement to explore a variety of physical activities. Instead of buying expensive equipment right away, put the money into rentals and some good instruction.

At the same time, the nonjock can be encouraged to develop other talents the team will value. The school paper is going to need reporters and photographers; the school band will need drummers, trumpeters, and tuba players. Parents may have to do some persuading to help kids see the many ways that people can participate without being captain of the basketball team.

Mike, who didn't make the baseball team, was really feeling out of it until his dad suggested he ask the coach if he could work as assistant manager. Mike may not be making home runs, but he's one of the guys and gets to go on all the trips with the team. Instead of ignoring the issue, his father helped him find a way to participate and value his nonathletic skills.

SPORTS—FOR EVERYONE

"Sports have changed. Girls are more accepted as equals now. When my older girls were this age (they're in college now), there was a real split between girls and boys. Now there are mixed teams, and Susie's proved herself. Girls are accepted in sports. It's nice."   —Mother of an eleven-year-old

Susie's mom is right. Attitudes about girls and sports have changed dramatically over the past few years. Some communities do sponsor mixed teams, while others have established separate (but equal) sporting programs. In large part, the influence of the women's movement brought about these changes and took the stigma off being a tomboy. Kids today are seeing female athletes compete in national and international sporting events, and young girls have new models of excellence to inspire them. In city parks and on country roads, children today see men and women jogging, riding bicycles, and working at keeping physically fit. A look at the world-record books for the last ten years shows that women are competing seriously, not just in traditional sports (like swimming) but in long-distance running and other sports formerly considered "unfeminine."

CAMP

These are the years when sleep-away camp is most appealing. Just consider what camp has to offer: a ready-made group of peers, a round of planned activities, a chance to try out new independence and spread those growing wings. Depending on your budget and your child's readiness to leave home happily, there are a multitude of summer-camp choices.

Like Katie, who doesn't like to "sleep over," your child may be happier with a day camp. Not only is it less costly than sleep-away camp, you'll still have weekends for family outings. Campers of this age are ready for team sports and new skills. Do check out the indoor facilities of the camp you are considering for safety and comfort on rainy days. Some camps offer an option of bringing lunch. That can lower the cost and suit your camper's eating style.

There are sleep-away camps that sign kids on for the summer, for a month, or even for a week. Although most camps offer a varied mix of sports and arts, some camps specialize in riding, music, dance, tennis, or computers. Children at the upper end of this age group may have strong interests in developing a particular skill. Such early specialization may be appropriate for some, but even the child who's working toward professional athletics would benefit from a program that includes other activities. Narrowing interests too early may limit the child's exploration of hidden talents and interests. Eight weeks at a computer or piano keyboard may be too much of a good thing. So check out the specialty camps, and make sure there's time allotted for exploring other activities, too.

Directories of camps and associations will help you zoom in on camps. If you can, make an on-site visit the season before; otherwise try to speak with parents who have had youngsters at the camps you're considering.

Ask about:

- *The staff:* What's their background? Do they have experience working with kids or is this just the only summer job they could find? A camping staff should include members with a solid base in child development.
- *The activities:* Are there choices, or must everyone follow the same program? Will this kind of program be comfortable for your child? Are there many offerings that will build his sense of success, or is he going to be struggling all season to conform and keep up?
- *The food and the physical plant:* Would you want to spend the summer in this setting? Are the grounds and swimming

area well cared for and supervised? Is there a choice on the menu, or must kids all eat what's presented? For example, at some camps peanut butter, jelly, and bread are available as an alternative if the child detests a particular meal. In other camps, kids have to eat what's offered or go without.

Sexual Stereotypes: New Patterns in the Old Mold

Despite women's changing roles, middle-years kids tend to remain essentially chauvinistic in their outlook and generally prefer the camaraderie of all-male or all-female groups. Psychologists see these separate societies as the kids' way of reaffirming their sexual identity. Of course, their gender identity has been in the making from infancy onward. Yet during the middle years, kids solidify their sense of themselves by joining with others like themselves. They do this by sex as well as by interest groups. Vis-à-vis adults, the peer group is a way of defining "us" as opposed to "them." Being one of the boys or one of the girls defines a different "us" vs. "them."

Parents and teachers certainly play a role in shaping stereotypical views by example and attitude. If Jennifer is talking about being an astronaut or Rob about being a nurse and the adults laugh, titter, and tease, then the message is sent and received. If they treat the ambitions as real possibilities, then that's the message the kids get.

Despite the seemingly old-fashioned separation of the sexes at this age, children are growing up with much broader concepts of what people of either gender can do. Recent reports indicate that teenage girls set their career aspirations for higher-level jobs than boys of the same age. In fact, one-third of the girls studied aspired to nontraditional jobs such as engineers, draftspeople, and welders. In the same group there were more girls than boys who hoped to be doctors and lawyers.

Physical Changes

Toward the end of this age span, as children approach puberty, a new awareness of real physical changes emerges. Girls tend to develop earlier than boys, and among them there is a lot of "body watching," as one mother called it. For those who are more physically mature than others, the change may not be altogether welcome. Given their attitudes about being "different," this reluctance should not be so surprising. Girls at the upper range of this age need assurance that they are not "freaks" because they do or do not wear a bra yet. The same is true for boys who may or may not have started their rapid growth spurt. Both boys and girls need honest and clear information about the physical changes that will affect both sexes. Since the old grapevine still abounds with a harvest of misinformation, parents play an important role in filling in the facts and pruning out the fancy.

At this age, nobody feels he or she is developing just right. Whether tall or short, rounded or flat, everyone suffers from fears of "too little" or "too much," "too early" or "too late."

And friendships may suddenly be ripped asunder when one child is "growing up" quickly and the other is left behind. A "little" sister can suddenly shoot up and tower over her big brother. A best friend may flaunt her development or taunt her less physically mature friend.

Kids need assurance that these inequalities even themselves out in time. A look through the family photo album may help your child see that even Mom and Dad went through a real metamorphosis, but turned out pretty normal, if not perfect. Parents can certainly help ease the pangs of being "left behind" by assuring the child that her big sister also went through a stage of being under- or overdeveloped. Stories from the parent's own erratic development may also help the child see that time will bring about some of those greatly desired changes.

Parents who feel uncomfortable about discussing menstruation or wet dreams may find it helpful to use a book to launch the topic. The *Girls' Book about Sex* and the *Boys' Book about Sex* are widely available in bookstores and libraries. Even if you think you've presented the necessary information, a straightforward book gives kids a chance to check out what they know and what they want to know privately and at their own pace. By the late middle years, kids who have not asked for information may warrant more concern than those who openly question parents. Many are too embarrassed to broach the subject of sex. That doesn't mean you should ignore it and assume they have no interest. For such children it is especially important for parents to find a way to open the channels of communication so the child does not have to look to peers for answers to important and natural questions.

Cliques, Clubs, and
Other Mutual Admiration Societies

"Allen doesn't have a best friend; it's more of a group, and a very clique-y sort of group. They're planning to have a club this summer. So far, the only purpose of the club is to meet every Friday."   —Father of a nine-year-old

In attics and cellars, in the backyard or the schoolyard, kids of this age are forever forming "clubs." Many have big plans for grand projects. They're going to put on a show or study the stars or build a treehouse. There's usually more talk than action. Indeed, the fights over who's in charge, when to meet and where, often take up more energy than the professed purpose of the group. For those who are "in" there are issues of power to be hammered out. Too much friction within the ranks frequently leads to a total breakdown of the organization or at least to the abrupt end of a meeting. Yet on one thing there is generally unity: these are closed clubs, with limits on "who's in" and "who's out."

These age-group cliques are the way kids guarantee their own place within a group. Those who are "out" are apt to salve their wounds by forming their own club and excluding others. While these groups have little permanence, they are a source of both happiness and misery for most children at one time or another.

THE BAD NEWS—WHAT PRICE ENTRY?

Not all groups are blessed with the old-fashioned innocence and wholesome values of an Andy Hardy movie. Tens and elevens sometimes come face to face with moral dilemmas that test conflicting value systems. Mark's initiation into the neighborhood gang is an example:

To become a member of the Eagles, Mark had to throw a rock at the first person to get off the bus. With the gang as witness, Mark clutched the ticket to admission in his hand, waiting for the next bus to pull up. "Here it comes," one of the members shouted, "get ready!" Mark froze. The first person off the bus was an elderly woman leaning on a cane. Mark couldn't do it. The price of admission was too high.

Mark's problem may seem extreme, yet the realities of peer pressure can't be brushed aside. Research shows that children today seem to be more intensely dependent on their peer groups at an ever-earlier age. Observers believe that this peer dependency has a lot to do with a distance kids feel in their relationships with adults. Current studies show that parents and other adults tend to be less available for comfort, advice, or companionship. In fact, children are frequently put in the position of advisor and confidant, playing the role of pseudoadult in their parents' marital, financial, and self-fulfillment crises. This turnaround in the parent-child relationship may actually push kids into situations they're not prepared to handle. When parents abdicate their role as stable and reliable advisors, children may look to the group to fill the void.

One ten-year-old's mother complained:

"It seems like everybody's too busy doing their own thing to be bothered with raising their kids. It's not just divorced parents or single-parent homes. Kids are supposed to take care of themselves and fit into their parents' schedule, instead of the other way around."

While greater independence and group acceptance are the great developmental tasks of the middle years, the strength of home and family ties must continue to be firmly established. With such ties parents can help their children keep a balance between sometimes conflicting value systems. They can encourage kids to continue building their individual talent without becoming slaves to conformity.

THE GOOD NEWS—ACCEPTANCE

Within these peer groups a lot of positive social learning is going on. Kids teach each other what's acceptable and unacceptable. Rules are important and so are loyalty and secrecy. Belonging is by no means easy. Acceptance often means some giving up of one's own ideas and giving in to the desires of others. It means listening as well as telling, negotiating instead of commanding, making concessions instead of demanding that things be done your way. Children of this age are not big on tact, but as a group they provide a sense of belonging that goes beyond individual friendships. It is from that sense of unity that kids find some of the strength they need to become independent and to build relationships outside their family circle.

Parents can lend their support to these childhood societies by making some space and privacy available. The back porch, attic, basement, or barn may need a coat of paint or some beat-up furniture for that lived-in feeling. In city apartments, a bedroom may have to do double duty. Projects may need some friendly assistance, a ride to the lumberyard, or a word of advice.

Kids of this age look to adults not so much for supervision as for a resource they can turn to when their ingenuity hits a snag. Having the club at your house doesn't mean you have to be a scout leader. It just requires a willingness to live with a little healthy hubbub and perhaps to provide a few extra snacks when kids need a boost.

MORE WAYS THAN ONE INTO GROUP LIFE

Aside from their self-made groups, children of this age are eager joiners of prepackaged groups—scouts, 4-H, religious groups, and community-based youth clubs.

> "Billy is the kind of kid who stands up when the teacher says
> sit down, but he loves the formal rules and rituals of scouting."
> —Father of an eight-year-old

Like Billy, middle-years children thrive on the built-in structure of groups. There are badges to be earned, and there is a formula for earning them. The rewards for following the rules and learning new skills are tangible. Success is attainable. Since the leadership is in the hands of adults, the group is less likely to fall apart or turn on single members. These activity groups are also often a child's introduction to the concept of social service, to contributing to the larger community. Projects that involve visiting nursing homes, making toys for children's hospitals, painting parkbenches, or cleaning up a playground give kids a sense of being useful members of the community in which they live. In fact, to insure a sense of success, many of these group and individual pursuits are structured with reasonable goals—an important ingredient to insure success!

Taking Lessons

"Katie took gymnastics, then ballet. Then she had had enough. She switched to skiing . . ."

—Mother of a ten-year-old

"Billy takes piano lessons and he loves them. He doesn't really practice much, but I don't make a big thing about it. I want him to play for his own pleasure, and he gets that. He's not going to be a concert pianist."

—Mother of a nine-year-old

"Adam goes to computer class once a week. He loves it. He wants to go to computer camp this summer with his friend. It's funny how many people in my office are terrified of the new technology, but these kids have none of that reluctance. It's all a fascinating game to them."   —Father of a ten-year-old

Whether it's computers or ballet or trombone, the appetite for learning new skills runs high. In some cases, the desire to join a particular class may have more to do with what friends are doing than with a real personal commitment. Katie flitted from gymnastics to ballet and then to skiing. Like most youngsters her age, Katie's interests change frequently. For many children, the initial enthusiasm fades when they discover the slow and frustrating side of acquiring new skills.

Billy's mom sees his lessons as an opportunity to balance group time with developing individual talents and interests. Billy may never play Carnegie Hall, but he may play for himself or at a party a few years from now, when the gang's all there. Rather than making an issue over an exacting practice regimen, his mom recognizes the pleasure he finds in playing and learning slowly on his own.

Though dabbling in the arts and testing the sciences may strike some adults as wasteful, exploration has real value to the middle-years child. Essentially there's no better way for kids to discover their own talents and test the strength of their commitment. Before buying expensive instruments, give it a test run with rented or borrowed equipment.

Forcing kids to take lessons against their will and getting locked into constant nagging over practice does nothing to enhance skills or communication on big issues. When interest lags, better to accept the inevitable and suggest a break from lessons for a while. There's no point in spending money on teachers and force-feeding reluctant kids. It may be that in six months or a year, your youngster will want to start again with a fresh commitment and a full understanding of what's involved by way of effort. If you think she might be ready to take up piano again, suggest it. Don't make her think that just because she got tired of it once, she can't have a second chance.

On the other hand, some middle-years youngsters see their lessons as training for a professional future. Without narrowing their sights by too much emphasis in one area, parents can give their children support and approval for their aspirations. Finding appropriate teachers and providing the space and equipment for practice are a parent's way of showing that he values his child's interests. At the same time, parents need to guard against pushing the child's achievements in order to bask in reflected glory. Sometimes kids get locked into pursuits that reflect their parents' lost dreams, rather than their own. Too much emphasis on one skill may lead the child to see himself too narrowly and rob him of the benefits of discovering other potential interests and talents.

"I Can't—I've Got _____ Today"

- Monday: Crafts
- Tuesday: Piano
- Wednesday: Tennis
- Thursday: Scouts
- Friday: Religious instruction
- Saturday: Dance/ski/computer class
- Sunday: Sunday school

These are the years psychologist Erik Erikson called the age of industry. Eager as they are to sign on, join up, and try out new skills, some middle-years children are definitely overindustrialized. The schedule above leaves little time for independent play and no time at all for just doing nothing. The value of unscheduled time should not be overlooked. Like all of us, children need time left over for exploration and daydreaming, time to reflect on their experiences with others and think about what they have done and what they hope to do.

"When Katie comes home she usually makes herself a snack and goes to her room. She plays around. She doesn't go to sleep. She's busy. But it's almost as if she has to be by herself for a good hour after a long day of being in the thick of things. It's 'down time.' "   —Mother of a ten-year-old

Katie isn't doing homework, chores, or practicing the piano—nor is she wasting time. Being alone is her way of taking a refreshing pause from the hectic pace of a normal day that is scheduled from the moment the alarm clock wakes her at 7:00 A.M. It may be time for nothing but woolgathering. Often we fail to see the value of daydreams because we can't see the tangible outcome or product of such excursions. Yet psychologists believe these moments may be the underpinnings of creativity and provide a healthy release from the rigors of here and now. Many children of this age find a different route to fantasy through books. Some are at the library every two days and read half a new book driving home from the bookstore. Others use their free time writing journals and diaries about the people and events in their lives. To encourage this kind of involvement, keep the reading fires kindled with frequent trips to the library and bookstore. For the writer, bring home colored pens, stationery, fabric-covered books, or a lockable diary for a surprise gift.

Leaving some time free gives children an opportunity to get to know the one person they are going to live with longer than anyone else in the world—namely, themselves. Knowing how to enjoy being alone is another dimension of being a social individual. But developing that ability is difficult if you never have time left free from scheduled events and constant companionship. A lack of such skills makes people a poor risk on the job or even in personal relationships. The ability to be a self-starter, to devise your own tasks or entertainment, is a resource needed throughout life.

Hanging Out

Once they have wheels (bikes, that is) and greater freedom in the neighborhood, kids are likely to find their own places for socializing. It may be the sandlot for a game of ball, the arcade at the mall, or the fast-food place. For most children, these small journeys into the bigger world provide a new taste of freedom heightened with adventure. With limited funds there are choices to be made about buying an ice-cream cone or playing Pac-Man. While some communities have banned young players from arcades or limited the hours they can play, others have left the control in parents' hands.

> "Katie gets an allowance of three dollars a week. I don't tell her what she can't use it for, but when we go to the mall, I tell her to take just a dollar, because if she can't resist the temptation of those dumb games, at least she won't have spent all her money. A couple of times she spent the whole three dollars and then she was upset, but I think she learned something from that."   —Mother of a ten-year-old

Katie's mom has given her a strategy for handling her money and time. Rather than making the games off limits altogether, she's helping Katie set her own limits. There will always be temptations out there, and Katie's mom won't always be around to say yea or nay.

Naturally, there are places and things parents have to say no to. If the local arcade is populated by unsavory characters or the neighborhood park attracts local stumblebums, you have to put that place off limits. If you explain why, kids will generally accept your concern for their safety, and though they may argue for a while, they'll usually comply.

Unfortunately, sometimes the gang ethic leads to unexpected behavior. Children often fall prey to "I dare you" games of petty thievery and vandalizing property.

> "Tommy came home and refused to go riding his bike. Robbie and two other kids were making a game of throwing rocks at anyone who rode down the next street. I don't like to fight

my kids' battles, but I called Robbie's house and his mom couldn't believe it."   —Mother of an eleven-year-old

Much as we hate to believe it, our own kids can do unacceptable things. If you find toys or candy or sports equipment you know they couldn't buy with their allowance, check it out. Don't threaten them with reform school, but do be clear and tough. Acknowledge the fact that "other" people may have dreamed up the mischief, but let your child accept his or her own share of the blame and the consequences. It's important that kids recognize their wrongdoing but also understand that they will be forgiven. Giving them space and privacy and greater freedom doesn't mean that parents should give license to the sometimes misguided group ethic. Unless kids learn to balance their own values against the group's, they will be in bigger trouble as the pressure to conform grows stronger during adolescence. In a sense, these small emergencies during the preteen years give parent and child a chance to work through family values in the face of growing pressures from the larger world.

Grooming and Dressing

"Probably our biggest hassles are over dressing and cleanliness. If I get Annie into a dress three times a year, that's a lot! Just getting her to take a shower, or to wash her hair, is rough. She has braces, and getting those teeth brushed several times a day—it's a problem! How do I handle it? We fight a lot. *And* we have a lot of discussions. Coming home from the orthodontist's, we talk. But not when the others are around. She's very sensitive, and she can't take criticism.
                    —Mother of a ten-year-old

While young children make a game of scrubbing teeth and bubbly lathers, soap suds seem to lose their appeal to middle-years kids. It's as if they haven't the time for such mundane matters as cleanliness. As with other routines and responsibilities, there is a big discrepancy between what they are capable of doing and what they actually do. So they need reminding and then more reminding.

While you and I may thank someone for a little reminder now and then, don't expect too much in the way of gratitude from kids this age. Try to keep your suggestions straightforward and friendly. It's just as easy to say, "Oops, your hair needs combing. Do you want some help?" as it is to say, "When are you going to learn to comb your hair? You look like a slob!" Pushed too far, the reminders can escalate into a power play between parents and child, which leads to neither cleanliness nor communication. It's better to tolerate a modicum of scruffiness that comes with the territory than to risk hardening the lines of resistance. Most grubbiness is superficial and not likely to jeopardize your child's health. Learning to take responsibility for one's appearance isn't an overnight process, and strong words and ultimatums from you probably won't hurry the learning.

For many parents, mothers in particular, it comes as something of a shock to find that their scruffy-looking child is nevertheless a critic in her own right. Suddenly, Mom can't be relied on to know what dress, shoes, or beads to wear. "You're not going to come to school in *that,* are you?" Try not to take the attack too personally. You don't have to conform to her suggestions, but it may help you to know what she doesn't like about something. At least give it a hearing. Probably you know more about what's appropriate for you and the occasion than she does, so talking may clarify things for her, if you keep it friendly. And often, you *can* follow some of your child's suggestions. Of course, kids of this age are not terribly tactful, and some parents really suffer from the slings and arrows that signal the parental fall from the pedestal. This "dethronement" of the formerly perfect parent is a necessary piece of becoming a separate person with individual tastes and opinions. Right now they don't want Mom or themselves to "stick out" or look different. You don't have to give in completely, but you can save yourself some anger if you understand where your child is coming from.

DRESSING TO FIT IN

Among the things kids learn at home (and in school) are the conventions of dress. So if your child is going to a jeans-and-sneakers school, don't send him off in a jacket and tie. Within limits of good taste and safety, the dress code of the group is a harmless nod to belonging. For your mother it meant penny loafers instead of Mary Janes; for you it might have been workboots instead of loafers. Each generation has its own look. Wearing your shirttails out or your sweatshirt inside out should not be seen as a disregard for one's appearance. Children of this age are essentially conservative, if slightly rumpled around the edges.

Naturally, there are limits of taste, place, and age-appropriate behavior that parents may need to take a stand on. There are family occasions when sneakers and shirttails are unacceptable. Dinner in the restaurant, a trip to the theater, or Grandma and Grandpa's anniversary may call for some "Thou shalt wear" pronouncements. If kids have a voice in selecting party clothes, they are usually less unhappy about dressing up for special events. Take your child shopping and, within reason, let him choose his own clothes. He'll be much more likely to enjoy the novelty of getting spiffed up.

KIDS WHO DON'T FIT

For the child who's overweight, shorter, taller, or in any way "different," the level of discomfort in a group, and the need to fit in, is no small matter. You may believe in the old adage "Don't judge a book by its cover," but research shows that both grownups and kids tend to judge people by first appearance.

We can help children to understand that some kids grow faster than others or that by adolescence the law of averages levels things out for most of us. We can also help the obese child begin to see the connections between eating habits and weight. Or course, all of these are long-range ideas, and what children want are quick solutions. Sometimes the family pediatrician or the gym teacher can get the message through better than parents can. After all, they're experts, and you're just ordinary people, telling your child something to cheer him up.

For immediate aid, it helps to take some extra time selecting clothes that help them "fit in." Oversized or undersized kids tend to end up with clothes that are either "too babyish" or "too old." It may mean more shopping around and some extra alterations, but the effort is worthwhile. Children who feel comfortable in their clothes are freer to forget them and to get on with the business of growing socially and intellectually.

Whether it's a special day or not, don't overlook the possibility of giving your child some positive feedback. Somehow, all of us have a way of noticing when necks are dirty or clothes mismatched. Too often, we take it for granted or forget to comment when kids have put themselves together and done it reasonably well. Yet praise can go a long way toward reinforcing exactly what you want to see.

Can Lisa Stay for Lunch? Dinner? Overnight?

"We live in an area where there are no children, so we import them. Their parents are very happy to drop them here and pick them up two days later."   —Mother of a nine-year-old

"Friday and Saturday nights they love to sleep over. Either Susie's friend sleeps here or she goes there. It's really no trouble. On Saturday they've got Little League practice or in the winter we go to the mall. They're so busy talking and playing games and enjoying the day, it's actually easier with company than if we're alone."   —Mother of a ten-year-old

This is the age when happiness is having a friend "over"—for lunch, dinner, or overnight. Sure, there are times when dinner just won't stretch or the schedule is too tight. But having guests and going visiting are an important part of a child's social development and provide an important experience on the road to developing independence. For an only child, hosting or visiting can offer a taste of what it's like to share one's personal space. Even on a limited basis, this is a real learning experience. Visiting gives kids an inside view of various life styles, family rules, and customs. There's no reason to fuss over special meals or company finery. In fact, your guests will be more comfortable if you don't. Just as you did when your child was younger, stick to the usual routine as much as possible. If your child has regular family responsibilities (setting the table, clearing it off, filling the pitcher), a friendly reminder may be called for. Your child's guest will probably enjoy pitching in and helping, too. Visiting children are often so solicitous and eager to help, they're too good to be true. Be gracious, but don't put your own child down with "See how Susie helps without being asked." Susie is trying on her company manners, just as your child will at Susie's house. Why not say, "It's so nice to have an extra pair of helping hands." Giving positive feedback to the guest need not be at the young host's expense. This is also not the time for extensive lessons in table manners or comparing kids' accomplishments at school. Save the lessons for when you are alone. Criticism is hard to take at any time, but in front of friends it is humiliating.

If your child's guest is staying overnight, chances are that bedtime will need delaying. Kids generally prefer to share a room, even if there's an empty guestroom available. Since overnights are generally not school nights, an exception to the rules-as-usual need not become a big issue. In fact, raids on the icebox and late-night giggles are part of the shared pleasure of sleepover parties.

However, for some kids, sleeping over is no pleasure at all.

> "Jennifer likes to go visiting, but she prefers to come back to her own house at night. She's tried to fight it and she's been successful a few times, but she prefers to have kids stay here. So when one of her friends doesn't want to stay, she'll say to me, 'I understand how Debbie feels.' Of course, she never tells other kids about her own fears, but she can put herself in their shoes, and that's a sign of growing up."
>
> —Mother of a ten-year-old

Jennifer's lucky. No one is pressing the issue and making her feel babyish. By making friends welcome, the parents avoid putting Jennifer into a situation that builds stress instead of social competence. Leaving home and liking it just comes later for some than for others.

Although they may talk about sleeping over or camping out, enthusiasm sometimes fades with the sunset. Mark's mother can always predict a telephone call around 10:00 P.M. "Hi," Mark says, "you know what I forgot?" It may be a toothbrush, socks, you name it. Clearly the item is not nearly as important as touching base with what Mark has not forgotten: the security of home and family.

Birds of a Feather

Friendships at this age tend to be based on mutual abilities and shared likes and dislikes. So physically active kids are more apt to befriend physical types than, say, a sedentary model builder. Although boys and girls may have playmates of the opposite sex, close friends are generally of the same gender and pretty much the same age.

Your friend is still your friend even though he lives on the other side of town. A friend is now someone you expect to depend on, to keep your secrets, and hold your place on the lunch line. Friends are no longer interchangeable and fleeting. There is more depth of caring and an expectation of loyalty and longevity.

Although friendships do tend to last longer, there are many reasons why friendships flounder, too.

Often, outside forces come between friends when families move and pals must part. For the child who is leaving there is real anxiety about being the "new kid" and finding a place in a new social circle. The child left behind often goes through a different, but no less lonely period of distress. Rather than ignoring the pain of loss, and cutting off the friendship, children may find some comfort in writing to each other or making occasional visits, if possible. In time, children who have had rewarding friendships will look for and find more of the same social pleasures with others. For most kids, however, this is not an overnight process. Losing a friend is not like losing a baseball glove or a bracelet, and parents can help by recognizing the importance of the loss.

Fighting and hurt feelings can also cause friendships to fall apart.

"In my day we called it flat-leaving. You know how that works. Somebody is supposed to be your friend and you go someplace and they leave you flat. My daughter has a friend like that—she tells Susie to come with her to so-and-so's house and when they get there, she has other friends and doesn't bother with Susie."   —Mother of a ten-year-old

More often than not, such fallings-out between friends are patched over with little need for parental interference. A sympathetic ear may soothe the ache and also help kids sort out their feelings. Rather than taking sides or casting blame, be a good listener. While the whole thing may strike you as insignificant, don't dismiss the whole matter as childish nonsense. Her feelings are running deeper, and it's important to let her know that you sympathize. You can't fight your children's fights for them, but you can often help them put things in perspective. Learning to get over hurt feelings is a part of growing up that can't be avoided.

"He's Not My Friend Anymore,"
or, "Nobody Likes Me"

While fights between friends are usually short-lived, sometimes broken bonds can't be repaired. As children's interests change, so too does their attachment to certain friends. Breaking off a long-standing friendship can be painful to both parties.

> "Billy and Jeff played together for two or three years, but when Jeff got involved with skiing and Billy didn't, Jeff found a new best buddy at the ski hill and Billy felt abandoned."
> —Father of a ten-year-old

Often the common interest that linked friends comes to an end when one friend moves on to a new and unshared enthusiasm. In a way, Billy and Jeff have outgrown each other, and Billy's parents may need to fill the void for a while. Although parents can by no means take the place of a best friend, they can ease the loneliness and lend assurance that the child will find a new best friend in time.

There's no point in saying, "Forget about Jeff. You'll find somebody else." The big message is not that friends are interchangeable, but rather that change is part of growing up. Don't minimize the feelings of hurt and anger. Listen without judging or casting blame on your child or his "nasty" friend. What the child needs least, right now, is a lot of criticism of his own shortcomings. Indeed, Billy may need some help focusing on which skills and interests he wants to develop. He may need some time alone or exposure to a group, or both, before he begins to forge a new "best" friendship. Painful as these times may be, most children learn a great deal about themselves and others in the process of losing a friend.

"Why Do You Play with That Kid?"

Parents are often distressed or mystified by their children's choice of friends. While friends are usually more alike than not, your child may seem to prefer kids who are absolutely unlike him. Randy, who's shy, may team up with Peter, the class clown. In their own way they are a perfectly balanced team. Randy is the ideal audience for Peter, and Peter does everything Randy would love to do.

Like magnetic poles, opposites often do attract because they satisfy a need in both kids. Unless your child is being bullied or led into danger, such relationships usually run their course without parental interference. On the other hand, there are times when parents may need to step in.

"Mark and his newfound friend, Ben, were constant companions after school. We figured they were out riding their bikes and doing the things kids always do. It wasn't until we got a call from the neighbors that we discovered the boys were doing a demolition job on a shed down the road. Our neighbor was mostly concerned about their getting hurt."
—Mother of an eleven-year-old

It would be hard to tell just who was leading or following, but the fact was both Mark and Ben were trespassing and destroying someone's property. Instead of breaking up the friendship, Mark's and Ben's parents dealt with the issue at hand. The boys gave up some of their allowance for several months to pay for the damages. Their parents also kept closer tabs on their after-school comings and goings.

Two on the Aisle: Theater, Ballet, Concerts

Actually, two in the balcony will probably give your child a better view over adult heads than costly orchestra seats. With their greater staying power, middle-years kids are now ready to go beyond the made-for-children shows. By this age, many are taking music and dance lessons, so a live performance holds new fascination and perhaps inspiration to practice. In addition to professional performances, don't overlook the possibilities of local high school or college concerts and theater.

Being part of a live audience is quite different from watching TV. There's no announcer setting the scene or filling in the story line. Although the program notes may include a synopsis, the print is notoriously tight and frequently hard to follow. So before and between the acts, you may need to read the notes and then do a little storytelling; try to set the scene and explain the drama that is about to unfold when the curtain goes up.

Between acts, take the opportunity to give your child a stretch, a cool drink, and a chance to get the wiggles out. The issues of social reciprocity and guidelines for theater-going (see Chapter 6) still apply for the older child, and anything that parents can do by way of explanation or preparation will make the experience more memorable all around.

Festive Occasions

Holidays and birthdays are special occasions in your child's social life. Some holidays center on the family and a gathering of the clan. Older kids often get lost in the shuffle of family get-togethers. After the first "My, how tall you've grown" and "What grade are you in?" grownups seem to run out of conversation. Once the sweet darlings and centers of attention, kids at this age are often expected to babysit for younger cousins or to blend in with the woodwork. Some responsibility is fine, but remember, it's their holiday, too. A bit of planning ahead can go a long way in making the day a happy one for everyone. See Chapter 6 for ideas that will contribute to family fun.

Whether it's an anniversary or a little sister's birthday, children enjoy the opportunity to do something tangible and festive for somebody else. Such events give them practice at thinking about what somebody else would enjoy. Selecting a gift, icing a cake, or stringing up streamers lets kids experience warm feelings that come from giving. Yes, they may need a loan or a helping hand, but they also need encouragement to do something for others.

Parties away from Home

When it comes to their own birthday celebrations, middle-years kids think big. You may need to scale things down to a size that fits your budget and space. By now the thrill of pin-the-tail-on-the-donkey and cake with candles may have worn thin. This is the age when going someplace new or doing something unusual has great appeal. A party at the roller-skating rink, the bowling alley, or the lake are just a few possibilities. Depending on where you live, your budget, and your child's interests, you can probably come up with many local attractions. Celebrating away from home may be especially desirable if your living quarters are tight, and it certainly simplifies preparations.

Naturally, you'll want to explore the possibilities with the birthday child. After all, whose birthday is it? Your child may really prefer taking six or eight friends out to a baseball game, rather than having a party at home for ten or more. Before you open the discussion, check out the going rates for bowling, skating, and other activities your child enjoys. Some places have group rates and certain hours when a party would be welcome. You don't want to sit around and wait at the bowling alley. Check, too, on the prices of pizza, burgers, and other snacks. It may be possible to serve a prearranged treat rather than trekking home for a meal. Ask if you can bring a cake and candles along to give the occasion a touch of tradition. If eating out will put a dent in the budget, start or end the party at home, with time for feasting and opening gifts.

Whether you buy or make invitations, be sure to indicate when the party begins and ends (two to three hours is plenty of time to celebrate). If driving everyone there and back is a hassle, why not have the guests dropped off and picked up at the place you're having the party? Give the birthday child a chance to pick out—or design—and fill in the invitations. For your own comfort, ask another adult to join you. Although you probably won't have an emergency, you must be able to leave the group if one child gets ill or injured.

PARTIES AT HOME

Of course, a party at home has more appeal to many parents and kids. This is the time for parties with a theme. If it's near a holiday you can borrow from the decorative possibilities of pumpkins, hearts, or patriotic banners. Your child's favorite hobby or sport may lend inspiration for invitations, decorations, and games. Be sure invitations indicate when the party is to begin and end. Mix and match some ready-made party goods with homemade fixings. Define the party room(s) by decorations that set the mood and provide enough space for action. Children don't need to run through the house, but they can't sit still the entire time, either.

To break the ice, have an activity set up for guests as they arrive. For example, if it's around Halloween, guests might enjoy decorating individual pumpkins with magic markers and toothpicks to add feathers, yarn, and buttons to the face. These become decorative favors for the table and you can give out prizes for the most beautiful, the funniest, or the scariest design. Since kids of this age are better able to handle competition, you can build a variety of contests into the day. Keep the prizes simple (and possibly edible), and be sure everyone gets something. A team game allows all the contestants to get prizes. In some games there could be winner, first runner-up, and second runner-up. Don't exclude the birthday child from contest prizes, or he'll feel left out of the fun of his own party.

When it comes to food, active kids generally have a hearty appetite. They enjoy "making their own," if it's not too complicated. Tacos or hero sandwiches are fun to customize—and *you* don't have to worry about who likes tomato and who hates lettuce. If it's strictly a dessert party, they'll enjoy making their own ice cream sundaes, with assorted toppings to choose from.

PARTY ACTIVITIES

Aside from the food, you'll want to plan (even overplan in case of a lull) a variety of games and activities. You may want to hire a teenage magician to perform tricks, or you might rent (or borrow) a projector and film from the local library or film supply. A restful diversion gives everyone a chance to digest and be together quietly. If it's a clear day, try a scavenger hunt or some outdoor games. But be prepared for rain, snow, and sleet, and have an indoor game-plan ready. You may want to try some variations on old favorites, to link them to your theme. You'll come up with great ideas by talking with your birthday child and/or checking a game book. Here are a few well-known games to get started:

CHARADES. Make up cards with phrases, titles, or words in advance. Each player draws one and must act out what his card says. If he stumps everybody, he gets a small prize (or point). If someone guesses, she scores. Charades could be based on the theme of the party.

This game can be played with teams, too. For team play, set a time limit. One member of the team reads the card and acts out the charade for his team. Each team gets a point for finishing before time runs out. The winning team has the most points.

FRUIT SALAD. An adult caller directs this game. Children sit on chairs in a circle. Caller names each child a specific fruit:

plum

apple	peach
peach	apple
plum	peach
apple	plum

You need at least two of each fruit. Caller arbitrarily takes one chair away. One child stands. Caller shouts name of a fruit. Those fruits must exchange seats. Standing child tries to capture a seat at this time. Caller shouts another fruit when all children but one are seated, and the game goes on.

Once everyone has a turn switching and playing, explain the new rule: the person left standing is out, and you're going to remove one chair each time.

The winning team will be the last fruit left in the game with a seat. Give prizes to all plums, or whatever. For other themes, use names other than fruits—e.g., goblins, witches, pumpkins.

RACES. Indoors or out, divide the group into teams, and run a few races. Try old-fashioned sack races, with kids jumping in pillow cases. Live dangerously—try racing with eggs (hard-boiled) in spoons. Tie your race in with a party theme for some extra pizazz.

COFFEEPOT. Choose one person to be *it*. *It* goes out of the room and the group picks an action word, like "eat." *It* then returns to the room and must ask questions: "Do people coffeepot?" "Do you coffeepot outdoors?" Limit the time or questions the group may ask. When *it* gets the answer, have *it* pick a new *it*.

You'll notice that the games for this age group call for more thinking strategy and listening skills. They also bring out and heighten the competition, and kids can handle it better than before.

Your child will certainly have other ideas of games to play and things to do. If it's summer, you might want to have a cookout. If you have space, you might plan a sleepover party. Letting the birthday child lend a hand through the planning stages actually extends this one-day occasion into days of anticipation that should lead to a special celebration.

Family Ties

"Susie chose to be on a team with her cousins. Her reason? So that the family wouldn't be split up. We could all root for the same team and not be pitted against each other."
—Mother of an eleven-year-old

For Susie and many other middle-years kids, the importance of family ties outweighs the influence of the group. In her close-knit family, Susie's cousins, aunts, and uncles remain the powerful hub of her growing social circle. By staying with her "family" team, yet additionally joining another, Susie has found a way to bridge both worlds.

Much as they enjoy being with friends their age, middle-years youngsters enjoy family outings and one-to-one experiences with parents. You don't have to take them to Disneyland or across a continent to spend time together. If you've got a couple of kids or more, why not try splitting up the gang occasionally? Try a trip with just one parent and one child, giving each other some time alone together that's qualitatively different from all-family outings.

Close-to-home and at-home activities give parents and kids an opportunity to share each other's company while working or playing. Often the pleasure of sharing a book is overlooked once children are able to read independently. The young reader, however, may still be limited in what he can tackle alone. Getting involved in longer books with chapters and more complex story lines is sometimes a formidable task for kids on their own. Reading out loud to them at this stage can keep the pump primed, enriching their language development and the delight to be found in books. Sharing the suspense of a book can become quality time after dinner or before bed. Unlike watching a sit-com, reading together provides a time when the child gets more personal attention.

Board games, too, are a good way of connecting and communicating. Kids this age are ready for games with more complex rules and a certain amount of strategy. A good many games use school skills—

word skills, math tasks, and logical thinking. You don't need to look for "educational" games or always turn time together into a direct teaching experience. Learning about winning, losing, and playing fair are social benefits that come with the simplest or most sophisticated game.

Nor does all "quality" time spent together have to center on fun and games. In every home there are jobs that you or your child can manage alone, but doing the task together opens the door to sharing on many levels. Whether it's washing the car, painting a railing, stirring a stew, or cleaning out the closets, there are opportunities for kids to feel they're making a contribution as helpmates doing real work for the general good of the family. At your side they can see the results and sense the rewards of cooperative efforts. It's not just showing them *how* to do things; attitudes about doing a job and doing it well get passed along in the process. These moments together also give kids an opportunity to open up and communicate about unrelated matters that are on their minds, but that they're more comfortable bringing up while something else is going on.

Researchers have found that kids' attitudes about work are rarely shaped by lectures or threats. Positive attitudes are formed when they see that the adults in their lives find rewards in their work, not just financial rewards, but personal pleasure in seeing a task through to fruition.

Too Much, Too Soon

Without romanticizing the good old days, childhood used to be a separate estate with clearer distinctions between being an adult and being a child. What kids lacked in power was balanced with a sense of security and protection. Divorce was rare; so were frequent moving and living behind locked doors. Tasks like cutting wood or lugging water from the well were purely physical. They were chores that required more strength than stress. Nor were children asked to assume such roles until they were physically ready. Older siblings were expected to tend younger ones, but adults were there to turn to when the going got rough.

Essentially, kids grew up in a relatively predictable and stable world. There were landmarks along the way that signified growing up: a later bedtime, a larger allowance, more freedom in the neighborhood, were privileges granted from the powerful adults in children's lives. There were also more subjects that parents talked about that kids were not privy to, subjects that grownups considered inappropriate for children.

In contrast, most kids today are on the fast track to growing up. The clothing they wear, the shows they watch, the things they hear, are rarely designed exclusively for children. It's not just what they see on TV. Within the home, in the name of being open and honest, there are few subjects reserved for adults ears only. Parental problems become everyone's, even though one of the "everyone's" may be just nine years old and hardly ready to solve his own problems, never mind Mom's or Dad's.

Studies now predict that 50 percent of our children will live in single-parent homes at some time in their childhood. Even if both parents are together, there is widespread concern among kids about the possibility of divorce, and many kids spend a lot of time wondering "what would happen if . . ."

For millions of children, the breakdown of the traditional middle-class family has become a reality, and with it comes a new set of expectations and demands for self-sufficiency. For some kids, however, the premature demands may produce more anxiety than independence. Doctors and therapists are reporting more stress-related illnesses and depression among ever-younger patients. Problems with drugs and alcohol are also becoming common among preteens. Our schools and communities have not caught up to the needs of working parents and their school-age children. A recent survey of working women indicates that 82 percent of them work because they need the money to support their families. So it's not a question of, "Should Mother work?" but rather, "Who will mind the kids while Mother is at work?" The answer in too many homes is simple: the children are minding the children, or the child is minding herself.

Much as we may wish to, we can't turn back the clock. Nor should we turn children into miniadults and rob them of their childhood. Expecting kids to help is appropriate, but demanding that they take charge of themselves and the household is too much, too soon. Teaching responsibility doesn't begin with a checklist of chores, but rather with parents who are responsible themselves and whose expectations are reasonable. Occasionally, letting children in on adult needs and feelings is a good thing, but expecting them to solve those needs is unrealistic and often harmful. All of us come home tired or irritable sometimes, but when kids get an image of adulthood as a dark round of insoluble troubles, it's hard for them to see the rewards of growing up or the pleasures that come from doing things for others.

Learning to read your child's signals and to guard against giving her too much responsibility is crucial. Kids may say they want to be on their own, without a sitter to care for them, because they want to prove how big they are to themselves and to you. However, many of these kids are not really prepared for prolonged periods of independence. Often they are trying to be grown up for your sake. They may go through the motions but at great cost to their feelings of safety and security. It may be important for parents to find a way of providing support, while still saving the child's face and feelings of dependency. This is a tall order for busy parents. You may need to invent a good reason for having someone at home when Kevin comes in from school. Or you may need to insist that if it's Monday, Kevin is to wait at Lisa's house until you pick him up. Kids may balk at some of these efforts on your part and tell you, "I'm not a baby!" But most of them know in their heart of hearts that they really want and need a support system. Few are really prepared at eight, nine, ten, or even eleven to be "on their own" for hours on end. Children who are expected to shoulder adult-sized responsibilities may develop a kind of pseudomaturity that robs their present as well as their future.

PROVIDING AFTER-SCHOOL ALTERNATIVES

"There's a woman down the street who sits after school for children of working parents. It's right around the corner from our store. Even though Laura could come to me, all her friends are there, so she got into the habit of going there and calling me on the phone. If there's homework to be done, they do it together, or they play soccer, or whatever. She's with her friends and that's the big thing."   —Mother of a ten-year-old

Small-town life and an accepting sitter make Laura one of the lucky ones. While she and her friends can spend the time socializing, for many middle-years children the hours after school are either feast or famine. Some are scheduled with lessons and meetings every day of the week.

There's little time for socializing with friends in a casual and unstructured way. For others, the hours after school are represented by a key and an empty house until five or six o'clock, when working parents come home. While some kids may be ready for such independence, many children are genuinely distressed by being on their own for prolonged periods of time. The potential for danger, real or imagined, is a source of anxiety for both kids and parents. One university operates a telephone help line that children can call when they're troubled by strange sounds in the house. Some schools and communities have set up after-school programs that offer both structure and supervision for kids. Ideally, such programs offer a mix of quiet time and physical activities, rather than merely tacking on more regimentation to the typical school day.

For communities that have no after-school programs, parents must be able to encourage schools or community-service organizations to sponsor supervised play times. Some families may need to rely on baby-sitters, relatives, and close friends. Often several working parents can set up networks to share the care of their children and to meet their social needs. Whatever the solutions, parents have to recognize that kids this age are still dependent on the adults in their lives. That doesn't necessarily mean being home with milk and cookies, but rather providing a comfortable alternative.

PLACES TO GO—THINGS TO DO

Despite the fact that kids are increasingly busy with their own friends, family time is still an important part of their social development. Indeed, going places with middle-years children can be an expansive experience for both parents and kids. It's as important as ever to get away from home, so that there are fewer distractions—no TV, telephone, or chores—to get in the way of being together. Whether you have a day, an evening, a weekend, or a week, there are more places you can go comfortably with your older child. He has more staying power and an appetite for new sights, tastes, and adventure.

Developmentally, children of this age have a better grasp of time and an interest in history. Trips to museum villages give them a sense of walking into a time machine and turning back the clock. It is through people rather than dates and events that they make their early connections with the past.

Since kids this age are usually avid collectors, museums of science and space, transportation, and sports are full of treasures to see and sometimes to touch. In the last few decades many museums have introduced special collections, Saturday programs, and hands-on exhibits that are designed for middle-years kids. Sometimes a news event, a television program, or school assignment can be enhanced by a visit to the planetarium, art museum, or nature sanctuary. By tuning in to children's new and growing interests in the world, parents can play an active role in selecting opportunities that give learning broader dimensions.

For the city child, a day in the country, a ride on the river, or a trip to the mountains can be an adventure and can lead to new discoveries. On a trip to an island where no cars are allowed, nine-year-old Tony was amazed to discover that both his parents could actually ride a bike, fly a kite, and enjoy tossing pebbles in the water. In our eagerness to make outings "educational," we sometimes forget the value of just having fun. A picnic and a change of scene with no teaching agenda may be a more positive experience and may be remembered longer than a costly trip to an amusement park.

For the country child a trip to a nearby city has great possibilities —everything from museums to zoos, botanical gardens to theaters, television stations to skyscrapers. Take a tour if you must, but don't overlook the adventure of public transportation and making your own discoveries.

Whether you live in the city or the country, kids have little contact with and great curiosity about how things are made or where they come from. This is a good age for an outing that takes you behind the secenes, to where industry's wheels are turning. Many companies have guided tours through bottling plants, pretzel factories, and power stations. Don't overlook the fun of picking your own produce at an orchard or farm. Outdoor concerts, county fairs, and craft shows are often annual events the whole family can enjoy together.

Often these excursions into the bigger world are enhanced by bringing along a friend. Much as you may long for the old days when you and your child walked hand-in-hand, kids at this age are just happier to have an age mate along to share giggles, snacks, and adventures with. To keep the outing happy, accept the fact that you may not see or do everything you planned. Take time for a break to sit down and bolster lagging enthusiasm with a cool drink and light snack. If there's likely to be a souvenir shop, leave enough time and spare change in the budget to cover a small keepsake as a happy reminder of the occasion.

PETS AND RESPONSIBILITY

School-age kids are often eager to own a pet. Certainly a child's relationship with another living creature can satisfy many needs. Pets are noncritical companions who don't talk back or tease. They're fun to play with and satisfy a need to give and get affection. Indeed, with a pet, a child has the chance of practicing a nurturing role with an affectionate and dependent creature. Recently, researchers have found that adults as well as children seem to be soothed by physical contact with pets. In some extreme cases, emotionally ill children who are unable to relate to people do respond with warmth and affection to animals.

Much as kids may want a pet, however, they are not quite up to taking full responsibility and sticking with it. As in all things, kids' interests may run high for a while and then suddenly fade. That doesn't mean you shouldn't have a pet. Rather, it may mean that you will have to fill in or take over occasionally, since the needs of a living creature are constant and your child's attention is not. The pet may be considered Jill's, but the adult should recognize that it's also a family pet and will from time to time require more than Jill's care. Often, after much pleading and promising, parents who basically don't want a pet give in out of a misplaced sense of parental duty. Then, when Jimmy doesn't follow through and neglects his longed-for furry friend, tempers flare and threats abound. Unless you're willing to occasionally share the care and see the greater good of having a pet, it may be better to veto ownership until later. It may not be a popular decision, but it will be an honest one. On the other hand, parents who have resisted getting a pet often find that they enjoy the animal at least as much as their child does.

WHEN I WAS YOUR AGE

From one generation to the next, kids have heard parents sigh and say, "When I was your age, I couldn't . . . ; I was expected to . . . ; I wouldn't have dared . . . ; I knew I had to . . . ," etc.

Of course, these words meant different things to your mother, your grandmother, and your great-grandmother. Most of us are far removed from the necessities of lugging water from the well, chopping firewood, gathering eggs, or slopping the hogs. But that doesn't mean that kids today have no responsibilities.

> "Katie really helps me around the house. She sets and clears the table, she folds the wash, and she polishes the furniture. Her brothers did the same jobs at the same age, but now they have outside jobs, so they do less around the house."
>
> —Mother of a ten-year-old

If Katie sounds too good to be true, you may find some comfort in what Tina's mom has to say:

> "She's really got a talent for dodging chores or ducking out when there's work around the house. My older kids get furious and say I let her get away with everything. Maybe they're right. Tina is the baby of the family, and sometimes I feel guilty about the way I handled the others. I really sat on them, and insisted on a lot of things I thought were important at the time. Now I've found they were not so important after all—you know, the timing for this and that. I used to say, 'You must do your homework immediately after school.' So Tina doesn't do it right after school. She does it a little bit later. It gets done."

In contrast with Tina's relaxed mom, eight-year-old Kevin and ten-year-old Julie's folks run a tight ship:

> "Since I work full time, they all have responsibilities around the house. We lay out clothes together the night before; they make their own breakfast; they listen for the bus and get themselves on it. I have to leave before they do, but my husband is here so they're not totally on their own. On weekends everybody helps clean the house. We don't go out until things are done. Everybody has a job, and nobody gets off scot-free."

Whether you work outside the home or not, middle-years boys and girls can and should be sharing some of the responsibilities in the home. True, they may not make hospital corners on the beds, and you might be able to fold the towels faster and neater, but the object is not perfection. Rather it's participation in a social system, lending a hand for the benefit of all. That doesn't mean hunting around for make-work and meaningless projects to teach your child a lesson. Kids of this age see babyish jobs that don't use their abilities as a put-down. They do want to learn how to do real things and to see tangible results. Cleaning out the car, shining the kitchen counter, scrubbing the bathroom tiles, are jobs they can roll up their sleeves for and get into. Cleaning off the table, taking the garbage out after dinner, cleaning their room, or making the bed fall under the heading of necessary chores that often require kind but firm reminders.

Routines are hard to glamorize, so be open to having kids do things in their own way. Allow them the autonomy of not doing things "the way they are supposed to be done." Often children have imaginative ways of getting chores done that are no less effective than traditional ways, and often more fun. Dusting the floor with rags on one's shoes may produce as clean a floor as a dust mop, and your child will enjoy the task. There's no formula for making housework hassle-free all the time. If there is constant friction over jobs undone, maybe a different schedule or a switch in jobs will work better. Talk it over with your child, and listen with an open mind. In Kevin's and Julie's house, brother and sister often trade jobs so no one feels stuck with something he hates doing. Cooperation is highly valued.

When kids have responsibilities that match their abilities, they may have things they'd rather do, but they're not facing insurmountable tasks. Living up to expectations from parents helps kids grow a sense of themselves as competent and useful members of the basic social unit of our society—the family. As Kevin and Julie's mom put it, "My kids have learned that I'm not going to be there all the time. I'm not capable of doing everything. They're discovering that we're all people here, that we need each other, and we have to help each other."

8

The New Society: Crisis and Change

Changing Customs, Changing Styles

Marriage is in. Marriage is out. Living together is in. It's out.

It used to be that children were raised according to family traditions handed down from generation to generation, like patterns for a quilt. But that no longer holds true. Now every generation, in some cases every half-generation, creates new life styles. Sometimes, it seems we make them up out of whole new cloth.

These new social ways, existing as they do side by side with older ones, are bound to affect the lives of children. And hard as it is for youngsters to make their way through these ins and outs, it's just as hard for parents.

Let's take a look at some of these changes and the ways they may affect children's social growth and development.

A CHANGE IN THE FAMILY

In today's world, relationships between partners change much more than they used to. One marriage in two fails. Live-in partners move out. People remarry and take on someone else's kids. All of this lateral movement doesn't make child-rearing any simpler. And whether it's the cause or effect of other changes is not clear. What is clear is that this new instability in parental relationships is a factor that needs to be considered in any discussion about raising a confident and sociable child.

What Will It Do to the Kids?

If we accept the importance of parents as models, anchors, and mentors, then it stands to reason that any major change in the family structure—like separation or divorce—will be bound to throw things out of kilter, at least for a while. Outgoing children may suddenly turn shy; happy youngsters may go moody and silent. Among preschoolers, toilet training may be a temporary casualty of adult breakups. Older children may protest family problems by flouting family rules and values. In short, family changes can cause sociable youngsters to turn antisocial and confident children to grow timid.

The more cheerful news is that children are wonderfully resilient. If love and attention are still coming from both parents, if the partners refrain from using the children as pawns in their war games, and if youngsters have other caring adults around during this hard time, they will usually adapt well in time to the new family situation. It may help to keep in mind that boys ususaly take longer than girls to make adjustments to new family life styles.

Obviously, parents must do what is necessary in their own lives. But it's important to remember that there are consequences for the kids. Remember, too, that the transition period is especially hard. It's wise during this period not to change drastically the way you interact with your youngster.

Don't do what Marge is doing:

Marge has just become a single parent. In her effort to pick up the pieces of her life, she is putting undue pressure on nine-year-old Eric. Besides giving him many new responsibilities, she has told Eric that she expects him now to be her helpmeet, her partner, and to share in some of the household decisions. Unconsciously, Marge is sending Eric the message that he must take his dad's place. Eric is not ready for that kind of responsibility, and certainly not at this time. He may seem to go through the motions of doing what is expected of him, like a "little man." But, in fact, it's unfair to ask Eric to give up a piece of his childhood this way. Especially now.

What about the flip side of the coin? Let's take a look at Dan, who feels so guilty about the breakup of his marriage and its effect on the kids that he suddenly puts all social limits and controls on hold. He showers his children with gifts, allows wheedling on former nonnegotiables, and tolerates tantrums and rudeness because of "the situation." This sudden switch of modes, coming on the heels of the other big change in their lives, is very disturbing to his children, who would have been more comfortable with familiar routines (even familiar arguments).

So what's the best stance for parents in a separation, divorce, or change-of-partners scenario?

- Be especially understanding and considerate about the children's temporary problems.
- Try not to make major switches in parenting philosophy while your child is sorting out the changes in the family.
- Arbitrate as many of the separation issues as possible in a civilized way so that children see a minimum of antisocial behavior from the parents.
- Make a special effort to keep in touch with friends and relatives during this adjustment period. Children (and adults) need the support system of loving family members and friends during crisis times.
- Be alert to the need for special counseling for your child, if he or she seems particularly depressed or if behavior problems seem to linger long after the breakup.

Death and Other Family Crises

A parent once called up a TV station to protest the fact that the network had shown a touching children's story about the death of a bird. The woman's youngster had seen the show and ended up in tears. Mom was protesting because she felt children should not be exposed to shows that make them cry. Children, she felt, should be spared sadness.

We all want our children to be happy. But life itself sometimes has a way of changing the design we had planned for ourselves and our children. Death, illness, and financial reverses are all facts of life. Should we shield our children from them?

The truth is, no parent can shield a child from what is real. Nor should we try. One of the ways children learn appropriate feelings is by going through a variety of experiences, happy and not so happy. By experiencing pain and loss and some of the very things that make them cry, children understand that sadness is something from which they can recover.

A DEATH IN THE FAMILY

A death in the family can be cause for profound sorrow for a nine- or ten-year-old. But it may have little meaning for a three-year-old. The important thing is to acknowledge that death is one of the most important occurrences in the whole repertoire of human experiences. It is so much a part of our social selves that to hide it from children is in a sense to make them socially handicapped.

> Three-year-old Jesse's turtle died. He felt sad, but was cheered by the ceremony of a turtle funeral and burial. A dignified death of a pet, taken seriously by the family, helps to shape a young child's understanding of human death, without at all demeaning it. Parents should never lie to a child of any age about the death of anything, or anyone.

> Six-year-old Michelle's aunt died. The family decided to take Michelle to the funeral. Relatives pressed the little girl to kiss her aunt in the coffin. Her parents perceived that Michelle was frightened by this expression of mourning. They quickly shielded her from what could have been a bad experience, one that Michelle wasn't quite old enough for.

> Ten-year-old Jeff didn't know his great-uncle well. But he asked to go to the funeral when the uncle died. Jeff was at an age when he was curious about all sorts of things. His interest in the funeral was not macabre. It was important for Jeff to go to the funeral to see what it was all about and how people behave when they say good-bye to a loved one.

. . . AND OTHER EVENTS

Family crises of all kinds need to be aired, with an eye both on the age of the child and his sensitivity. Sometimes frank talks aren't appropriate for the particular stage the youngster is going through. The child who is worrying about things that go bump in the night probably should not be told about the robbery in the next block. But ordinarily, dealing clearly and openly with social problems and crises is the best way, whether you are telling young Tim that Dad has lost his job, that the family is moving, or that Grandpa is dying of cancer.

Kids who have learned gradually to deal with a variety of life situations—both bad and good—are often much more able to cope than those who are completely sheltered.

The real question a parent has to ask is, How much is my child ready to handle?

As a general rule, young children should not be burdened with *lengthy* explanations. "Grandpa died yesterday. He was sick for a long time," is probably enough information for a three- or four-year-old. But if a child of any age asks for more information, it should be given.

Older children need to know more, and even to see grownups grieving or angry, so they will know how to *care* in appropriate ways. Sometimes parents make an effort to hide their own feelings of grief or anger at the sickness or death of a loved one. But this can be more frustrating than beneficial to the young people in the family.

Children and Machines

Machines have certainly changed the social framework of both children and adults. The very fact that children spend so much of their time sitting—first in school, then in front of TV, and most recently, in front of computers—is bound to have an effect on their minds, if not on their physical development.

Children are exposed to a wealth of stimuli. Some of it is useful and enriching information, which they can incorporate into their growing body of social skills to their great benefit. But it's not all to the good, and parents need to keep an eye on what their youngsters are seeing on TV or doing on their computers.

TV AND KIDS

Television is basically a passive sport, and it has already had a huge effect on how kids play. In some suburban neighborhoods where children once played outside, the backyards and sidewalks are empty. Where are the children? They're inside, glued to the television set.

They're substituting watching for doing, a vicarious experience for hands-on experience.

It's sometimes tempting to listen to the siren song of the TV baby-sitter-pacifier. But a little TV goes a long way. The best spectator-sports program is no substitute for playing the game yourself. And no sit-com can take the place of a sit-down family dinner where real people are talking to one another. We need to think seriously about whether TV is, or should be, a child's best friend, and whether Angie and Andrew shouldn't be getting out more.

There's nothing wrong with limiting TV time. The earlier you set up the pattern, the better. Limits on the content may also be in order. Some TV programs may clearly work against positive social development. Programs that are scary, violent, or sex-filled are not fare for children. You can be firm on this subject and feel you are doing your youngster a real service.

COMPUTERS AND KIDS

What about the computer? It can be angel or devil, depending on how it's used. Its big virtue is that it is not passive. In other words, in order to get something out, you must put something in. Right away it's a cut above the television set, at least as far as *interaction* goes. The other thing about the computer is that it can bring children together to work on projects cooperatively. In fact, recent research at Bank Street College has indicated that the social benefits of the computer may be among the best things about it.

A computer, used wisely, can be a powerful learning and entertainment medium. But overdone, the computer becomes one more piece of technology keeping a child from a healthy interaction with other children and other parts of the environment.

From Social to Socially Responsible

Perhaps here is a good place to pause and take another look at this social design we've been working on. How are we doing? Is the pattern of our children's sociability what we had in mind, or are there still some rough spots? More important, do we feel comfortable with what has happened so far? And are our children as confident as we had hoped they would become?

Every family has its own principles, so the answers to some of these questions will vary. But when all is said and done, most of us want pretty much the same things for our children. By the time youngsters are at the edge of adolescence, the overall texture of these social goals will be visible.

These are some of the things we hope to find in place: Sammy and Sue are by now affable and unusually poised young citizens. They get along well with their peers and even with most adults. They have probably graduated from the camp of the unwashed to being compulsively clean preteens. They even take the hair out of the bathtub after they shower. And they shower endlessly. They behave well in a three-star restaurant. They are learning what to say and what not to say. There is little need to censor portions of their conversations, at least when they are out in public. They have been known to take out the garbage without being told. And they write to their grandparents.

On balance, you could certainly say that there has been forward movement on many fronts. Does this mean that Mom and Dad can assume that the job is done? Not really. Because some of the things we feel so good about are only the visible signs of the social process—the trappings, in a manner of speaking. Underneath is the real stuff we're after—the warp and woof of this social design we're working on. And it is these underpinnings that give it real form and shape.

There is more to being confident than meets the eye. What we've been after with all these bits and pieces of social behavior is to help our children to become not only *socially acceptable,* but more importantly, *socially responsible.* Developing a sense of social responsibility is a key to confidence that may be your child's greatest asset.

We're glad Sammy is considerate of his grandmother. But perhaps equally important is that he's on his way toward feeling concern for *all* older people.

It's great that Sue takes out the garbage in her house. Someday soon she may feel impelled to do something about the garbage in the larger environment.

Right now we want Sam and Sue to be popular. But might it not be terrific if someday they also had the strength to be *unpopular* once in a while, in matters of principle?

To sum up—both Sam and Sue have already acquired a healthy social sense. First they learned how to operate within the family group.

Later on they learned how to behave among friends and among strangers. The final and perhaps most important step will be for them eventually to feel *for* and be at home *with* the whole human family. Then they will be truly social people.

BIBLIOGRAPHY

Activities to Learn By. Lillian and Godfrey Frankel. New York: Sterling, 1974.

Baby Learning Through Baby Play: A Parent's Guide for the First Two Years. Ira J. Gordon. New York: St. Martin's, 1970.

Between Parent and Child. Dr. Haim G. Ginott. New York: Macmillan, 1965.

Bringing Up Children. Grace Langdon. New York: John Day, 1960.

Child Behavior. Frances L. Ilg, Louise Bates Ames, and Sidney M. Baker. New York: Harper and Row, 1981.

Child Development and Education: A Piagetian Perspective. David Elkind. New York: Oxford, 1976.

Child Development and Socialization. Jere Brophy. New York: St. Martin's, 1977.

Childhood and Adolescence: A Psychology of the Growing Person. Joseph Church and L. Joseph Stone. New York: Random House, 1979.

Childhood Socialization: Studies in the Development of Language, Social Behavior, and Identity. Norman K. Denzin. San Francisco: Jossey-Bass, 1977.

Children's View of Themselves. Association for Childhood Education International membership service bulletin 104, 1959–60.

Child's Eye View. Carol Tomlinson-Keasey. New York: St. Martin's, 1980.

A Child's Journey. Julius Segal and Herbert Yahraes. New York: McGraw-Hill, 1978.

The Child under Six. Jesild Hymes, Jr. Englewood Cliffs: Prentice-Hall, 1963, 1971.

The Complete Question and Answer Book of Child Training. Ester L. Cava. New York: Hawthorne, 1972.

Dealing in Discipline (study guide). Margaret Verble. Lincoln, Neb.: University of Mid-America, 1980.

Developing Responsibility in Children. Constance J. Foster. Chicago: Senior Research Associates, 1953.

Developmental Tasks and Education. Robert J. Havighurst. New York: McKay, 1955.

Discipline without Fear. Loren Grey. New York: Hawthorne, 1974.

Don't Push Me, I'm No Computer. Helen L. Beck. New York: McGraw-Hill, 1973.

Don't Push Your Preschooler. Louise Bates Ames and Joan Ames Chase. New York: Harper and Row, 1981.

Effective Parents, Responsible Children. Robert Eimers and Robert Aitchison. New York: McGraw-Hill, 1977.

Every Child's Birthright: In Defense of Mothering. Selma Fraiberg. New York: Basic Books, 1977.

The Family Book about Sexuality. Mary S. Calderone, M.D., and Eric W. Johnson. New York: Harper and Row, 1981.

The Family Guide to Children's Television: What to Watch, What to Miss, What to Change, and How to Do It. Evelyn Kay. New York: Pantheon, 1974.

The Father's Almanac. S. Adams Sullivan. Garden City: Doubleday, 1980.

The First Relationship: Infant and Mother. Daniel Stern. Cambridge: Harvard, 1977.

Friendship and Peer Relations (vol. 4 of *Origins of Behavior*). Michael Lewis and Leonard A. Rosenblum. New York: John Wiley, 1975.

Growing with Your Children (pamphlet). Herbert Kohl. Boston: Little, Brown, 1979.

The How and Why. Aline Auerbach. New York: Child Study Assn., 1957, 1969.

How to Help Your Child Start School: A Practical Guide for Parents and Teachers of Four- to Six-Year-Olds. Bernard Ryan, Jr. New York: Putnam, Perigee, 1981.

How to Play with Your Children, and When Not To. Brian and Shirley Sutton-Smith. New York: Hawthorne, 1974.

The Integration of the Child into a Social World. Martin P. Richards, ed. New York: Cambridge, 1974.

Kindergarten and Early Schooling. Dorothy H. Cohen and Marguerita Rudolph. Englewood Cliffs: Prentice-Hall, 1977.

Language Art: An Idea Book. Mary Yanaga George. Novato, Calif.: Chandler and Sharp, 1970.

The Learning Child. Dorothy H. Cohen. New York: Pantheon, 1973.

Learning for Little Kids: Parents' Sourcebook for the Years Three to Eight. Sandy Jones. Boston: Houghton Mifflin, 1979.

Love and Discipline. Barbara Brenner. New York: Ballantine, 1983.

Loving and Learning: Interacting with Your Child from Birth to Three. Norma J. McDiarmid, Mari A. Peterson, and James Sutherland. New York: Harcourt, 1977.

The Magic Years: Understanding and Handling Problems of Early Childhood. Selma Fraiberg. New York: Scribner, 1959.

The Middle Years of Childhood. Patricia Minuchin. Monterey, Calif.: Brooks-Cole, 1977.

The New Extended Family: Day Care Programs That Work. Ellen Galinsky and William H. Hooks. Boston: Houghton-Mifflin, 1977.

The New-Fashioned Parent: How to Make Your Family Style Work. Eleanor Berman. Englewood Cliffs: Prentice-Hall, 1980.

New Season: The Positive Uses of Commercial Television with Children. Rosemary Lee Potter. Columbus, Ohio: Merrill, 1976.

Parenting: A Guide for Young People. Sol Gordon and Mina Wollin. New York: Oxford, 1975.

The Parenting Advisor. Princeton Center for Infancy, Frank Caplan, ed. Garden City, N.Y.: Doubleday, Anchor, 1977.

The Parent's Encyclopedia. Milton I. Levine, M.D., and Jean H. Seligmann. New York: Crowell, 1973.

The Parent's Guide to Everyday Problems. Eda Le Shan. New York: Scholastic, Four Winds, 1981.

Parents' Guide to Everyday Problems of Boys and Girls. Sidonie M. Gruenberg. New York: Random House, 1958.

Partners in Play. Dorothy Singer and Jerome Singer. New York: Harper and Row, 1978.

The Pleasure of Their Company: How to Have More Fun with Your Children. Bank Street College. Radnor, Pa.: Chilton, 1981.

Psychology and Education: An Introduction. Jerome Kagan and Cynthia Lang. New York: Harcourt, 1978.

Raising a Responsible Child. Dr. Don Dinkmeyer and Gary D. McKay. New York: Simon and Schuster, 1973.

Raising Children with Love and Limits. Psyche Cattel. Chicago: Nelson-Hall, 1972.

The Show and Tell Machine: How Television Works and Works You Over. Rose K. Goldsen. New York: Dell, 1978.

Social Behavior from Fish to Man. William Etkin. Chicago: Phoenix, 1967.

Social Development in Childhood: Day-Care Programs and Research. Hyman Blumberg Symposium on Research in Early Childhood, 1974, Roger A. Webb, ed. Baltimore: Johns Hopkins, 1977.

Straight Talk (pamphlet). Drug Fair, Inc., Alexandria, Va., 1980.

A Sympathetic Understanding of the Child: Birth to Sixteen. David Elkind. Boston: Allyn and Bacon, 1978.

Teaching Social Behavior to Young Children. William C. Sheppard, Steven B. Shank, and Darla Welson. Champaign, Ill.: Research Press, 1973.

Television and the Preschool Child: A Psychological Theory of Instruction and Curriculum Development. Horney Lesser, ed. New York: Academic, 1977.

Television: How to Use It Wisely with Children. Josette Frank, ed. New York: Child Study Assn., 1976.

Toddlers and Parents. Dr. T. Berry Brazelton. New York: Delacorte, 1976.

Total Child Care: From Birth to Age Five. Lorisa M. DeLorenzo and Robert J. DeLorenzo. New York: Doubleday, 1982.

Total Learning for the Whole Child: Holistic Curriculum for Children Ages Two to Five. Joanne Hendrick. St. Louis: Mosby, 1980.

Tough Love. Community Services Foundation, Sellers, Pa., 1980.

TV On-Off: Better Family Use of Television. Ellen B. DeFranco. Santa Monica, Calif.: Goodyear, 1980.

Understanding Children: A Parent's Guide to Child Rearing. Richard A. Gardner, M.D. Cresskill, N.J.: Creative Therapeutics, 1979.

Understanding Your Child from Birth to Three: A Guide to Your Child's Psychological Development. Joseph Church. New York: Pocket Books, 1973.

What Every Child Needs. Lillian Peairs and Richard H. Peairs. New York: Harper and Row, 1974.

The World of the Child: Clinical and Cultural Studies from Birth to Adolescence. Toby Talbot, ed. New York: Doubleday, Anchor, 1967.

Young Children Learning: Reaching Out. Alice Yardley. New York: Citation, 1973.

A Working Mother's Guide to Child Development. F. Philip Rice. Englewood Cliffs: Prentice-Hall, 1979.

Your Child from Six to Twelve. U.S. Department of Health, Education, and Welfare, Office of Child Development, Washington, D.C., 1966.

Your Two-Year-Old. Louise Bates Ames and Frances L. Ilg. New York: Dell, 1980. (Also by the same authors and publisher: *Your Three-Year-Old; Your Four-Year-Old; Your Five-Year-Old; Your Six-Year-Old.*)

INDEX